THINKING ON THE page

A College Student's Guide to Effective Writing

Praise for *Thinking on the Page*:

"As chair of a large university English Department at an enormous university and a regular recipient of review copies of writing manuals, I know that such a deeply thoughtful, broadly expert, and terrifically useful volume is a rare achievement in an ever more crowded genre. With patience, clarity, respect for their readers, and an inspiring commitment to the craft of writing, Gwen Hyman and Martha Schulman demystify and defuse fears about the writing process, and they do so beautifully, with the wit, range, sureness, and creativity of the best teachers. *Thinking on the Page* abounds with smart, practical advice, model writing strategies, and a treasure house of savvy, wide-ranging literary analysis, showing how to put this wonderful book's guidance into action.

"Students could not do better than to have these authors with them through college or university. I'll happily go further than that: Directors of university writing-intensive courses should count on this book as they plan their classes. I will be doing so from here on in."

—Professor Jonathan Warren,
Chair of the English Department
at York University

THINKING ON THE page

A College Student's Guide to Effective Writing

WD

**WRITER'S DIGEST
BOOKS**

WritersDigest.*com*
Cincinnati, Ohio

GWEN HYMAN & MARTHA SCHULMAN

For more resources for writers, visit www.writersdigest.com.

19 18 17 16 15 5 4 3 2 1

Distributed in Canada by Fraser Direct
100 Armstrong Avenue
Georgetown, Ontario, Canada L7G 5S4
Tel: (905) 877-4411

Distributed in the U.K. and Europe by F&W Media International
Brunel House, Newton Abbot, Devon, TQ12 4PU, England
Tel: (+44) 1626-323200, Fax: (+44) 1626-323319
E-mail: postmaster@davidandcharles.co.uk

Distributed in Australia by Capricorn Link
P.O. Box 704, Windsor, NSW 2756 Australia
Tel: (02) 4577-3555

ISBN-13: 978-1-59963-869-0

Edited by *Rachel Randall*
Designed by *Bethany Rainbolt*
Cover illustration by *Olive Panter*
Production coordinated by *Debbie Thomas*

ACKNOWLEDGMENTS

This book has grown out of our work with students, both in our classes and in the Center for Writing at The Cooper Union, and it would not exist were it not for our amazing, dedicated, gifted Center for Writing colleagues, past and present—the fantastic teachers of writing we're lucky enough to work with and learn from every day.

We are so very grateful to William Germano, the Dean of Humanities and Social Sciences at The Cooper Union, for his unflagging support and his clear-sighted and timely advice.

An eternal thank-you to Rachel Randall, whose early enthusiasm and on-going advocacy and support for this project made all the difference, and to all the people at Writer's Digest who worked on this book and made it look like our vision—only better.

A million thank-yous to Kimberly Witherspoon, our amazing and endlessly generous agent at Inkwell Management, and her fantastic crew—in particular, the intrepid Allison Hunter and Nathaniel Jacks.

Our great thanks to Olive Panter, our brilliant illustrator (and former student!), who transformed our words into pictures with great skill, patience, and enthusiasm.

Gwen thanks her husband, Andrew Carmellini, as always, for everything. Martha thanks him for putting up with her presence at his dining table for years on end.

ABOUT THE AUTHORS

GWEN HYMAN is the Director of the Center for Writing at The Cooper Union for the Advancement of Science and Art in New York City. She has trained dozens of writing teachers and mentored countless new professors on the ins and outs of writing pedagogy. She earned her PhD in English at Columbia University in New York and has taught writing, literature, cultural studies, and food studies at the college level for nearly two decades. She is the author of *Making a Man: Gentlemanly Appetites in the Nineteenth-Century British Novel* (Ohio) and co-author, with Andrew Carmellini of *Urban Italian* (Bloomsbury) and *American Flavor* (Ecco).

MARTHA SCHULMAN has been teaching writing, including developmental writing and English as a Second Language, for over a decade. She directs the Cooper Union Summer Writing Program, an intensive college-preparatory course for high school students. She is a Senior Associate and a consultant to faculty on writing pedagogy at the Center for Writing at The Cooper Union and has taught writing to American-bound college students in China. She holds a Masters of Fine Arts (Fiction) from Columbia University and a Masters of Arts in Teaching from Brown University. Her fiction, essays, and reviews have been widely published.

TABLE OF CONTENTS

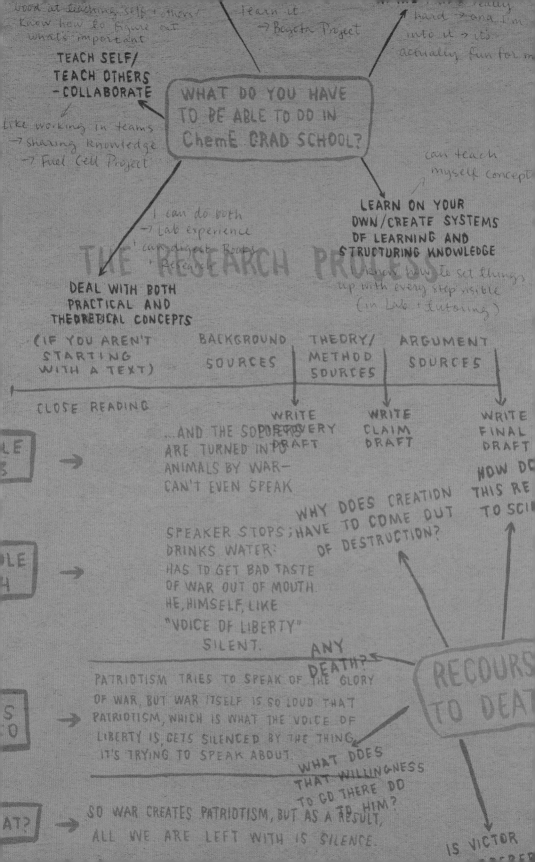

good at teaching self + others
know how to figure out
what's important

→ learn it
→ Bogotá Project

...this was really
hard → and I'm
into it → it's
actually fun for m

TEACH SELF/
TEACH OTHERS
- COLLABORATE

like working in teams
→ sharing knowledge
→ Fuel Cell Project

WHAT DO YOU HAVE TO BE ABLE TO DO IN ChemE GRAD SCHOOL?

can teach
myself concept

↑ can do both
→ Lab experience
↑ can digest Books
+ Research

LEARN ON YOUR
OWN/CREATE SYSTEMS
OF LEARNING AND
STRUCTURING KNOWLEDGE
I know how to set things
up with every step visible
(in Lab + tutoring)

DEAL WITH BOTH
PRACTICAL AND
THEORETICAL CONCEPTS

THE RESEARCH PROCESS

(IF YOU AREN'T STARTING WITH A TEXT)	BACKGROUND SOURCES	THEORY/ METHOD SOURCES	ARGUMENT SOURCES

CLOSE READING

WRITE DISCOVERY DRAFT

WRITE CLAIM DRAFT

WRITE FINAL DRAFT

...AND THE SOLDIERS
ARE TURNED INTO
ANIMALS BY WAR—
CAN'T EVEN SPEAK

HOW DO
THIS RE
TO SCI

WHY DOES CREATION
HAVE TO COME OUT
OF DESTRUCTION?

SPEAKER STOPS; DRINKS WATER:
HAS TO GET BAD TASTE
OF WAR OUT OF MOUTH.
HE, HIMSELF, LIKE
"VOICE OF LIBERTY"
SILENT.

ANY
DEATH?

RECOURS
TO DEAT

PATRIOTISM TRIES TO SPEAK OF THE GLORY
OF WAR, BUT WAR ITSELF IS SO LOUD THAT
PATRIOTISM, WHICH IS WHAT THE VOICE OF
LIBERTY IS, GETS SILENCED BY THE THING
IT'S TRYING TO SPEAK ABOUT.

WHAT DOES
THAT WILLINGNESS
TO GO THERE DO
TO HIM?

AT?

SO WAR CREATES PATRIOTISM, BUT AS A RESULT,
ALL WE ARE LEFT WITH IS SILENCE.

IS VICTOR

ANYONE CAN LEARN TO WRITE

This book is founded on one fundamental belief: Writing is hard, but it's not mysterious and it's definitely not impossible. There are specific techniques and approaches to writing effectively, and they can be learned. This means that **anyone can learn to write well**.

By *anyone*, we mean anyone who thinks he's not a good writer, anyone who feels like what's in his head is smarter than what ends up on the page, anyone who feels like he loses his own voice when he writes, anyone who's bored with essay writing that feels formulaic, anyone who suspects that writing can't really be so different from other hard things he's learned to do. In other words, this book is for anyone who writes. And in particular, it's for all writers in search of new approaches or techniques to help them write more effectively.

THE MYTH OF BAD WRITERS

As teachers, we've encountered plenty of people who've been told that they're "bad writers." But we don't believe there's such a thing as a "bad writer"—just writers who haven't found the approaches and techniques that work for them. Some are writers who don't see the world as a series of narratives or linear stories. They may think in equations or images instead of words, or they may think in 3-D. Others aren't native English speakers, and expectations of writing are different in their first languages. Some are multitaskers who find it tough to concentrate on one thing at a time, so they wander all over the place, linking disparate ideas as they come to them. Others like to get all of their ideas straight before putting them on the page.

Maybe you fall into one of these categories. But let's be clear: Thinking spatially or in numbers or in images doesn't make you a bad writer. It just makes you a writer who needs a set of approaches that works for you. This book will offer you new ways of thinking about the various processes and stages of writing, as well as a wide range of techniques and lots of examples. Our aim is to help you banish the very idea of the "bad writer" by putting you in charge of your writing process.

WRITING IS HARD

Many people think they're "bad" writers because they find writing tough: They imagine that "good" writers just sit down in front of their computers and come up with perfect, polished prose. As people who write and teach others about writing for a living, we wish it worked like that, but unfortunately, **the perfect writer with the perfect method is a myth.** File it with the Easter Bunny and Santa Claus. Know instead that any writer with the right techniques and a realistic sense of what's required can write a good essay, whether it's about a literary text or economics or the best way to design an airplane.

All writers—even professional writers—struggle with the writing process. They often don't know where to start, write a lot of drafts, get stuck, outline and re-outline and reverse outline, go back to the text or whatever they're writing about again and again, talk to other people about their work, question themselves, get frustrated and throw stuff out, get angry when they have to throw stuff out, and get excited when things come together. That's because **writing is thinking. And real, worthwhile thinking isn't easy.** Saying something meaningful is complicated and challenging. That's why it's worth doing.

WRITING IS NOT ABOUT FORMULAS

Because writing is hard and time-consuming, people tend to rely on formulas. There are lots of these formulas around—the most common version is called the "five-paragraph essay"—and they have one thing in common: They tend to rely on repetition. For instance, a frequent piece of formulaic writing advice goes like this: *Tell your audience what you're going to tell them, tell them the thing you're telling them, and then tell them what you told them.* But this advice assumes that you and your audience aren't very bright—otherwise, how would you be able to keep repeating the same concept without boring yourself or your readers? And it also assumes that you don't have anything interesting to say. We don't buy either of these assumptions. We know that when our students have the tools, they come up with ideas and questions we would never have thought of ourselves. And as teachers, we find it much more interesting to read an essay that takes us somewhere than to read one point repeated over and over.

WRITING IS A PROCESS

The most common formulas reduce writing to a straightforward act of reporting information (more specifically, "right" information or "right" answers). But that's not very helpful when your task is to think hard about something and communicate your analysis to your audience through writing. **Effective writing isn't just an act of reporting: It's a series of operations involving learning, asking, investigating, and working things through on the page.** You're not just writing down what you already know or what everybody knows or what you think the professor wants. You're writing to figure out what you think about the topic or the question or the text. And to do that effectively, you have to accept that writing is a process, because you can't figure out what you think via a formula. In this book, we'll take you through many steps in the writing process and show you different options for working through the different stages of that process.

WRITING IS READING

Good analytical writing often starts with noticing something you don't understand about your subject. The subject may be a film, an experiment, an event, an image—but in college, it's most often a written text of some kind. And this means that **effective reading is integral to effective writing**. In a strong essay, the writing process starts not when you sit down at the computer, open a new document, and start writing your essay but much earlier. In fact, it starts when you begin reading the document that you'll eventually write about.

When faced with a text in a college-level class, students don't always know what to do with it. Texts in college classes are usually assigned before the class meetings in which those texts will be discussed; with little advance guidance, a student can feel lost when she starts to read. Unsurprisingly, she falls back on what she knows: She reads for content, perhaps making notes; she thinks about the text in terms of her own personal experience; she evaluates it (I liked it/I hated it; it's good/it's bad). This is about the limit of what many students think can be done with a text: summary, evaluation, comparison to one's own experience or stories in the news. But these approaches won't give you much to work with because you're not really thinking about the text.

Some of the work you do in reading and writing for college will seem familiar: You'll still need to read for plot, events, and facts. When you write for a college class, you begin by understanding the text in terms of its genre, its historical moment, its content, and the moves it makes. But this kind of summary work is only the beginning. At the college level, once you've done this baseline work, you need to go further. *Analysis*, not summary, is the cornerstone of writing for college. In order to analyze a text, you need to zoom in on specific passages or "moments," read them closely and carefully, and ask questions about what you see. This questioning process, and the thinking it lets you do, constitute analysis.

When you understand how to read a text closely and ask questions of it, you open up a lot of possibilities. There are many directions you can take and any number of ways of looking at a text and making claims about it. Students often find this freedom daunting at first. But once you know what you're being asked to do and you learn the techniques that let you do it, you can move beyond summary and do real work.

Close Reading

In order to figure out the moves a piece of writing is making, you'll need to engage in a process called *close reading*. This involves choosing a particular moment in the text and looking carefully and closely at its building blocks—its overall structure, grammar, syntax, sentence structure, and individual words. Close reading involves looking at a text very attentively in order to avoid assumptions and generalizations. This gives you the opportunity to say something significant about what you see going on.

Close reading is about finding the places where there are gaps or differences between what you understand when you read on the surface and what you see when you look at this granular level—and then asking questions about what's going on. It requires that you look at a given passage multiple times, from every possible angle, recording what you see and think as you go. You might choose a moment because it seems particularly interesting—or because it's so weird you can't figure out what you think about it at all. What's important is that you're finding material that looks intriguing to you and then exploring it. This process allows you to come up with interesting, thoughtful, evidence-based ideas about the text. Close reading is the essence of analytical reading—and the basis of analytical writing—across all fields and disciplines.

Asking Questions

When you read closely, you generate a lot of questions. You may find yourself wondering, for instance, what it means when a character repeatedly uses a particular word or phrase—and what that repetition might indicate about the character or his motivations. You may notice patterns and begin to think about their meaning. You may find gaps between what a passage seems to say at first glance and what you discover when you look more closely at the specific language of the passage. In other words, you start asking the kinds of questions that don't have definitive or "right" answers. That's good: It means your questions are analytical, as opposed to questions that can be answered with summary, with opinion, or with obvious or generally accepted ideas. And that, in turn, means that when it's time to start writing, you'll be able to generate noteworthy material to work with.

WRITING IS THINKING

As we said before, one reason that writing is hard is because ideas don't arrive on the page perfectly formed. **In fact, it's the act of writing that lets you explore what you don't understand; by writing, you learn about your subject, about what you think about your subject, about how your ideas build on one another.** Doing so requires you to take some risks, of course. Many people find it safer to figure out their ideas in their heads before they put them down on the page (or state them out loud); we know many students who have spent endless hours sitting with their fingers poised over the keyboard, waiting for the sentences to arrange themselves perfectly before they write them down. Others cross out or delete as soon as they write because they demand that every word be perfect. But that inevitably means that lots of interesting work gets abandoned because it can't be made neat and tidy in your head before it goes on the page.

Good writing is messy, just like thinking is messy. When you're trying to figure out what you really think or make meaningful connections between ideas, you will inevitably go down roads that don't lead anywhere, come up with concepts that you discard, come up with incomplete ideas, circle around your point, and so forth. And you won't end up keeping everything that you produce because not everything you produce will be useful. That's okay. People who write for a living write lots of garbage and throw a lot of material away—but they recognize this as part of the process of figuring out their ideas. As the writer E.M. Forster once said, "How do I know what I think until I see what I say?" **Getting your thoughts out of your head and onto the page, where you can see them, is the crucial move that lets you test your ideas.** When you've seen what you think, you can challenge yourself by asking more questions and thinking harder. And that leads to better work.

This is what we mean by thinking on the page: The process of moving from close reading through process writing (the notes and questions and messy, risky stuff) is what allows you to figure out what you initially don't understand, what you come to think about that confusing or difficult or interesting thing, and how you want to express what you think. The final essay is a chance to demonstrate a streamlined version of that process to your reader so that she's convinced by your argument. This kind of work is harder and takes longer than fitting pieces into a formula—but it's also much more rewarding. Instead of jumping through a series of hoops, you're thinking every step of the way.

Communicating Ideas, Telling a Story

The best way to demonstrate your thinking on the page is to approach your essay as you would a story. Think about what happens when you tell a story to a friend: What you're engaged in, really, is a process of convincing your listener that what you're saying is worth listening to. You try to get your ideas across logically and clearly so your listener understands what you're talking about. You choose language that highlights what you're excited about and emphasizes what's important in your particular telling. You avoid saying things that are obvious, and you try not to repeat yourself because repetition is boring. All of this is equally true of essay writing. You want your listener to get your point, to stay with you, and to trust that you know where you're going. At the same time, if there are no surprises or discoveries, he'll be bored. **Good writing, in any field or genre, carries a reader along and gets a point across by creating a compelling and logical narrative.**

WRITING IS REWRITING

It's not so simple, though, to write a narrative that takes your reader somewhere—especially when that narrative is derived from your questions about the most confusing or difficult spots in your text. If you're doing this kind of complex, thoughtful work, you can't expect to get it all on the page in the right order the first time around. **The process of writing takes time: You need to do a lot of writing and a lot of different kinds of writing in order to be a successful writer**. You need to figure out where in the text or material you're focusing and why, look hard at that material and ask questions about it, and then write through your ideas and organize them. And while the product of all this work is a linear, logical essay, the process of writing it is messy and nonlinear and difficult.

WRITING AND READING BEYOND YOUR ENGLISH CLASS

You may be thinking that this discussion only applies to English and composition or expository writing courses. That's one of the great myths about writing in college: that other disciplines don't require writing or use writing as a means to think through ideas. (Students have often said to us: "I chose my major so that I'd never have to write anything again!") But just about any field requires writing as both process and product. Whether you're a biologist or a chef, an artist or an astronomer, you're going to need to communicate about your work in writing, both in school and afterward.

You'll also find that talking to yourself on the page is a critical way of thinking things through and making your work better in the studio, the lab, the kitchen, the shop … . We've seen students use writing productively to gain some distance from their hands-on work in all kinds of fields and in all kinds of ways. An art student might freewrite about the direction his recent paintings have taken. A group of engineering students may find that by trying to create an abstract for their project, they figure out what they're really working on. An architecture student can use writing to explore the ways her models may not yet completely express her ideas. In every field, writing can make the work you do more thoughtful and fruitful because this process of looking closely, actively engaging, analyzing, and drawing conclusions lets you step outside of the work you're engrossed in, think it through, and come to fresh conclusions.

While forms and disciplinary language may be field specific, there are fewer differences than you'd think when it comes to ways of reading, analyzing, and coming to conclusions through writing. As you move through this book, you'll encounter a range of different types of texts and we'll show you how to use our approaches to work with them. This book is a toolbox you can carry with you through your college experience and beyond.

ABOUT THINKING ON THE PAGE

This book will take you through all the steps of thinking on the page, from your first encounter with a new text to your final edits of the paper you hand in. We'll discuss active reading and what that means; process writing, in which you deepen your questions and analysis as you go; assessing your drafts; doing research and incorporating it into your work; and finally, editing and polishing your final product.

As you move through this process, you'll generate summaries, questions, graphs, and outlines, probably in forms that are new to you. You'll ask yourself a lot of questions about the phenomenon you're exploring in your moment in the text, and you'll respond by exploring that phenomenon more closely and carefully, using a range of techniques. You'll draft, take stock of what you've done, and draft again. You'll take risks and ask hard questions to generate uniquely interesting ideas—and you'll get some practice in testing your ideas and in trusting your own thinking. You'll learn how to tell a story in essay form so that your ideas are clear and engaging to your readers: There's no point in having a new idea if others can't understand it. In the end, you'll produce work that's thoughtful, analytical, and meaningful both to you and your readers.

NO BAD WRITERS

A lot of students come to college thinking they'll never be good writers. They don't like writing, don't think they're good at it, wish they didn't have to do it, don't see the point of doing it. But with the right approaches and techniques, anyone can learn to write effectively and persuasively. We know this for sure because we've worked with a lot of students on reading and writing. We've seen them make false starts and get stalled and forget where they're going; we've seen them try out structures and techniques that help them look critically at their own work; we've seen them read and rewrite and reread and rewrite again. The process is messy, challenging, and complicated, but when students come to understand that the moments when they feel stuck are part of the process, they're less frustrated. When they have techniques and approaches to draw on, they can move on productively. And when they really let themselves think on the page, asking themselves questions and challenging their own assumptions, something amazing happens: They figure out what they think and how to get it across to others. They find their voices. We hope this book will help you find yours.

CHAPTER ONE
READING

This book is about writing—but if you want to write well, you need to know how to read effectively. And while you might reasonably assume that you know how to read by now (after all, you've made it to college), reading effectively at the college level requires a different set of skills. Knowing how to read the words isn't the same as knowing what you're actually expected to do with a text, especially in courses in which you're asked to write about those texts. Reading isn't a single operation: There are many ways of reading. When you're reading in order to write about what you've read, you need to read in a way that suits that purpose.

When you walk into the first day of a college class, no matter what the topic is, you'll probably walk out with a reading assignment. Often the only instruction you'll receive about the reading is the range of pages you're responsible for. Understandably your first instinct will be to put the reading skills you acquired in high school into play. But many students quickly find that those skills aren't sufficient to help them *do* anything with the texts they're assigned.

You might, for example, come to college with the habit of scanning the assigned reading for the information you'll need for the test or the paper. That's a useful skill, and one you'll continue to use, but it isn't enough on its own. In college, you're generally reading assigned texts not just to glean information but to do something with that information. This is as true of the reading for your biology class as it is of the material for your English class.

KNOWING WHAT YOU'RE READING AND WHY

The first move when you're reading to write is figuring out what you're reading and why you're reading it. Once again, this might seem pretty basic—but reading in college classes, as we said, is often assigned without explanation, and a single course can involve many different types of reading material, assigned for many different purposes. Picking up a text you've never seen before and that you know little or nothing about can be intimidating, especially since college-level texts are often significantly more complex than those you read in high school. Many people react to this by reading in a hurry, getting frustrated, or not reading at all. None of these approaches sets you up to understand the text you're reading or to notice things about it—steps that are critical if you're going to do anything with the text in front of you. So it's useful to ask yourself these questions when you first pick up a text.

1. What Kind of Text Am I Reading?

Genre and time period are important. In an assignment for a history class, for example, you may find yourself reading documents from the historical period you're studying, a textbook providing a time line and basic summary of events, or a historian's take on these events. In each case, you need to be clear on what type of material you're reading so you can decide how to use it. Though a textbook, a political speech, and a soldier's letter home might all talk about the same battle, they'll do it in different ways and for different purposes.

Similarly, you read a poem with different expectations than you do a novel and a novel with different expectations than you do a nonfiction essay or a piece of scientific or philosophical writing. Is the text you're reading attempting to convince you of the soundness of an idea? Is it creating a fictional world? Exploring a concept through metaphoric language? What work is the text trying to do?

Sometimes the genre of the text you're reading may not be entirely clear at first glance. For example, take a look at this opening excerpt from Charles Darwin's *On the Origin of Species by Means of Natural Selection*.

> When we compare the individuals of the same variety or sub-variety of our older cultivated plants and animals, one of the first points which strikes us is, that they generally differ more from each other than do the individuals of any one species or variety in a state of nature. And if we reflect on the vast diversity of the plants and animals which have been cultivated, and which have varied during all ages under the most different climates and treatment, we are driven to conclude that this great variability is due to our domestic productions having been raised under conditions of life not so uniform as, and somewhat different from, those to which the parent species had been exposed under nature. There is, also, some probability in the view propounded by Andrew Knight, that this variability may be partly

connected with excess of food. It seems clear that organic beings must be exposed during several generations to new conditions to cause any great amount of variation; and that, when the organisation has once begun to vary, it generally continues varying for many generations. No case is on record of a variable organism ceasing to vary under cultivation. Our oldest cultivated plants, such as wheat, still yield new varieties: our oldest domesticated animals are still capable of rapid improvement or modification.

This is one of the most famous books in the history of science—but it might not read like any scientific writing you've ever encountered, and the differences created by the passage of time can really throw you off as a reader. The moment we've chosen here seems to begin in the middle, but it's the very beginning of the book. Darwin doesn't introduce or explain the scientific concepts or terms he's working with. He keeps saying *we*, referring to the reader and the writer as one group—something that would almost never happen in twenty-first-century scientific writing. He also doesn't include a summary at the beginning or a declaration of the topic. In other words, the norms and expectations for science writing in the time in which this was written make it really difficult for modern readers to recognize the genre. If you can't figure out what the text you're reading is, it's hard to find a way to fit it into the narrative of your class or research or to make sense of it and then make use of it.

WHAT IS A "MOMENT"?

We use the word *moment* instead of *page* or *paragraph* or *scene* because it better reflects the way a text catches a reader's interest. When you think about a text, after all, you probably don't think in paragraphs or pages: Instead you think about an interaction, a conversation, a description ("when the narrator listens to his mother play piano," "that part where he talks about hand-washing in hospitals," "the point about cultivated plants versus the ones growing in the wild"). That's what we mean when we talk about a *moment*.

WHAT IS AN "EXHIBIT"?

Sometimes you will be asked to write about an *exhibit* rather than a moment in a text. When we say *exhibit*, we mean anything that you're looking at and analyzing that isn't a passage in a text (for example, a frame in a movie, an artwork, a microscope slide of a virus).

Basic Tools for Reading

You can begin to figure out what you're reading by taking a look at parts of the book you might otherwise skip. It's a good idea to read the blurb on the back of the book (or on your e-reader's summary page). For example, if you're reading Darwin's *On the Origin of Species*, it's helpful to know that the text was written in England in 1859 as a scientific treatise: That information will help you place the text in a context (during the Industrial Revolution, for instance) that may inform your reading. Once you know this, you can read with certain expectations in mind, which will help to minimize confusion and misdirection.

The back of the book isn't always helpful: For example, the back cover of the Norton edition of Mary Shelley's *Frankenstein; or, The Modern Prometheus*, another text we'll be working with in this book, gives us a lot of information about other materials the editors have included but not too much information on the text itself. But the introduction quickly lets you know some key facts—for instance, you immediately discover that *Frankenstein* is a novel written in 1818. The introduction also helps you avoid some serious misreading since it corrects something most readers assume: that the term *Frankenstein* refers to the monster. (It actually refers to the Swiss scientist, Doctor Victor Frankenstein, who sets himself the task of creating a human being.) You'll also find it useful to look at the table of contents, if there is one, because it gives a quick overview of how the book is divided up and what ground it will cover. (Darwin's table of contents breaks down every topic the text will cover so you can see the shape of the discussion before you get going.) This, too, will help you figure out exactly what you're reading.

If you've talked about the text in class at all, you'll also want to make use of your syllabus and your class notes. It's a good idea to look over this material before you start reading to remind yourself not only about the basics of the text but how it might fit into your overall course structure. For example, if you're reading e.e. cummings's "next to of course god america i" (we'll look at this in some depth later), your professor might have noted its year of publication, given some details about the author, or maybe even discussed some connections to poems you've read earlier in class. All of this will help you figure out how to read this piece.

Sometimes the genre of the piece is made clear by its context: If you know where the text is published, this will help you figure out how to read it. For example, it's helpful to know that the Atul Gawande essay on hospital practices we look at below, "The Checklist," was published in *The New Yorker*, which is dedicated to long-form journalism. Your approach to a piece in a popular magazine like *The New Yorker* will necessarily be different than your approach to, for instance, an essay on hospital practices in a peer-reviewed academic journal written by and for experts in the field. The subject may be exactly the same, but the venue matters because it affects the language used, the tone, the length, and so forth.

All of these things shape the way you read and the work you expect the text to do. Both pieces on hospital practices, for instance, may be trying to convince you of something—but while Gawande's is trying to inform a general public about a problem and a potential solution in an engaging way, an academic essay on the same subject may assume its readership understands a great deal about hospital practices, is familiar with specialized terminology, and understands current debates on the issue. Gawande's piece makes an argument, but it can carry readers along with storytelling instead of foregrounding its point up front; an academic piece needs to make its argument clear. By understanding the context of a piece, you can understand something about who it's written for and how it will set about convincing you of something.

2. What Is This Text About?

This may seem like an easy question, but it can actually be pretty tough to figure out what a text is talking about—especially when it's written in very formal or old-fashioned language, or it seems to begin in the middle of things. (Take another look at the Darwin excerpt, or cast your eye over the excerpt from John Milton's epic poem *Paradise Lost*, which appears later in this chapter, to see what we mean.) The work you've done to figure out what you're reading will help you here, of course, **but to find the subject of the text—the thing it's preoccupied with—you may still have to do some work.** You might start by reading the beginning of the text for key words. Darwin's text, for example, begins with repetitions or variations of the words *plants*, *animals*, *cultivation*, and *variation*. Just by noting the repetition of these words—even if you know nothing else about the text—you can start to figure out what Darwin's text is interested in. When you encounter a passage that seems to include a number of key words, it's a good idea to reread it, highlighting each key word that you've spotted so far. (The key words may change as you keep reading. That's okay—you're mapping your understanding of the text as you go.) You can figure out more about the text you're reading by asking some very preliminary questions. **Every text is its own world, with its own language, rules, and concerns.** You have to find your footing in this new world before you start forming ideas about what you're reading. You might ask questions like:

- what does this text seem to be emphasizing?
- what's its tone?
- what issues or concerns or subjects keep coming up?
- what's left out?

These first-order approaches will help you ground yourself in the world of the text, understand its preoccupations, and find its direction and argument. These are the "facts" of the text—and the entry-level data that you need in order to do anything at all with it.

PRACTICING: ASKING INFORMATIONAL QUESTIONS OF A TEXT

Note and keep track of basic information about your text by using a chart listing questions and answers. Try something like this.

QUESTION	INFORMATION
When was this text written?	
Where was it published?	
Who's the author?	
What's the genre?	
What audience does it seem to be written for?	
What's the book about?	

While every question may not be relevant to every text, these are the sorts of questions you should be able to answer quickly as you start reading. There is also a second order of summary questions to keep in mind as you move through a text for the first time. They might look like these.

If the material is nonfiction, what is the author's take on the topic?	
If the material is fiction or poetry, what are the preoccupations of the text?	
What's missing?	

READING ACTIVELY AND SUMMARIZING EFFECTIVELY

Active reading is the process of engaging with the material you're reading instead of letting the words slide passively by. It means asking questions as you read, tracking ideas and plot events, looking up words, listing, and charting. Active reading means reading with a pen in your hand, a habit that's useful in every field. Whether you're reading a novel, a history book, or a nonfiction essay, keeping track of the material and your ideas about it will always give you a firmer foundation from which to move forward.

The first step in active reading is keeping track of what's going on. This is where summary comes in. Summarizing is the act of telling the story of the text to yourself. This, too, may feel pretty basic, but that doesn't mean it's a step you should skip. If you're not confident about events and characters, or about the key points of a nonfiction piece's argument, you won't be able to read closely because you can't place a passage in context or understand its questions and implications. Missed plot pieces or relationships can be fatal to an effective analysis. For instance, if you're reading *Let the Great World Spin* by Colum McCann and you miss the fact that Corrigan is the narrator's brother, as the opening paragraph (found later in this chapter) indicates, you'll have difficulty following what's going on as the novel moves forward.

Here are some tools for summarizing well.

MAKING THE TEXT YOUR OWN: ANNOTATING AND MARKING

Unless you have a photographic memory, note taking is integral to effective summary. It's the first step in tracking what happens in a text and recording your initial ideas about it. An effective note-taking system records information that you can **go back to** (by reviewing passages you found interesting and reminding yourself of your thinking) and **move forward from** (by using your notes and summaries as a starting point for asking more questions of the text).

You'll want to make different kinds of notes as you read and create summaries each time you stop reading. These notes will be really helpful down the line. And even though this note-taking process will slow down your reading a bit, it will save you time later: Instead of searching for passages you were sure you'd remember or trying to figure out your thoughts on a particular topic, you'll have a record of your responses and ideas. These will be the starting point for your essay.

The basic moves of annotation are:

- underlining or highlighting interesting lines or words.
- making marginal notes about what you've marked (quick definitions, basic summaries or paraphrases, notes or questions about what you're reading, and connections you've noticed to other parts of the text).
- doing "wrap-ups" at the end of each reading session.

Underlining, Highlighting, and Making Notes in the Margins

If you're like most students, you're probably already accustomed to doing a fair bit of underlining or highlighting in your books. These are crucial operations—but they're not sufficient on their own. If you don't make notes next to that underlining, you're wasting your time, because you'll end up doing the work twice. When you're reading, you think you'll remember why you highlighted a particular sentence, but by the time you start working on your paper, chances are you'll have forgotten. You'll have to read the passage again to remind yourself of its context and the basics of what it's talking about, and you still might not be able to retrace what interested you.

Effective marking always includes your own words—in the margins, at the top and bottom of the page, and (if you've got something more to say) inside the front and back covers. The more you write in the book, the more material you'll have to work with as you move forward. Books are a sea of typed text; your written notes will stand out and provide a quick way to remind yourself of what you know or what you want to know. A lot of students don't like to write in their books—but if you want to say something about a text, you need to. (This is why it's a bad idea to share a text with your roommate or to use a library book: You need a copy you can write in. The same holds true with electronic formats. Don't use an e-reader unless it has an annotation or note-taking function.)

Another reason to write in your text is to break down its authority. When you're reading a text that's been around for a long time or carries a lot of weight, it can feel presumptuous to question or analyze it. You might feel as though everything has already been said about it. That's especially true with famous and difficult texts like *On the Origin of Species* or *Paradise Lost*. But **when you make notes in the margins, ask questions, and jot down ideas, you start talking back to the text. This breaks down its authority and gives you permission to say something about it.**

To take effective notes, **start by briefly summarizing in the margins.** Your comments can be as short as a word or three: For instance, in reading the first paragraph of McCann, it might be worth noting, "narr's family: piano." Summary notes serve as a map of what happens and when: They can save you a lot of time otherwise spent flipping through your book, trying to remember where a particular event occurred. They're also very helpful in assessing whether you're actually "getting" the text: Do you understand what's going on? If you can't summarize, that means you need to reread the passage at hand. It may very well mean that you need to look up words or concepts or references you aren't sure about, and it's often a sign that you need to go back to an earlier point in the text where you knew what was happening and start again from there. It's easy to get carried along by a text and end up missing stuff. Note taking in the margins can help you avoid that.

Even at the summary level, engaging effectively with a text can be pretty complicated. Let's take a look, for example, at the opening to *Paradise Lost*.

> OF Mans First Disobedience, and the Fruit
> Of that Forbidden Tree, whose mortal tast
> Brought Death into the World, and all our woe,
> With loss of Eden, till one greater Man
> Restore us, and regain the blissful Seat,
> Sing Heav'nly Muse, that on the secret top
> Of Oreb, or of Sinai, didst inspire
> That Shepherd, who first taught the chosen Seed,
> In the Beginning how the Heav'ns and Earth
> Rose out of Chaos: Or if Sion Hill
> Delight thee more, and Siloa's Brook that flow'd
> Fast by the Oracle of God; I thence
> Invoke thy aid to my adventrous Song,

That with no middle flight intends to soar
Above th' Aonian Mount, while it pursues
Things unattempted yet in Prose or Rhime.
And chiefly Thou O Spirit, that dost prefer
Before all Temples th' upright heart and pure,
Instruct me, for Thou know'st; Thou from the first
Wast present, and with mighty wings outspread
Dove-like satst brooding on the vast Abyss
And mad'st it pregnant: What in me is dark
Illumin, what is low raise and support;
That to the highth of this great Argument
I may assert Eternal Providence,
And justifie the wayes of God to men.

On first read, Milton's opening may look impenetrable. But it's possible to figure out what's going on, even in an archaic and difficult text like this one. You can try the following basic operations to help you find some ground beneath your feet and begin summarizing a new text.

- **READING OUT LOUD:** saying the text to yourself so you can better grasp the meaning
- **REARRANGING:** reordering the language of the text so it reads more like standard modern-day English
- **DEFINING WORDS:** looking up words that are totally unfamiliar—as well as those that are used in unfamiliar ways
- **PARAPHRASING:** restating the text's language in your own words
- **TAGGING:** keeping track of speakers and shifts in the action

Reading Out Loud

The first step in analyzing new material is to read it out loud. Reading a text out loud gives you another means of letting the language sink in. Saying the words and hearing their rhythms will make them more familiar; often your ear will recognize a word your eye might not. Many words in old texts are still part of our common language, though in slightly different forms. For example, *illumin* may look foreign on the page, but when you say it out loud, it sounds a lot like *illuminate*.

READING VS. LISTENING

People learn language by using four operations (or competencies): reading, writing, speaking, and listening. You're most likely to learn and understand written material when you make use of all of these. But different people learn in different ways: For example, some people find reading aloud much more effective than reading on the page, while others find that they comprehend better when they read silently. Try out a variety of operations to see what works best for you. If you find that hearing a text read aloud is helpful, you may want to get it in audiobook form. Most classic works assigned in college can be found in this format. However, listening to an audiobook doesn't mean you can skip the kinds of note taking we're talking about here. You need to read along as you listen to the text and make your notes on the page. And you still need to do the wrap-ups we talk about later in this chapter each time you stop.

A key rule to keep in mind when reading poetry aloud is that you shouldn't stop reading at the end of a line unless you come to a period or other end-of-sentence punctuation. And when you start breaking the poem down, punctuation can provide you with clues about how words may be grouped together.

Rearranging

When you're reading a text like Milton's, you might start by rearranging the words so that they sound like the kind of English you're accustomed to. Modern-day English usually proceeds like so: subject, verb, object. For example:

He [*subject*] hit [*verb*] the ball [*object*].

Milton often reverses this order so that the subject is last and the object is first. In our example, that would read like this.

The ball hit he.

Knowing this will help you rearrange his words so they read more easily. For example, in the last stanza, Milton says:

What in me is dark Illumin.

In this phrase, the order is:

What in me is dark [*object*] Illumin [*verb*].

We can reorder the phrase so that it's in the order we're used to.

> Illumin [*verb*] what in me is dark [*object*].

The subject in this sentence is implied: Milton is talking to something or someone that he hopes will do this "illumining." Similarly,

> what is low raise and support

becomes

> Raise and support what is low.

This may seem pretty simple, but sometimes the sentence parts that need reordering are spread across a much longer span. Check out the opening of Milton's
epic again.

> OF Mans First Disobedience, and the Fruit
> Of that Forbidden Tree, whose mortal tast
> Brought Death into the World, and all our woe,
> With loss of Eden, till one greater Man
> Restore us, and regain the blissful Seat,
> Sing Heav'nly Muse,

In this very long section of this very long sentence, the subject and verb are five
lines below the beginning of the object phrase. If you were to make sense of this
in modern-day English, you'd have to move the verb and its subject all the way
up to the very beginning of the sentence. It would then read like this.

> Sing, Heav'nly Muse, of Man's First Disobedience, and the fruit of that
> forbidden tree …

To figure out how the sentence works, we began with something that you may
have noticed right away: In contemporary English, sentences don't start with *of*.
It would sound very strange, for instance, to say, "Of chocolate I am fond." That's
because the subject is *I*, the verb is *am*, the object is *chocolate*, and the word *of*
alerts you to the object. (*What is it I'm fond of? Oh, yes. Chocolate. Without that* of,
I would be merely fond.) When you see a sentence that begins in this way, it alerts
you to the fact that you need to find the verb that goes with the object. Finding
the verb will lead you to the subject. Finding the verb, in fact, is often the key to
what's going on in all kinds of convoluted sentences.

Because sentences like Milton's are so confusing, it can be useful to bring some visual clarity to them: It's helpful to designate a highlighter color for subjects, another for verbs, and another for objects and to mark the parts of speech as you go along. Since texts like *Paradise Lost* are often printed in small, dense type, it can also be useful to type out sections of the text you're working with on a separate page, triple-spaced, and mark the parts of speech that way so they're easy to see. We highlighted the objects in purple, the subjects in blue, and the verbs in green.

> Of Mans First Disobedience, and the Fruit
> Of that Forbidden Tree, whose mortal tast
> Brought Death into the World, and all our woe,
> With loss of *Eden*, till one greater Man
> Restore us, and regain the blissful Seat,
> Sing Heav'nly Muse

Defining

Once you've rearranged the sentences so they make sense, the next step is to define any words that are unfamiliar or that are used in an unfamiliar way. Looking up words is as basic and useful a tool as turning on the light when you walk into a room. If you don't know the meaning of a word in a passage you're examining (the general meaning, the way it's used there, the range of meanings a word may have), you can't read the passage closely: If you're guessing, approximating, or defining from context, you aren't being precise enough.

With many texts, you can use a standard dictionary, but Milton wrote *Paradise Lost* in 1674; a lot of words have changed meaning or have fallen out of use. Look up old-fashioned words in the *Oxford English Dictionary*, which not only defines the word but gives you examples of how it was used in the past. Here, for instance, the OED says that *illumin* (which it spells *illumine*) is a verb meaning "to light up, to shed light upon; to shine upon or into." It also says that this verb is the same as *illuminate*. (The easiest way to use the OED is in electronic form. Most schools subscribe to the OED online.)

Let's look at that first part of the sentence again, the one we started rearranging above. Here's what it looks like rearranged and written as if it were a regular sentence rather than poetry.

Sing, Heavenly Muse, of man's first disobedience and the fruit of that forbidden tree whose mortal taste brought death and all our woe into the world with loss of Eden, until one greater Man restore us and regain the blissful seat.

It's already clearer and more approachable, but some of the words and phrases still don't make sense. Another way of defining unfamiliar language or concepts is to use the information included in the book, usually found in either footnotes or endnotes.

In this edition, for instance, the notes tell us that *man* in the first sentence doesn't refer to an individual man but to all of humankind. They also tell us that when Milton says "one greater Man," with *man* capitalized, he's talking about Jesus. *Muse* refers to the Greek idea of the nine muses (music, dance, theater, poetry, and so on), but since Milton is writing an explicitly Christian story, he needs a Christian muse who's up in Heaven. According to the notes, he's talking to the Holy Ghost. Odds are you know what *Eden* is, but just in case, you might want to look it up. It's defined as the home of Adam and Eve and also as Paradise.

As we mentioned, when you encounter words that you know but that are used in unexpected ways, you should make your way to the dictionary. Milton often uses words that are still part of modern English but that meant something very different in his day. *Seat*, for instance, obviously means something like "chair" to modern readers. But in this passage, it's used in an unfamiliar way; if you tried to make the sentence work using the familiar meaning, it wouldn't make sense. The note in the text reveals that in Milton's day, *seat* meant both *home* and *throne*, so it has the sense of a great, elevated home. If there's no note, the OED is your go-to.

Paraphrasing

Paraphrasing means putting the language of the text in your own words, and doing this will help you engage with the text. It's also the simplest way to see if you understand what you're reading. It doesn't change the poem; it's just a way for you to get a better handle on it. The text is much less fragile than you may think, and your work with it won't break it. You don't need to change every single word when you're paraphrasing for yourself: If you're sure you understand what something means and you don't have a better word for it at hand, it's okay to leave it be.

But it's important to paraphrase any word whose meaning seems at all unclear to you so that you're certain you understand what you're looking at. Be sure that you're actually rewriting a given passage in your own words: When you're summarizing a chunk of text and you leave a significant piece unchanged, it can be a sign that you're not really engaging with the text. We'll talk about this more in the wrap-up section.

It's much easier to paraphrase after you've rearranged the text so that it reads like modern-day English. When all the pieces are in order, you can ensure that you address all of them in your paraphrase. Here's a paraphrase based on the rearrangement above.

> Tell, Holy Ghost, how humans first disobeyed God by eating the forbidden fruit from the tree of death and how that brought death and all our sorrow into the world and made mankind lose paradise until Jesus brought humans back to paradise.

Now that you've paraphrased this passage, you understand a critical part of the story Milton's telling: It's about how Adam and Eve disobeyed God by eating the fruit from a tree that was prohibited to them. Not only does this disobedience cost them their home in Paradise, but according to Milton it also brings death and all of humankind's sorrow into the world.

Tagging

Paradise Lost is a particularly complicated text, and characters' voices sometimes run into one another, so it's a good idea to keep track of the basic setup: who's speaking, to whom, and when. A text doesn't always provide dialogue tags like "he said" or "the snake said to Eve"; even when it does, the tags may not always be clear, so it can be easy to get mixed up. If you attach a name to each change of speaker in a particularly confusing section of your text, you'll have a quick visual cue of who's speaking when.

This can be useful even when there isn't direct dialogue. Sometimes, for instance, the narrator may be speaking for him- or herself, while at other times he or she may be recounting what someone else has said. It's helpful to keep track of this as you go so that when you return to the text, you know who is speaking and you don't mistakenly attribute an opinion or idea belonging to one character to another.

Another form of tagging that's useful in texts that have very long sentences—whether in poetry or prose—is the tagging and tracking of pronouns. Just in case you missed it in your high school grammar class, here's a quick primer in pronouns, which are words that stand in for nouns.

> Michael threw the ball to the other boys. They caught it and threw it back to him.

In this example, *they* stands in for *boys*; *it* stands in for *the ball*, and *him* stands in for *Michael*. *They*, *it*, and *him* are pronouns that replace *Michael*, *the ball*, and *the other boys*. When that happens, the nouns that the pronouns replace are called antecedents.

In old-fashioned writing, a pronoun can be very far away from the noun it's standing in for; if you take the time to explicitly link the pronoun to its antecedent, you'll have a much better understanding of the sentence. The guideline to keep in mind when you're doing this work is that the pronoun is always in the form that matches the form of its antecedent.

For instance, in the sentence above, *the other boys* needs a plural pronoun. A single male pronoun means you're looking for a male name. Pronouns also have to indicate whether they're functioning as subjects or objects. (As a reminder, a subject is the word in the sentence that is doing an action: In "The girl threw the ball," the subject is *the girl*. An object is the word that is receiving the action: In "The girl threw the ball," the object is *the ball*.) An object pronoun replaces an antecedent that is an object of the sentence: "The girl threw **it**." Similarly, a subject pronoun replaces an antecedent that is the subject of the sentence: "**She** threw the ball."

The simplest way to keep track of who's who is by highlighting each pronoun and its antecedent. In this example, the antecedent is highlighted in purple and the pronouns are highlighted in blue. (This passage is from later on in Book I of *Paradise Lost*.)

> Th' infernal Serpent. He it was, whose guile
> Stird up with Envy and Revenge, deceiv'd [35]
> The Mother of Mankind, what time his Pride
> Had cast him out from Heav'n, with all his Host
> Of Rebel Angels, by whose aid aspiring
> To set himself in Glory above his Peers,

He trusted to have equal'd the most High, [40]
If he oppos'd; and with ambitious aim
Against the Throne and Monarchy of God
Rais'd impious War in Heav'n and Battel proud
With vain attempt. Him the Almighty Power
Hurld headlong flaming from th' Ethereal Skie

In this case, all the pronouns (*he, him, his, himself*) go back to *Th' Infernal Serpent* (their antecedent). In this example, the pronouns aren't all that confusing—there's no one else in the passage they could refer to—but it's still useful to do the tagging since, for example, that last *Him* is more than ten lines away from the antecedent (*Th' Infernal Serpent*). This kind of tagging and tracking will also help as you rearrange the text: Seeing that *Him* is an object pronoun reminds you that it needs to go after the subject (*the Almighty Power*) and the verb.

Reading Old-Fashioned Nonfiction

Just as reading a poem written hundreds of years ago can be challenging, reading nonfiction from earlier eras can also be difficult. In part this is because the author naturally assumes that his readership is beginning from the same readerly assumptions that he is. Since writers in historical periods before our own (or from different cultures or languages) expect that their readers will be able to interpret their references and cultural asides, they may start their work in what feels to a contemporary reader like the middle of things because they assume that readers of their time know where the author's work fits into existing discussion of the issue. (We do this, too: Think of all the times you've read a blog post that begins with something like, "You know that guy that did that thing everybody's been talking about?" Well, you only know because you're part of the culture.)

Take a look once again at the excerpt from Darwin's *On the Origin of Species*. This section is at the very beginning of the first chapter, "Variation Under Domestication," which comes after Darwin's historical sketch and introduction. The first section of the chapter is titled "Causes of Variability." Here's how it starts out.

When we compare the individuals of the same variety or sub-variety of our older cultivated plants and animals, one of the first points which strikes us is, that they generally differ more from each other than do the individuals of any one species or variety in a state of nature. And if we reflect on the vast diversity of the plants and animals which have been cultivated, and which have varied during all ages under the most different climates and treatment, we are driven to conclude that this great variability is due to our domestic productions having been raised under conditions of life not so uniform as, and somewhat different from, those to which the parent species had been exposed under nature. There is, also, some probability in the view propounded by Andrew Knight, that this variability may be partly connected with excess of food. It seems clear that organic beings must be exposed during several generations to new conditions to cause any great amount of variation; and that, when the organisation has once begun to vary, it generally continues varying for many generations. No case is on record of a variable organism ceasing to vary under cultivation. Our oldest cultivated plants, such as wheat, still yield new varieties: our oldest domesticated animals are still capable of rapid improvement or modification.

The concept Darwin is talking about here is not actually that complicated: He's saying that plants and animals cultivated by humans adapt to fit their human-made environments over several generations. But it can be tough to figure this out, especially if you're launching yourself into the text with no real understanding of what it's supposed to be about. There's no "Here's what I'm talking about" statement; he goes straight into "When we compare the individuals …" as though we're all busy comparing individuals among plants and animals all the time and fully expect him to talk about it. (Darwin's theory was controversial even in his own time, so he was careful to align it with other work that was already published on the topic of what we now call evolution. By starting in the middle, he gives the impression that he's not breaking new ground here: He's just picking up a conversation that's already ongoing.)

The language of the text is old-fashioned and formal, and the sentences are quite long, with many subordinate clauses, so it can be tough to follow the line of thinking. Take this sentence, for example.

> And if we reflect on the vast diversity of the plants and animals which have been cultivated, and which have varied during all ages under the most different climates and treatment, we are driven to conclude that this great variability is due to our domestic productions having been raised under conditions of life not so uniform as, and somewhat different from, those to which the parent-species had been exposed under nature.

This is not exactly a straightforward expression of the idea that different types of cultivation lead plants and animals to adapt in different ways. Even the look of the text can be off-putting since Darwin's work is often published in an old-style, dense typeface unfamiliar to modern readers. All of this can mean that when you begin working with this type of material, you may find that you read right over it because you're waiting to figure out what's going on. Or you may get bogged down in individual words and phrases, which keep you from deriving meaning from the whole thing. Both approaches waste your time and ensure that you'll have to read the material again just to figure out the basics of what's going on. So here are some tips for reading this kind of work more effectively.

- **READ THE SUPPORTING MATERIALS FOR THE TEXT.** As we noted earlier, supporting materials can help you find your feet in working with a new text—and that's definitely true with *Origin*. Most versions of *On the Origin of Species* include the author's own introduction. As is the case with many classic texts, a modern introduction is usually included as well. Most modern introductions to *Origin* cover some history, the basics of Darwin's argument, a sense of how people responded when the book first came out, and its place in discussions today. The table of contents gives you a broad sense of what the text is trying to cover or discuss, as do Darwin's chapter headers, which have a lot of subheadings (common in nineteenth-century texts). It's useful to remind yourself of how the text fits into the course progression; if your professor has introduced the material in class, you should also look back at your notes.

- **READ IN LARGE CHUNKS, AND THEN GO BACK.** If you stop at every word you don't understand or every reference you don't get, you'll never get through the reading—and you'll be so busy sweating the small stuff that you probably won't understand the bigger picture. In this case, for example, you might get stuck on that reference to "Andrew Knight"—who's he?—and lose the thread of the discussion. If you pause to look up "uniform" on a first read, the same thing happens. Similarly, if you find yourself confused by the language of a text, you may find that you focus on isolated chunks that seem clear to you. But when you do this, you run the risk of taking these pieces out of context, which can lead you to misread the text.

When you first read a historical text, you need to trust yourself a bit. Get through a chunk of it, and then note what you think is happening in that piece. You'll find you often understand more than you think—and sometimes obscure meanings become clearer as you move on. (This is particularly true of philosophical and theoretical texts, which often begin with very confusing principles and then give examples that make everything much easier to understand. In the case of Darwin, those long sentences with the multiple clauses become much clearer when you read all the way through to the end of each sentence.)

Older texts are often very wordy, and while that can be annoying, it also makes reading for comprehension *easier*, since these texts generally say the same thing several times over. This paragraph of Darwin's, for example, basically consists of several variations on the idea that cultivated plants and animals adapt over several generations, depending on conditions. It's worth marking words or concepts you don't understand with a particular color so that, if this bit turns out to be significant, you can look things up.

- **AT THE END OF EACH CHUNK OF READING, NOTE QUESTIONS THAT COME UP.** If you see something strange, write it down. For example, the reference to food seems sort of random—does it make sense in terms of the idea of variation Darwin is talking about? If he's suggesting that cultivated plants and animals are different from those in the wild because the conditions of cultivation are different, is that the same as how much food a plant or animal has? Read skeptically: Sure, Darwin was a world-changing, amazing scientist, but that doesn't mean every one of his ideas holds water. Look for the places where the argument seems strange or doubtful.

In general, when you're reading nonfiction, you always want to:

- figure out what the central argument or claim is, even if it's only implied.
- think about what you think about the argument. Go beyond "I agree" or "I disagree": What questions do you have about the claim? Does it contain conflicting ideas? Does it contradict itself? How is the claim set up in terms of logic and ideas? Think through what makes sense and what doesn't and why.

- look at language. For example, you may notice that while Darwin's text uses formal language, it also uses *we*, *our*, and *us* a lot—from the very first sentence. How might this affect the way you read the piece and think about the ideas? What work does it do in terms of advancing—or detracting from or complicating—the point the text is making?

Reading Contemporary Poetry

Poetry, even the contemporary kind, can seem fairly intimidating because readers often feel like they need to determine the "right" reading of a poem and fear they're not "getting" it. Poetry plays with metaphor and simile more than other types of literature, it may or may not be narrative, and it's often elliptical, leaving out connections between words, lines, or ideas. But you're not expected to "make sense" of a poem by turning it into a coherent narrative. Like any other literary form, poetry invites interpretation, not "solving" for a single right answer. And the very strangeness of poems can actually help you out: Because they don't read like natural language, they force you to pay attention, and because they don't hide their strangeness, it's easier for you to find material to focus on.

Look, for instance, at this well-known poem from 1927 by the American poet e.e. cummings.

> "next to of course god america i
> love you land of the pilgrims' and so forth oh
> say can you see by the dawn's early my
> country 'tis of centuries come and go
> and are no more what of it we should worry
> in every language even deafanddumb
> thy sons acclaim your glorious name by gorry
> by jingo by gee by gosh by gum
> why talk of beauty what could be more beaut-
> iful than these heroic happy dead
> who rushed like lions to the roaring slaughter
> they did not stop to think they died instead
> then shall the voice of liberty be mute?"
>
> He spoke. And drank rapidly a glass of water

When you read this poem straight through for the first time, it can look like nonsense, a flood of words and partial quotes—"land of the pilgrims," "oh say can you see by the dawn's early"—all jammed together. There seems to be something about America and patriotism going on, and maybe something about fighting for your country—but that's just a cloud of meaning rather than a clear sense of what the poem's about. And beyond those few semifamiliar phrases, this poem still seems fairly random.

To take the poem apart and analyze it, you'll need to slow down.

- **WRITE DOWN YOUR FIRST IMPRESSIONS.** Jot down what you think the poem is about and any strange or interesting things that you notice about it (anything is fair game).
- **NOTE ANY INFORMATION YOU HAVE ABOUT THE POEM, SUCH AS ITS HISTORICAL MOMENT, THE POET, AND SO ON.** Knowing something about when a text is written helps you contextualize it. (You might read this poem differently, for instance, if it had been written during the war in Iraq.)
- **READ THE POEM LINE BY LINE; READ IT OUT LOUD AS WELL AS SILENTLY.** Because poetry is a genre that often depends on the ear as much as the eye, it's always useful to listen to it as well as read it.
- **THINK ABOUT WHAT THE POEM LOOKS LIKE.** Poems are visual as well as aural, and some poets treat their chosen form like visual art. How long are the lines, for example? Is there a particular pattern? Some poems have a very particular shape; some seem uniform except, for instance, for one long line. Look at the spacing between lines: Is it consistent? If not, where does the consistency break down?
- **LOOK AT ANYTHING THAT SEEMS STRANGE IN THE POEM.** Where are the line breaks? How does the punctuation work? For example, did you notice on your first reading that up until the last line, the poem is mostly in quotation marks, indicating a single speaker? What about the fact that almost nothing is capitalized? What about the fact that none of those phrases you recognize is finished?

These tools will help you begin thinking about the poem you're reading. You might also want to look at poetic devices. For example, take a look at the rhyme scheme. Some poems don't rhyme at all; others have a very rigid or traditional rhyme scheme.

In the cummings poem, it's easy to miss the rhyme scheme entirely—it doesn't look like it rhymes—but if you pay careful attention, you'll notice that *i* in line 1 rhymes with *my* in line 3, while *oh* in line 2 rhymes with *go* in line 4. Then the rhyme scheme gets weird: *worry* doesn't exactly rhyme with *gorry*, and *beaut* definitely doesn't rhyme with *slaughter*. This breakdown of the rhyme scheme is worth paying attention to because it's a place where the poem is disrupted: It's like a flashing light, telling you to look carefully at what's being said and how it's being said. Noting this now will help you out later, when you're working on your essay.

Reading Narrative Fiction

Sometimes the hardest text to read closely is the simplest, most straightforward one. It's easy to see weird things when the writing is weird to start with—when you're reading poetry, for instance, or really conceptual writers like James Joyce or Virginia Woolf. But when the prose seems straightforward, it can be hard to get beyond the surface or to do more than just read for content. Take this passage, for instance—the first paragraph of Book One in Colum McCann's 2009 novel, *Let the Great World Spin*.

> One of the many things my brother, Corrigan, and I loved about our mother was that she was a fine musician. She kept a small radio on top of the Steinway in the living room of our house in Dublin and on Sunday afternoons, after scanning whatever stations we could find, Radio Eireann or BBC, she raised the lacquered wing of the piano, spread her dress out at the wooden stool, and tried to copy the piece from memory: jazz riffs and Irish ballads and, if we found the right station, old Hoagy Carmichael tunes. Our mother played with a natural touch, even though she suffered from a hand which she had broken many times. We never knew the origin of the break: it was something left in silence. When she finished playing she would lightly rub the back of her wrist. I used to think of the notes still trilling through the bones, as if they could skip from one to the other, over the breakage. I can still after all these years sit in the museum of those afternoons and recall the light spilling across the carpet. At times our mother put her arms around us both, and then guided our hands so we could clang down hard on the keys.

There's more than one way to read fiction like this. If you're reading for leisure, you might just read it through and move on, passively swallowing it rather than engaging with it. Nothing wrong with that—but it's generally not useful in college. On the other hand, your high school classes might have gotten you in the habit of reading for plot or theme or character—in other words, for summary of one sort or another. As we've said, summary is useful—it's the critical first work you do before going on to more analytical work. But the kind of summary we're talking about here is more concerned with figuring out what's going on in the text than with playing a "Where's Waldo?" game of finding themes. That's because when you decide that a piece of fiction has a particular theme, it's easy to feel like your work is done—when the reality is that identifying a theme doesn't offer you much of an opportunity to ask questions or think through your ideas.

Here's a basic summary of the passage.

> The narrator is recounting a memory of his or her mother playing piano, copying songs from the radio, while Corrigan (the narrator's brother) and the narrator listen. Their mother, the narrator recalls, was a good piano player even though she had a hand that had been broken. Sometimes she helped the narrator and Corrigan bang on the keys.

So far, so good. You might also note where the story is set (Dublin) and when (sometime when people listened to the radio on Sunday afternoons and heard a lot of jazz, so a while ago). It's a good idea to keep a running tally in the margins of what's going on and to do a wrap-up of what you've read each time you stop. (We spend more time on wrap-ups later in this chapter.)

But in this case, straightforward summary doesn't do much work for you because the text seems so transparent that you often just end up rewriting what's already on the page. This won't help you very much as you move toward essay writing. If you don't slow down and pay attention with a text like this, it's easy to let crucial details pass you by. (One trick to help you slow down, if you tend to read quickly: Cover the page with a piece of paper, and move the paper down beneath each line you read. That will stop you from skipping ahead quickly and missing things.)

In reading this kind of text, you might look for strange or missing things on the level of events in the text. You might note, for example, that you don't know anything about the narrator: He or she doesn't bother introducing him- or herself. You have some idea of where and when the memory the narrator is recounting takes place—but where and when is the narrator speaking *from*? We don't really know anything about Corrigan, either, though we do learn some things about the mother. And a central fact about the mother—that she's a musician whose hand has been "broken many times"—is also unexplained. These are the kinds of things that are worth noting in the margins or inside the front cover of the text.

Even at this early stage, you might want to ask some basic questions about the language used to express events. For example, if the mother is guiding the kids' hands, why are they "clanging down hard on the keys"? That's strange given the fact that she's serious about her playing. It's also useful to pay attention to tone: "the lacquered wing of the piano" has a different tone from "she was a fine musician." "Lacquered wing" is poetic language, whereas "she was a fine musician" is straightforward. The piano seems to resemble a stuffed bird, which is also strange.

You might also note words or references you don't understand ("Radio Eirann," for instance, or "Hoagy Carmichael"). And you might look up words that you think you know but that are used in strange ways in the section you're reading (like *trilling*, for example).

Not every passage requires close attention. But opening passages are particularly important because they set up the story, give you some preliminary information, and pull you into the narrative. If it turns out, for instance, that Corrigan and the narrator's mother are central characters, this opening scene will begin to shape the way you read them, so you want to note it. And if it turns out that they don't matter at all, then it might be worth going back to the opening and thinking about what they're doing there, right up front.

Reading Contemporary Nonfiction

Like contemporary fiction, a work of contemporary nonfiction may seem pretty straightforward, but it's not always clear what you're expected to do with it. Once you've figured out what it's about, the summary of what it says, and whether or not you agree with—or like—its premise, what else can you do?

Take, for instance, Atul Gawande's article "The Checklist," published in *The New Yorker* on December 10, 2007. The title implies that this story is about some sort of list, but Gawande takes his time getting to his point. First he talks about how amazing modern medicine is, and then he gives an example, the story of a three-year-old girl who fell into a frozen fishpond and was underwater for thirty minutes. Where, you might ask, is all of this going? It's not until a column into the second page that Gawande seems to get to the idea he's really talking about: He tells us that keeping the little girl alive was really complicated and that because medicine is so complicated and hospitals are such complex places, things go wrong and people make mistakes.

But then Gawande leaves checklists behind again. He tells a story about a patient of his who nearly died in the ICU because the lines feeding drugs into his body were infected; he talks about specialization and then goes on to discuss an airplane competition in Dayton, Ohio, in 1935. And that story, finally, leads to a discussion of the development of the checklist in medicine—five pages into a nine-page article. But a clear argument about checklists is still not evident: We get, instead, the history of how a doctor at Johns Hopkins decided in 2001 to try to implement checklists in ICUs to stop line infections.

This article is interesting; it's easy to read, and the stories are pretty good. But what are you supposed to do with it? You're not picking it up as an interesting piece of leisure reading, after all. Perhaps your engineering or biology professor has assigned you this piece, along with your usual textbook reading, or perhaps you're reading it in a composition class. In either case, you're expected to have some ideas about the piece, and you may have to write about it. How do you read this type of nonfiction for a college class?

To begin, you might treat this form of nonfiction the way you would a piece of historical nonfiction like the Darwin piece. *The New Yorker*, where the article is published, does a lot of long-form nonfiction storytelling. Knowing that, you can presume that, even if you're reading this for a pre-med or engineering class, the author isn't making a technical argument or providing a block of information to be learned. That tells you something about what to read for: If this piece isn't full of data, you must have been assigned it for some other purpose.

As with historical nonfiction, read in chunks and note a few words of summary after each chunk (a few paragraphs, a page, a section—whenever you stop reading). This will help you think through the purpose of each section without getting bogged down in details. This kind of wrap-up can be really useful when you're ready to return to the article after your first read and think it through analytically and structurally.

As you read, think about tone. For example, the text uses terms like "he is the kind of guy who …" but it also has sentences like "… they helped with memory recall, especially with mundane matters that are easily overlooked in patients undergoing more drastic events." If you pay attention to these tone shifts instead of just taking them in stride and reading past them, you can start to ask about the effect of these different tones. What do these shifts do?

It's also critical to look for the argument or claim the piece is making. Nonfiction writing usually makes a claim, even when that claim is hard to see. As you move through the article, look for places where the text is asserting something. How do those places relate to one another? The overall structure of a nonfiction piece can be as important as the language it uses in setting up arguments. Gawande's piece doesn't deliver its argument up front: Does that approach help to get you on the side of the piece's argument somehow? Does it soften you up?

Above all, think about questions. Once you know what the piece is saying, where do you see strange things or things that seem extraneous or contradictory? Are there gaps between what you see as you scan through the piece and what you notice when you look closely? Instead of just thinking about the overall argument and whether or not you're convinced, look closely and specifically at each instance of claim making and think through what you see at each point—then think about what it all adds up to and whether the sum is really convincing.

Choosing What to Pay Attention To

No matter what kind of text you're reading, you will inevitably make choices about what seems interesting and important to you and what falls lower on your list of priorities. To a casual reader, every event in a text might carry equal weight as part of the story, but your job, when you're reading to write, is to make choices about what you think is important or interesting or strange. Your choices may not be the same as those of other readers—even other readers in your class. That's okay. Everybody reads differently.

For example, as you work with the cummings poem, you may find yourself wondering about the following lines.

> in every language even deafanddumb
> thy sons acclaim your glorious name

… and you may find that you're paying much less attention to all the partial quotes from patriotic American speeches and songs. That's fine. If you give everything equal significance, or, worse, if you take someone else's word about what's important in a given text or passage, you'll have a hard time coming up with a compelling question or idea and you won't be able to tell your own story about the text.

MAKING LANGUAGE VISUAL: GRAPHING, LISTING, CHARTING, AND DRAWING

If you tend to be a visual learner, it's useful to get into the habit of graphing, drawing, or charting information as you move through the text. The idea here is to see your learning style as a strength and use it to work with the text effectively and efficiently. People have a bad habit of labeling themselves as "science and math people" or "English and history people" or "visual people," and they tend to assume that those skills are entirely separate. In fact, all kinds of readers can use visual methods to better understand their ideas and turn them into words. And people who are particularly drawn to the visual may find these methods especially useful.

Here's an example of what we mean: An architecture student recently showed his professor a draft of a grant proposal he was working on. He wanted to study the use of tools. When the professor asked the student why he wanted to do this, he said, "Because tools encapsulate something important about being a human being."

This felt kind of vague to the professor, so she asked him to explain. He said, "I know what I mean, but I don't have the words to explain it."

So she sketched this drawing and said to the student, "Tell me what happens if a tool comes into the picture."

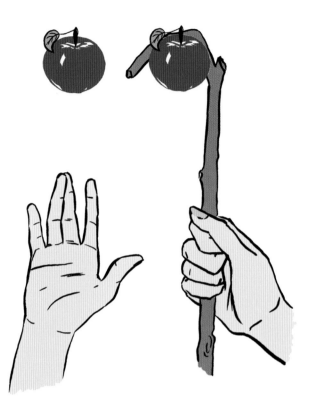

The student drew a stick and then narrated a story about how the tool let the man get what he wanted.

That one word, *wanted*, crystallized what he thought was important about tools and let him write the missing sentence.

> By letting people obtain or achieve things they otherwise could not, tools are a measure of human desire.

This sentence lets his readers know why he was so interested in tools and why he thought they were worth studying. And the student found the words to express this crucial information by using a simple drawing that helped him focus on the relationship he was exploring.

Thinking spatially or in numbers or images doesn't make you a less capable reader or writer—it just means that you have another set of methods at your disposal.

There are innumerable ways to make a text visual. For example, to keep track of things, you might decide to create a genealogical table or list, or to chart events as you read. This is especially useful when you're reading a novel, where the relationships between characters can be confusing. By the end of the third chapter of *Frankenstein*, for example, your list of characters might look something like this.

List of Characters So Far
- Capt. Walton: the adventurer, writes the letters at the beginning
- Mrs. Saville: Walton's sister, the person he writes to
- the gigantic being on the raft??
- ~~the stranger~~ Victor Frankenstein: the main character → mostly the speaker
- Mr. Frankenstein: Victor's father
- Caroline: the orphan Mr. F. saves/his wife/Victor's mother??
- Elizabeth Lavenza: Victor's cousin, "playfellow," foster sister, and girlfriend?
- Henry Clerval: Victor's friend
- Krempe: prof of natural philosophy
- Waldman: prof of chemistry

If it's clearer for you, you might create a graph or drawing showing relationships between characters.

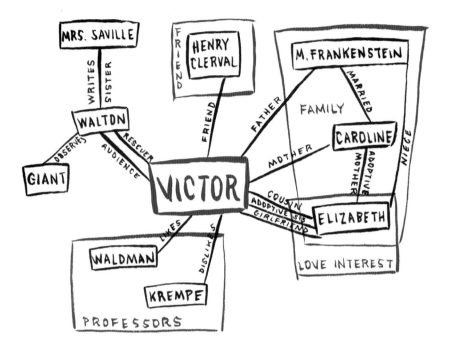

You might also want to create a time line, either in narrative form or as a graph or drawing (or both, if that's helpful to you). In *Frankenstein*, this is particularly useful, since the book begins more or less at the end and then jumps back to the beginning.

Time Line

- Victor's family background
- father adopts Elizabeth to rescue her from evil stepmother
- happy childhood
- age 13: finds book by alchemist, father tells him it's "sad trash"
- Victor is 17: mother dies
- V goes to the university at Ingolstadt, meets profs; M. Krempe says "you've wasted your time" reading alchemists
- gets interested in where life comes from, studies it by studying dead bodies

—— [gap: these things happen later even though they come first in the book]:

- Dec 11, 17—? Walton's first letter: prepping for trip
- March 28, 17—? Walton's second letter: still prepping for trip
- July 7, 17—? Walton's third letter: on his way (he's in Archangel)
- Aug 17—? Walton's fourth letter: stuck in the ice; see the big guy; rescue the stranger
- Aug 13: becoming friends with the stranger
- Aug 19: the stranger starts telling Walton his story (the stranger is Frankenstein)

You can also create pictures or charts or graphs representing events or relationships in the text and what you think about them. Even very simple visualizations can help in making sense of complicated moments or ideas.

If you're writing about a nonfiction text, think about how visual practices can help you clarify what's going on. You might create:

- a time line of advances in a field or of events in a historical progression.
- a list of key categories.
- a graph of relationships between ideas.
- a chart of key actors in an event.

PRACTICING: MAKING LANGUAGE VISUAL

Choose one of the visual techniques we've shown you, and use it to organize and clarify information in a text you're working with. You might want to experiment with more than one technique to find one that works best for you.

WORKING IN THE LANGUAGE OF THE TEXT

While visual techniques are productive and important, always make sure you're still working in the language in which the text is written. You don't want to translate, whether it's from one language to another or from words to symbols. That's because language holds meaning: Words don't necessarily have direct correspondences in other languages or in visual symbols. This makes it very difficult to translate a piece of writing word by word from one language to another (as you know if you've ever tried your hand at translation). The nuances of meaning may be lost, and those nuances are exactly the stuff you need to work with, even when you're just talking to yourself in the early stages of the writing process. So it's important to try to read and write about the text in the language in which it's been assigned.

If you're not a native speaker of English, the temptation to make your notes in the language you know best may be strong. But if you can resist it, you'll find your life will be much easier down the line since you won't have to translate everything—the text, your notes, your ideas—back into English as you write.

Some students "translate" texts into the "language" of their disciplines. For instance, a student who reads "next to of course god america i" and sees a strong relationship between patriotism and war in it might express the relationship like this.

$$P = W$$

But there's a problem here. In a mathematical equation, the aim is to set up the numbers and symbols so that they have only one possible meaning. But when you translate a language-based idea into a mathematical equation, you run the risk of reducing a complicated and nuanced relationship to its lowest common denominator. Math is a different language than writing. And just as a mathematician solves an equation with equations, you should use language to respond to language.

This is true for images as well. You'll note that all of our examples of charts, graphs, and drawings employ words rather than entirely replacing words with images. That's because images are a form of language—and that language isn't the same as the one the text is written in. Even as you make your text visual, be sure to keep working with words.

WRAP-UPS

Once you've reached a stopping point in your reading, spend a few minutes skimming your notes and then writing down what you remember about the text, as well as any thoughts or impressions that occur to you. You can also note any questions you have, but remember: You aren't trying to answer them yet.

Take a look, for instance, at this section from Gawande's article. He's talking here about the recovery of the little girl who fell in the frozen pond.

> What makes her recovery astounding isn't just the idea that someone could come back from two hours in a state that would once have been considered death. It's also the idea that a group of people in an ordinary hospital could

do something so enormously complex. To save this one child, scores of people had to carry out thousands of steps correctly: placing the heart-pump tubing into her without letting in air bubbles; maintaining the sterility of her lines, her open chest, the burr hole in her skull, keeping a temperamental battery of machines up and running. The degree of difficulty in any one of these steps is substantial. Then you must add the difficulties of orchestrating them in the right sequence, with nothing dropped, leaving some room for improvisation, but not too much.

For every drowned and pulseless child rescued by intensive care, there are many more who don't make it—and not just because their bodies are too far gone. Machines break down; a team can't get moving fast enough; a simple step is forgotten. Such cases don't get written up in *The Annals of Thoracic Surgery*, but they are the norm. Intensive-care medicine has become the art of managing extreme complexity—and a test of whether such complexity can, in fact, be humanly mastered.

Here's a quick wrap-up of this section of the article.

What's amazing about the girl's survival is that everything went right. In the ICU everything has to be done right, in the right order, by a bunch of people. Lots of patients die in the ICU because of machine or human error; in fact, their dying is routine, because people can't be expected to always handle such a complicated series of procedures.

You might also note some thoughts about this passage.

- sounds like surviving the ICU is just about luck in everybody getting everything right
- I don't really understand this thing about "improvisation"—it's never explained. What does it mean? Why do you need space for it if this is all about systems?
- crazy that it's "the norm" that people die from human error in the ICU. What's that about?

This wrap-up shouldn't be a completely fresh take on the passage: It's just the material that stays with you now that you've finished reading and the ideas and questions that seem important to you at this point. The quick choices you make about what's worth noting will help you identify your own interests in the text as you move forward—and when you're ready to make decisions about where to focus your paper, they'll be really useful.

This passage from Gawande's essay is fairly short; when you choose a short passage like this to wrap up, it usually means you see something particularly interesting in that moment in the text, and that will help you make choices about where to focus your energy down the line. (You wouldn't want to summarize every short section as we've done here—if you did, you'd never finish reading.) When you do a wrap-up of a longer section, the choices you make about which points to put in your wrap-up tend to come from the moments you find most compelling, and that, too, will help you narrow things down later. In either case, be sure to read and wrap up in sections. If you try to read the whole text at once, or to finish the book before you start taking notes, you'll likely end up confused about events and miss or glaze over interesting and important material. Plus, you'll be exhausted.

Wrap-ups shouldn't take very long to do; for one thing, you don't need to worry about grammar, spelling, or sentence structure. But don't skip them: They're a useful step as you're reading, and they'll also be useful to you when you start writing.

PRACTICING: WRAP-UPS

1. Choose a passage from your text that you've read and marked up. If you're working with a short piece like the cummings poem, wrap up the whole thing.
2. Write a brief wrap-up of your passage. You can write in narrative form or use bullet points.
3. Note any questions or thoughts that occur to you about your passage.

PITFALLS AND PROBLEMS: WHEN SUMMARY GOES WRONG

Summarizing is a crucial step, but not all summaries or wrap-ups are equally effective. Here are some that don't work very well. In each case, we're looking at a section of *Frankenstein* (excerpted below) where Victor Frankenstein has arrived in Ingolstadt to start university and has just met one of his professors. (This is before he's created his monster.) He's talking in part about some books of science ("natural philosophy") that he was obsessed with as a boy: They're centuries old, and they present ideas that were thought of as magic (or nonsense) in Victor's day. Here's the passage, followed by several problematic summaries.

> The next morning I delivered my letters of introduction, and paid a visit to some of the principal professors, and among others to M. Krempe, professor of natural philosophy. He received me with politeness, and asked me several questions concerning my progress in the different branches of science appertaining to natural philosophy. I mentioned, it is true, with fear and trembling, the only authors I had ever read upon those subjects. The professor stared: "Have you," he said, "really spent your time in studying such nonsense?"
>
> I replied in the affirmative. "Every minute," continued M. Krempe with warmth, "every instant that you have wasted on those books is utterly and entirely lost. You have burdened your memory with exploded systems, and useless names. Good God! in what desert land have you lived, where no one was kind enough to inform you that these fancies, which you have so greedily imbibed, are a thousand years old, and as musty as they are ancient? I little expected in this enlightened and scientific age to find a disciple of Albertus Magnus and Paracelsus. My dear Sir, you must begin your studies entirely anew."
>
> So saying, he stepped aside, and wrote down a list of several books treating of natural philosophy, which he desired me to procure, and dismissed me, after mentioning that in the beginning of the following week he intended to commence a course of lectures upon natural philosophy in its general relations, and that M. Waldman, a fellow-professor, would lecture upon chemistry the alternate days that he missed.
>
> I returned home, not disappointed, for I had long considered those authors useless whom the professor had so strongly reprobated; but I did not feel much inclined to study the books which I had procured at his recommendation. M. Krempe was a little squat man, with a gruff voice and repulsive countenance; the teacher, therefore, did not prepossess me in favour of his doctrine. Besides, I had a contempt for the uses of modern natural philosophy. It was very different, when the masters of the science sought immortality and power; such views, although futile, were grand: but now the scene was changed. The ambition of the inquirer seemed to limit itself to the annihilation of those visions on which my interest

in science was chiefly founded. I was required to exchange chimeras of boundless grandeur for realities of little worth.

The Summary Is Too Short

Victor doesn't like the natural philosophy professor. Victor's disappointed with modern science.

As you can see, this summary is very short. When the student who wrote it looks back at it, she won't know why Victor dislikes the professor or why Victor looks down on modern science. She won't know how (or if) the first sentence connects to the second one. In other words, she's lost both the plot connections and whatever it was that caught her attention in the first place.

The Summary Is Too Long

Prof Krempe calls Paracelsus and the other old authors a waste of time. He tells Victor that each moment he spent reading those books was wasted. Krempe is just as dismissive of them as Victor's father was, calling their work out-of-date garbage. Krempe can't believe that in these modern times, someone's still reading these guys. He tells Victor he'll have to start his studies all over again. He gives Victor a list of books to read and tells him to come to hear his lectures and those of another prof (Waldman). Victor goes home and says he's not disappointed because he already knew those old books were useless, but he seems pretty mad at Prof. Krempe. Calls him ugly and disgusting and says he doesn't even want to study natural philosophy anymore, not if it's this guy who teaches it. According to Victor, modern natural philosophy is also garbage: At least the old guys thought big even if they didn't achieve it; these modern guys, what do they do? They just put down the old dreamers who were the reason Victor was interested in science to start with. Just when he's supposed to be beginning his scientific study, he already thinks it's pointless since he's required, he says, to give up the power of the old stuff for this weak new science since old science was bold but made-up/imaginary, whereas modern science might be reality-based but isn't worth much.

This summary, on the other hand, is almost as long as the original. By including everything (sometimes twice), the student has failed to make any decisions about what's important. If he doesn't think about what matters to him in the passage and what doesn't, he's just retelling the text. When he rereads his notes, he'll basically be reading the text all over again—which is a huge waste of his time.

The Summary Is Too Close to the Text

> Professor Krempe makes fun of Victor for having read out-of-date guys like Paracelsus. Krempe tells Victor that each moment he wasted with those books is totally and completely lost. Victor seems pretty mad: He calls Krempe "repulsive." Then he starts talking about what's wrong with scientists of his time. He says the old scientists at least thought big (they were looking for "immortality and power"). He now thinks science is pointless since he's required, he says, "to exchange chimeras of boundless grandeur for realities of little worth."

This summary is problematic because it's not always in the student's own words. For example, she quotes a big chunk of text at the end of her summary. She doesn't define the words she's quoted, she doesn't try to restate them in her own words, and she doesn't say why she thinks they're important. When you're paraphrasing to understand, it's okay to retain some of the words in the original, but if your wrap-up includes large, unchanged chunks of text, you're letting the text stand in for your own work. That's a slippery slope, as you can see here: By quoting instead of summarizing, this student has missed the opportunity to think about what's interesting to her and perhaps to note a question or idea about it.

And it's not just the direct quotes that are problematic. Here's the language from the text.

> "Every minute … every instant that you have wasted on those books is utterly and entirely lost. …"

And here's the student's language.

> Krempe tells Victor that each moment he wasted with those books is totally and completely lost.

As you can see, the student has more or less lifted the language of the text into her notes, changing a word or two but keeping the structure, syntax, and sound of the original. This suggests she doesn't feel comfortable making decisions or offering ideas about what she's reading—and that will be a problem when she tries to figure out what she wants to say.

This type of partial borrowing of the text's language also creates a potentially dangerous situation. It's easy for the student to forget what she said versus what the text said; when she rereads her notes later, she'll likely think that all the language is her own. She may end up using borrowed words and phrases in her paper without attribution—and as a result, plagiarizing without realizing it. Plagiarism—presenting the language of the text as your own—is the most serious violation of the rules of academic writing. Even if you plagiarize by mistake, it can result in significant repercussions. We'll talk more about plagiarism and how to avoid it later on.

PRACTICING: EVALUATING SUMMARIES

1. Look back at the summary you wrote in the Wrap-Ups section.
   a. Use different colored highlighters to mark:
      - material that actually seems interesting or important to you.
      - repetition.
      - quotation.
      - extra stuff that doesn't belong.
   b. Then evaluate your work.
      - Is your wrap-up too short to show plot connections and areas of interest?
      - Is your wrap-up too long, meaning that you haven't made any choices?
      - Is your wrap-up full of quotation or near-quotation instead of summary?
      - Does your wrap-up help you focus on what's interesting to you in the text?

2. Swap summaries with another person.
   - Mark up your partner's wrap-up as you did your own.
   - Evaluate your partner's wrap-up as you did your own.
   - Discuss with your partner.
      - Which parts of the wrap-up served as good summary and why?
      - Which sections seemed confusing or extraneous and why?
      - What seemed to be most important in the wrap-up? Least important?

THE NEXT STEPS:
CLOSE READING AND ANALYSIS

You've read your text, noted, charted, summarized, even made some preliminary decisions about what interests you. You may never have generated so much material about a text before, but you still have a lot to do before you're ready to write the paper. That's because you still don't know what you want to say. In the next section, we'll talk about how to start figuring that out by asking questions, reading closely, and analyzing.

CHAPTER TWO
READING (WRITING)

The baseline reading work you've done so far constitutes the crucial first step in approaching a text for a college class—and for getting ready to write about it. So now that you know a fair bit about the text and you've started to figure out what interests you about it, what's the next step? Baseline reading is about acquainting yourself with the text; once you've done that, the next set of moves involves homing in on language and asking questions. That's what will let you move on to analysis. In this chapter, we'll give you an idea of what this process looks like. (We'll get into more detail about how to do it, and we'll show you more techniques for getting it done, in the following chapters.)

The French writer Roland Barthes makes a distinction that's useful here: He talks about the difference between *consuming* a text and *playing* it. When you consume a text, it's like consuming a meal: You've read (eaten) it, and now you're done. Since you read it for a class, you may need to show that you consumed it. This often means showing that you can summarize what you've read, that you have an opinion about it, that you know the information in the text, or that you can identify a number of key ideas in the text. Essentially, it's an act you perform to show the teacher that you've read the book.

But what does it mean to *play* a text? Think of it, Barthes says, the way you'd think of playing a piece of music on a piano. When you're trying to learn a musical composition, you break it up into manageable pieces so that you can understand the motifs, the patterns, the kind of composition it is. It takes time and effort to get the piece into your brain and for your fingers to know it. It's only after you've done all of this that you have a real sense of how the piece works. That's when you can start playing the piece—and playing *with* it, thinking about what parts to emphasize or de-emphasize, or the feel you want to give the piece.

A piece of music is made up of notes; a piece of text is made up of words. This may seem obvious, but students often overlook the importance of the specific language in a text, focusing only on the ideas, the plot, or a message or moral they think the text or its author is sending. Analysis, however, requires a balancing act: You have to know about the ideas or the plot, but if that's all you have to talk about, everything you have to say will be obvious. In order to analyze a text, you need to think about the language it's made up of.

Consider the different kinds of texts, from newspaper reporting about Internet privacy to the novel *Frankenstein* to a scientific article about cloning. Each of these can be boiled down to the idea that technology is problematic and potentially dangerous. When you lump all of these different kinds of texts together and extract only the shared general ideas, you overlook the important specifics and differences—you end up with nothing more than a blurry overview of the subject. To bring back Barthes's metaphor, when you generalize you're just humming a vague version of the text's melody. But when your discussion of a text comes from its language, you're playing its notes.

Focusing on the words—the language of the text, its syntax, tone, the multiple meanings words can have—lets you play the text with authority. **Authoritative ideas about a text are those that are both consistent with the facts of the baseline reading** (you can't make up a whole new version of the text or overlook elements that are clearly there) **and based on a close reading of the language of the text.**

This kind of close reading means thinking not just about what is said but also about how it is said. In other words, your task is to go beyond asking what the most important ideas are so that you can explore how those ideas are expressed and look at the gaps between the ideas and their expression. These are the kinds of questions you ask when you're beginning to read closely:

- What word choices are used at critical junctures in the text, and what do you make of those choices?
- What's the effect of using that one particular word?
- Does the text seem to switch direction suddenly?
- Are there moments when the text says it's going to do X but, on closer inspection, it actually does Z?
- Are there moments when the text confounds your expectations by describing something in language that seems at odds with the thing it's describing?

These sorts of questions will take you deeper into the text and let you start figuring out what you have to say. **This is how you move from opinions to ideas.** Remember that the text is not a closed system in which you cannot intervene. When you aren't just taking a text's ideas or structure or plot at face value, you have more space for your own thoughts. Playing a text means looking at it not as a monolithic thing with an agreed-upon reading but as a set of many possible meanings. This is analysis.

Sometimes this process flummoxes students because they're accustomed to the idea that every text has an agreed-upon reading—a "right" answer. That's a really attractive idea because it makes things simpler: If there's a right answer somewhere, you just need to work hard enough to find it, and then you'll have the security of knowing you're correct. But complex texts have multiple meanings, in large part because words have multiple meanings. This can be frustrating, but it's also liberating. The fact that a text can't be pinned down to one meaning allows each reader to come up with her own way to play it, instead of simply looking for something somebody else has already thought of.

READING (QUESTIONING)

Let's take a look at a text to see how this works. In chapter one, we talked about the basic moves you need to think about when you're reading a poem. Now we'll build on those moves and start to play the text. Here's the e.e. cummings poem again.

> "next to of course god america i
> love you land of the pilgrims' and so forth oh
> say can you see by the dawn's early my
> country 'tis of centuries come and go
> and are no more what of it we should worry
> in every language even deafanddumb
> thy sons acclaim your glorious name by gorry
> by jingo by gee by gosh by gum
> why talk of beauty what could be more beaut-
> iful than these heroic happy dead
> who rushed like lions to the roaring slaughter
> they did not stop to think they died instead
> then shall the voice of liberty be mute?"
>
> He spoke. And drank rapidly a glass of water

One of the great things about poems is that because they're usually fairly short, you can read every word closely if you want to. For our purposes, though, we'll just look at a few areas.

As we said earlier, this poem is, at first glance, confusing. But we've taken you through some base-level reading of this text in chapter one, so you have some idea of what's going on and you're ready to really explore it. You do that by asking questions. The act of questioning lets you figure out what you think is going on in the text. And as we said before, a good place to start questioning is when you see something that sticks out to you as odd or interesting or surprising.

For instance, when you return to the poem, you might be struck by the word *deafanddumb*—a fairly strange compound word—and you might come up with a question about it.

> Why does cummings make the speaker say "in every language even dea-fanddumb/thy sons acclaim your glorious name"? *Deafanddumb* isn't a real language—or even a real word.

This is a reasonable thing to want to know, but before you respond, it's useful to step back and look at the question itself. If your question is really asking why the author does X or says Y, you'll hit a dead end because it's impossible to come up with an authoritative answer. The author's not here to ask—and even if he were, he might not know or remember why he wrote things a certain way. More important, this method of approaching the language of the text doesn't really give you anything to say: It just returns all authority over the text to the author. If the answer is "because cummings thought X," there's no room for interpretation or analysis. So let's start by rephrasing the question.

> When the speaker says that he's talking about "every language" and then chooses one to exemplify what he's saying, what's the effect of referring to *deafanddumb* as if it were an actual language?

This is a good question because it doesn't have a definitive answer: Different readers may very well come up with different responses to what *deafanddumb* does in this moment in the text. And as long as they're all based on the evidence in the text itself, all of them may be equally valid. If there were only one right answer, it would mean there was only one right way to play the text. To return to Barthes's music analogy, that would mean that all musicians who played a piece of music well would play it in exactly the same way, with the same emphases and pauses and pacing—which would mean there was only one definitive way to hear and interpret the piece of music. We know that's not the case. And, though it may be a bit harder to see, the same is true of language.

So how do you approach this question about *deafanddumb*? The first order of business is to respond to the question you've set yourself. One way to do that is by *freewriting*. This means sitting down at a computer or with a notebook for a set period of time (five minutes, ten minutes, twenty minutes) and writing down everything you're thinking about your question. The process is called "freewriting" because you're freely writing down any idea that strikes you, without worrying about grammatical correctness or complete sentences. There's no stopping and thinking, no deleting or crossing out or rewriting. You're not writing this for public consumption, so you don't need to evaluate or edit your ideas or try to make them coherent; **you're just talking to yourself on the page. The idea is to use writing as a means of thinking.**

It can be useful to put your question at the top of the page and then start by responding to it. A freewrite on our question might look something like this.

> When the speaker says that he's talking about "every language" and then chooses one to exemplify what he's saying, what's the effect of referring to *deafanddumb* as if it were an actual language?

> *Deafanddumb* the way he's using it, is a way of saying the language that people who can't see or hear use. So in that way, it's like Italian or whatever. But he doesn't say sign, he says *deafanddumb*, so even though he's saying it as an example of a language, what really sticks out is the idea of NOT being able to speak, being dumb. So in every language, even silence, people affirm your (america's?) glorious name, but if you're doing it silently, it can't be heard. And if it can't be heard, maybe you're not doing it at all. So in one phrase is the idea of speaking to affirm glory and NOT speaking or not being able to speak.

When you've finished your freewrite, it's a good idea to walk away to clear your head and give yourself some perspective. When you come back, reread what you've written and see what stands out to you; you may want to highlight any ideas that seem worth pursuing. In this freewrite, for instance, you might notice an interesting idea: Using *deafanddumb* as an example of a language is different than using an actual language (like, say, Italian) as an example because *deafanddumb* includes the idea of not speaking or being unable to speak. That's a fairly strange way to talk about language, which is usually made up of some kind of speech. So the poem is saying something about language that goes beyond the way we generally think about it. That's interesting: You've gone beyond noticing some strange wording in the poem to thinking about what that strange wording does. This is a critical step in close reading.

But you can't stop there because you haven't really done any analytical work yet. To get to analysis, **you need to do something with what you've noticed**. In other words, you need to think about the way the phenomenon you've noticed affects how you think about this section of the poem. So the next move is to go back and reread the poem to see if your observation about *deafandumb* relates to anything else that you see in the text. (In a longer text, you might just reread the rest of the phrase you were looking at, the whole sentence it's in, or the paragraph.)

When you read the poem with *deafanddumb* in mind, what strikes you? Maybe you notice the word *mute* in the line "then shall the voice of liberty be mute," and you wonder why liberty would be silent. You could also notice that the "heroic happy dead" are, by definition, incapable of speaking. Making this connection can open up more questions. For example:

- Is there a connection between the dead and liberty?
- Is there a relationship between "think[ing]" (or not thinking) and being "mute"?

You'll notice that this question sequence has moved us away from literal connections (*mute* really does mean not speaking) and into less literal ones. The move away from literality is a hallmark of the work of interpretation and analysis.

You might also think about how the concept of being *silent/mute/deafanddumb* functions in a slightly larger way in the poem. For instance, what about the speaker? He's talking throughout the poem, and then, right at the end, he stops and we hear about his actions from a narrative voice instead. And it seems like his stopping is important because the narrator tells us about it in two ways.

1. First he says, "he spoke," which, since it's the past tense of *speak*, means, of course, that the speaking is over.
2. Then he says, "And drank rapidly a glass of water," which, unless the speaker is a ventriloquist, means he must have stopped talking.

So maybe the speaker is out of words? Or maybe he's said what he came to say? Or maybe he's been rendered silent by what he has said?

Each of these options, and probably others, could be substantiated through evidence from the text, and each will have different implications for the way you read the poem in terms of the role of speaking and silence—the topic you've chosen to focus on here.

You can also think about how the poem's **form** relates to its **content**. You might, for example, notice that the period after "He spoke" is the only one in the whole poem. The general structure of the poem involves sentences that run together, but that's not the case here. If the only time the poem comes to a full stop is right after the speaker has stopped speaking, that might raise some questions for you about speech and silence in the poem.

And all of this work came from looking at one word: *deafanddumb*. You can see how thinking about just one word in a text can open up a passage in a number of ways, helping you find your way into issues that interest you in the poem. Of course, you're still not ready to write (sorry about that): In the case of our example, you don't yet know what you think about this whole issue of silence in the poem. And there are still many parts of the poem that we haven't touched on. You might want to think, for instance, about how the idea of silence and speech relates to the American phrases in the poem.

It's a good idea to raise as many questions as possible about a text before you start writing about it. You want to look at the text from as many angles as possible, explore lots of different ideas about language and form, and give yourself as much material as you can find. Once you've raised a lot of questions and chosen those that strike you as most interesting, your next step will involve responding to those questions through writing and rereading (we'll talk more about this in later chapters). For now, what's important is that you can see how asking questions that come from the language of the text opens up the text and starts you on the path of analysis.

FINDING STRANGENESS IN FAMILIARITY

Not every text is as strange as the cummings poem, of course. And when a text doesn't seem strange, it's easy to get carried along by the narrative and to overlook opportunities to ask questions or examine the language closely. That can happen because (as in the Gawande article) the text tells a story smoothly and provides information, even fairly technical information, without jargon that might stop the reader in his tracks. Or it can happen because (as in the McCann excerpt) the text isn't obviously strange or filled with old-fashioned language that slows him down so he can notice things. And it can also happen when a text is so well known that we take it for granted.

Martin Luther King, Jr.'s "I Have a Dream" speech, delivered at the March on Washington in 1963, is an excellent example of this type of text. Even if you've never read or heard the whole speech, you would probably recognize its language: It's the one in which King talks about his dream of his children living in a world where they would "not be judged by the color of their skin but by the content of their character." King's speech is one of the most famous texts of the Civil Rights era, and it's usually read as a statement of hope. But when you take a closer look and ask questions, instead of letting the speech's familiar cadences roll over you, it's possible to find a great deal of complexity beneath the surface.

King starts by talking about the Emancipation Proclamation, which freed the slaves. Then he says, "But one hundred years later, the Negro is still not free," and goes on to list a series of ways black people are not treated equally. Having set the stage, King gets to why he and the hundreds of thousands of people listening to him are at the March. He says, "We have come here today to cash a check." Let's look at that whole section.

> We have come here today to cash a check. When the architects of our great republic wrote the magnificent words of the Constitution and the Declaration of Independence, they were signing a promissory note to which every American was to fall heir. This note was a promise that all men, yes, black men as well as white men, would be guaranteed the unalienable rights of life, liberty, and the pursuit of happiness.
>
> It is obvious today that America has defaulted on this promissory note insofar as her citizens of color are concerned. Instead of honoring this sacred obligation, America has given its colored people a bad check, a check that has come back marked "insufficient funds." We refuse to believe that the bank of justice is bankrupt. We refuse to believe that there are insufficient funds in the great vaults of opportunity of this nation. So we have come to cash this check, a check that will give us upon demand the riches of freedom and security of justice.

When you isolate this moment in the text and read it on its own, King's metaphors about checks and money probably jump out at you much more than they would if you read the speech as a whole. You might ask:

What's going on with this set of metaphors about money?

That's a pretty vague question. But at this stage, this vagueness is actually useful. We've barely started our investigation; we don't want to predetermine its results, so we frame the question in the most neutral way possible. We've noticed that something is going on with all these financial references; now we're going to try to see what that something is, moving step by step.

The first step is to go back to the text and underline or highlight all the financial words.

> We have come here today to cash a check. When the architects of our great republic wrote the magnificent words of the Constitution and the Declaration of Independence, they were signing a promissory note to which every American was to fall heir. This note was a promise that all men, yes, black men as well as white men, would be guaranteed the inalienable rights of life, liberty, and the pursuit of happiness.
>
> It is obvious today that America has defaulted on this promissory note insofar as her citizens of color are concerned. Instead of honoring this sacred obligation, America has given its colored people a bad check, a check that has come back marked "insufficient funds." We refuse to believe that the bank of justice is bankrupt. We refuse to believe that there are insufficient funds in the great vaults of opportunity of this nation. So we have come to cash this check, a check that will give us upon demand the riches of freedom and security of justice.

This lets you see at one glance just how frequently King is using these monetary terms. Once you've seen that, you can start to work with these words. Begin by **defining** words you aren't sure about. For example, you might not be sure of what *promissory note* means. According to *Merriam-Webster*, it means "a written promise to pay at a fixed or determinable future time a sum of money to a specified individual or to bearer." Write the definition down near the word so you don't forget it.

As we said in chapter one, it's a really good idea to look up words that you think you know but that are used in unexpected ways. You may find that while these words have the meaning you expect, they also carry other meanings or nuances: It's often surprising how many ways a single word can be read. Discovering multiple plausible meanings gives you more material to work with. For example:

The phrase "fall heir" sounds strange because "heir" is usually used as a noun. According to *Merriam-Webster*, an heir is "one who inherits or is entitled to inherent property."

That's not the way King is using the term here, though: If you "fall heir," that's like "falling ill" or "falling down," like it's an accident.

So in this case, the dictionary confirms that the usage is strange, and this lets you ask some questions about what work the usage is doing here: How might you read this section of the text differently with this new definition in mind?

Now that you've made the sheer number of monetary terms visible, it would be easy to conclude that each usage of monetary language is more or less a repetition of the others. But your task here is to look closely, to see if you can, in fact, find difference in apparent repetition and sameness. **When you're reading closely, repetition is a flashing light**: You always want to pay attention to it because when a text repeats itself, it's revealing something about itself and its preoccupations.

A really simple but useful way of detailing subtle differences and changes in meaning and implication is to make a chart of the repeated terms—in this case, the monetary terms in the passage and their meanings and connotations. On the left side of the chart below, we've listed each of the monetary terms in the passage. On the right side, we've thought through the particular way the term operates. Building a chart like this will help you distinguish between near matches and terms or phrases that seem similar but actually do different work. These subtle distinctions are a key part of analysis because they let you say something that is not immediately apparent.

"cash a check"	If someone writes you a check, they better have the funds to pay it. Otherwise they're in trouble.
"signing a promissory note"	Same as *check* (promise to pay money) but in a way even stronger because it has the sense of a promise.

"fall heir"	*Heir* means there's a legal aspect because a will is a legal document that you can't just blow off because you don't feel like it or it's inconvenient. Note: "fall heir" is a weird usage; it sounds like people are heirs accidentally, not through any merit of their own.
"defaulted" on the "promissory note"	When you default, you fail to do something you were obligated to do. So they broke their promise.
"a bad check"	A bad check is a check that the person who wrote it can't cover. It's a check that will bounce.
"a check that will come back marked 'insufficient funds'"	Exactly. The check is no good because the person who wrote it doesn't have the money.
"We refuse to believe that the bank of justice is bankrupt."	That check, though, isn't for money; it's for justice ... and King says that he doesn't believe that bank doesn't have the funds to pay.
"We refuse to believe that there are insufficient funds in the vaults of opportunity."	King (and everyone else there, because he says "we") doesn't believe that there isn't enough money in the bank vaults. But now the money is justice, it's opportunity.
"We have come to cash a check ... riches of freedom and security of justice."	Same as the beginning, but now we know what the check is for.
"a check that will give us upon demand"	A check is a legal document: If you wrote it to me, I have the right to demand the money.

Once you've charted all the terms and their connotations, you can really see the differences that can be found in similarity—which lets you see that there's more going on than you might initially have thought. And now that you've spelled out what you're seeing, it's easier to home in on a particular set of ideas or terms and ask questions about it.

You could, for instance, decide to focus on the way that King talks about that check. Here are some questions you could ask.

- What currency is it in?
- What exactly is owed? Is it money or justice or opportunity or freedom?
- What's gained by using these financial metaphors?

Just as with the cummings poem, you can see that once you focus on something that you notice and really start looking at it, all kinds of lines of inquiry open up. Suddenly this text that you thought you knew looks a lot richer and more complicated than it seemed.

READING PAST THE OBVIOUS

Sometimes a straightforward text doesn't offer you rhetorical clues like repetition. In fact, it may appear to be so direct that it seems as if anything you'd say about it would be obvious. But that doesn't necessarily mean you're out of options. Once you're sure you can paraphrase the text, you can move on to thinking about not just what is being said but how it's being said.

Consider this excerpt from *Ways of Seeing* by John Berger, which is a book about looking at art. Here Berger is discussing the nude—not a particular painting of a nude but the category as a whole. This is how he starts the discussion.

> To be naked is to be oneself.
> To be nude is to be seen naked by others and yet not recognized for oneself. A naked body has to be seen as an object in order to become a nude. (The sight of it as an object stimulates the use of it as an object.) Nakedness reveals itself. Nudity is placed on display.
> To be naked is to be without disguise.

Here's what the summary might look like.

> Nudes and naked people are different even though they both don't have clothes on. The nude is there to be seen and looked at. The nude is always on display, while a person who is naked is simply him- or herself.

If you stop with this summary, all you've done is consume Berger's ideas. In order to play the text, you need to start asking questions about how Berger makes his argument and what is implied or suggested by the way he proceeds.

To do this, it's useful to go back to freewriting, but this time, try a question/response format. In this approach, as you can probably guess, you ask yourself a question and then do some writing to respond to the question. This can be useful because it lets you move piece by piece and it helps to ensure that your ideas stay connected to each other instead of jumping all over the place.

Naked/Nude:

Q: Why start with naked?
R: Nudes, are, by definition, naked, so it makes sense to start there. But he doesn't just start with nakedness, he starts by defining it. He says to be naked is to be oneself.

Q: If nakedness is the condition of being oneself, what's that about?
R: A person who is dressed is, somehow, not as purely him- or herself as a person who is naked? Hmm. That's interesting.

Q: He also says that "to be naked is to be without disguise." What's going on with that?
R: If "to be naked is to be without disguise," that kind of suggests that at all other times (i.e., anytime you're wearing clothes), you're disguising or hiding your true self. *Merriam-Webster* defines *disguise* as clothing "designed to conceal one's true identity" or as a "form misrepresenting the true nature of something." That means that nakedness is the condition not only of being without clothes but of being without a screen. When you're naked, you are your true self because at all other times you're hiding something.

Q: Wow. So what does this say about clothing?
R: Clothes don't just hide your naked body, but they allow you to hide yourself, to represent yourself as something you may not be.

Now that you've worked through nakedness, you can start to think about nudity.

> Q: What does Berger say about nudity?
>
> R: Nudity is the condition in which you are "seen naked" but "not recognized for oneself." Wait, didn't he just contradict himself? Before, he said being naked WAS *being yourself.*

Sometimes when students find a contradiction, they stop. They think: *Aha! Caught you in a contradiction, Mr. or Ms. Author. Game over.* But here's the thing: Seeing a contradiction is just the beginning. **Contradictions are actually rich places to investigate and ask questions because they're places where the text reveals a lot about itself and its preoccupations.**

In fiction, a contradiction usually indicates a place where you might want to pay attention to the text. For instance, when a narrator contradicts herself, that can lead you to question her motivations in that moment, think about what's "true" in the story, and so forth. In nonfiction, contradiction often appears at a point where an argument gets complicated. It may in fact mean that a problem exists with the argument—in which case you need to think through what is contradicting what, why it matters, and what this does to the argument. But it may also indicate that more than one thing is true at the same time, which makes things really interesting for you as a reader.

For example, you might begin to explore Berger's apparent contradiction through a series of questions, beginning with one that lets you see what the text actually asserts.

> Q: How can it be that the nude is naked but not "recognized as oneself"?
>
> R: According to Berger, it's because the nude is a naked person that's been "placed on display" and "seen as an object."

> Q: So what?
>
> R: Well, naked people are themselves, but objects don't have selves.

> Q: Wait a minute: Does that mean that Berger is saying that a nude is a thing? That painting a person nude turns that person into a thing?

As you can see, you've come up with some really interesting ideas by looking carefully at what the text says and how it says it. The questions are logical and specific, and they come straight out of the text. Raising these questions showed you the complexities in a text that seemed straightforward and let you see how much you could say about that text. You're now in a position to start analyzing what you've seen. In the next chapter, we'll show you how to do that.

CHAPTER THREE
DOING ANALYSIS

In chapter one, we demonstrated how to use summary to really understand what a text is about. In chapter two, we addressed the process of noticing what's happening beyond the literal level in the text and asking preliminary questions about what you've seen. In this chapter, we're moving on to real analytical work.

Analysis asks questions about a phenomenon you've noticed in the text so that you can eventually come up with a set of ideas about that phenomenon. **When you analyze, your job is not to accept the text at face value: It's to look for the places where it contradicts itself, gets weird, or uses unexpected language or sentence structure.** You're exploring the material that isn't clear or straightforward, that troubles you, that doesn't seem to make sense.

In general terms, analysis requires you to:

- seek out the places where the text seems to be strange or troubling or inconsistent or contradictory.
- ask questions about these strange or troubling things.
- explore these questions by looking at specific language in the text.

WORKING WITH UNCERTAINTY

Analysis is challenging because it involves working with uncertainty: going straight to the places you'd rather avoid because you don't understand them. This can be intimidating because you're plunging right into the part of the book or material that's causing you the most trouble. It may feel counterintuitive—but think of it, for example, like diving. If the water you dive into isn't very deep, you can't try too many tricks or speed along underwater because you'll hit the bottom too soon. On the other hand, if you gather your courage and dive into the depths, you'll have a long way to enjoy the ride, and by the time you reach the surface, you'll have discovered all kinds of things that are new to you.

No Right Answer

Since analysis involves working with uncertainty, you're always trying to figure something out, which means you're always asking questions. To ask productive questions of a text, as we've said, you need to give yourself permission to delve into the stuff you don't understand. Often, though, students prefer to avoid questions that reveal what they don't know. Instead they might ask:

- What's the right way to think about this passage/character/event/book?
- What's the most important part of this book?
- Who or what does this character represent?
- What does this symbolize?
- What's the major theme?
- What did the author have in mind?
- Doesn't the text just mean exactly what it says?

… all of which are variations on the question students really want to ask:

> What's the right answer?

But when you're asking questions about problems in the text, there's no such thing as a right answer.

Different Questions, Different Readers

One reason there's no one "right" answer is because, as we said when discussing the cummings poem in chapter two, every reader reads a given text a little bit differently. There's no such thing as the universal person or the universal mind: Each reader reads through the lens of his own experiences and interests, so everybody experiences a text in his own way. And this means that even if two students write about exactly the same moment, their readings of that moment, and therefore their essays, will be different.

That doesn't mean students in a given class have nothing in common. For one thing, they've all taken part in the same discussions, so they have a common fact base and probably some overlapping ideas. But each student will understand even these common elements through the lens of her own point of view and interests.

Let's look at *Frankenstein* to see how this works.

This excerpt is from a very early part of the book, before we've met Victor Frankenstein or heard about his interest in science. Here British explorer Robert Walton is trying to find a passage to the North Pole. He writes his sister a series of letters; this passage comes from one of these letters (with some sections excerpted, as indicated by ellipses).

> But I have one want which I have never yet been able to satisfy; and the absence of the object of which I now feel as a most severe evil. I have no friend, Margaret: when I am glowing with the enthusiasm of success, there will be none to participate my joy; if I am assailed by disappointment, no one will endeavour to sustain me in dejection … I desire the company of a man who could sympathise with me; whose eyes would reply to mine. You may deem me romantic, my dear sister, but I bitterly feel the want of a friend. I have no one near me, gentle yet courageous, possessed of a cultivated as well as of a capacious mind, whose tastes are like my own, to approve or amend my plans. How would such a friend repair the faults of your poor brother! I am too ardent in execution, and too impatient of difficulties. But it is a still greater evil to me that I am self-educated: for the first fourteen years of my life I ran wild on a common, and read nothing but our uncle Thomas's books of voyages. At that age I became acquainted with the celebrated poets of our own country … Now I am twenty-eight, and am in reality more illiterate than many schoolboys of fifteen. It is true that I have thought more, and that my day dreams are more extended and magnificent; but they want (as the painters call it) keeping; and I greatly need a friend who would have sense enough not to despise me as romantic, and affection enough for me to endeavour to regulate my mind.

Different readers may well have different responses to this passage. For instance, one reader finds this line very interesting: "But it is a still greater evil to me that I am self-educated." Her attention is arrested by this; she wants to know more about what the line means, why self-education is such a great evil to Walton, and what it has to do with his desire for a friend. How are education and friendship related here?

A different reader might choose a different part of the passage. For instance, he might focus on this sentence.

> I have no one near me, gentle yet courageous, possessed of a cultivated
> as well as a capacious mind, whose tastes are like my own, to approve
> or amend my plans.

He might ask what it means that these particular qualities are the ones Walton wants in a friend. He might wonder why Walton gives such power to a (hypothetical) friend—why does Walton need a friend to "approve" or "amend" his plans?

A third reader might choose this passage to home in on.

> It is true that I have thought more, and that my day dreams are more
> extended and magnificent; but they want (as the painters call it) keeping.

She asks, *What does "keeping" mean here? If it has something to do with things being under control, why would the daydreams of an explorer need that? Shouldn't they be "magnificent"?*

These questions aren't particularly deep or meaningful—they're first responses. But you'll note that each set of questions takes up a different topic or issue. Each of these beginning investigations has the potential to be the seed of a good paper. That's because each **emerges directly from the language of the text and connects to the reader's interests without leaving the text behind.**

You'll note, too, that all of these responses are phrased as questions. That's very important. If you're asking productive questions, you're not looking for some predetermined "right answer." Instead you're interrogating, investigating, exploring possibilities, opening things up, and thinking hard—and the focus of all this hard thinking is the text.

CHOOSING A MOMENT

To start the process of analysis, you need to make choices. You've probably generated quite a bit of material in your summarizing and preliminary work, but you can't use it all. If you try, you may never finish writing your paper. And in any case, you can't really write an interesting and engaged paper about an entire book. It's just too big.

That's why the first step in analysis is finding a place in the text where you'll focus your question-asking. It's most useful to begin your analysis with a limited section of text. Just as you might, in a lab class, look at a bacterium under the microscope in order to understand it (and, in turn, to understand something about the way it interacts with other bacteria, which will lead you in turn to think about this interaction in a particular environment), so, too, you want to begin textual analysis by looking very closely at a small piece of the whole: a moment.

Students often want to look at very long sections of text when they start their analysis. A student may worry that if he chooses a brief moment, he won't have enough to write about. But choosing a long section of text doesn't really help you write a longer essay—in fact, it may result in too much summary and generalization and not enough close analysis. When you have more material than you can really work with at the granular level, it's easy to get overwhelmed.

And the truth is, you don't need a lot of text to generate a lot of material. When you're reading closely, it's entirely possible to write a whole page about five words: what they mean, what their effect is, why that matters. So if you're a writer who struggles to fill pages, here's a good reason to really engage with analytical writing: analysis, done well, requires a lot of space.

How do you decide on the moment you'll begin with? You'll want to keep two things in mind.

1. The Prompt: Your Assignment

- How much latitude do you have in terms of topic and approach?
- What limitations or requirements has the professor given you in terms of choosing a starting point?

In some cases, the professor will choose the moment for you; when that happens, it's your job to delve into the moment to see what questions you can ask about it. In other cases, you may have a set of moments to choose from. And sometimes you can choose any moment you like. While that can be freeing, it can also be overwhelming: As Eleanor Roosevelt once wrote, with freedom comes responsibility. In that case, you need to choose a moment that will be productive for you and that fits the parameters of your course and assignment.

2. Your Own Interests

We've talked about how different readers may see the same text in different ways, depending on their backgrounds and interests. The same is true when it comes to choosing a moment. Within the confines of the prompt, you'll want to think about **the moments or questions in the text that are most puzzling or compel-**

ling to you. Sometimes students hesitate to make these choices because they don't feel qualified to decide on any one part of the text or because they're not sure how to know if a moment is rich enough to base an essay on. But if you've been doing the work of summarizing and noticing, you've already given yourself a lot to base your decision on. Here's how to do it.

Begin by going through your summary materials. Your marginal notes, endpaper notes, summaries, charts, graphs, and questions are your guides here. Remember that you created these in part so you'd have a useful map of the text and your interests. Now it's time to look back in order to move forward—to remind yourself of what caught your attention so you can start organizing and making choices. Skim the text, looking for places where you've done the most marking. Don't feel obliged to read in depth: Instead, look for the stuff that makes you go, "Hmm." Read over what you've written, highlighting and marking points or moments that continue to interest you.

Things to ask:

- Are there issues or problems that keep coming up in your markings?
- Do these moments have anything in common?
- If there are several issues here, which is the most interesting to you?

Problems in the Text Are Your Friends

In analytical writing, a moment you find strange or confusing will give you lots of material to work with *because* it's strange or confusing. You want a piece of text that on first reading, and even on second or third reading, doesn't resolve itself into clarity.

Students often find this a little mind-bending, but actually a lot of creative work proceeds this way. Consider how scientists work: Rather than beginning with a solution, they start with a problem. They ask questions about that problem, and they see where those questions lead them. In college writing, you're doing exactly the same thing.

Let's look at *Frankenstein* again to see how this works. We've chosen a moment that occurs not long after the encounter between Victor Frankenstein and his professor, which we looked at in chapter one. Here Victor describes how he became interested in chemistry, what he calls "the principle of life" at university, and his experiments with the creation of life from dead matter. Here's the whole moment.

Whence, I often asked myself, did the principle of life proceed? It was a bold question, and one which has ever been considered as a mystery; yet with how many things are we upon the brink of becoming acquainted, if cowardice or carelessness did not restrain our inquiries. I revolved these circumstances in my mind, and determined thenceforth to apply myself more particularly to those branches of natural philosophy which relate to physiology. Unless I had been animated by an almost supernatural enthusiasm, my application to this study would have been irksome, and almost intolerable. To examine the causes of life, we must first have recourse to death. I became acquainted with the science of anatomy: but this was not sufficient; I must also observe the natural decay and corruption of the human body. In my education my father had taken the greatest precautions that my mind should be impressed with no supernatural horrors. I do not ever remember to have trembled at a tale of superstition, or to have feared the apparition of a spirit. Darkness had no effect upon my fancy; and a churchyard was to me merely the receptacle of bodies deprived of life, which, from being the seat of beauty and strength, had become food for the worm. Now I was led to examine the cause and progress of this decay, and forced to spend days and nights in vaults and charnel houses. My attention was fixed upon every object the most insupportable to the delicacy of the human feelings. I saw how the fine form of man was degraded and wasted; I beheld the corruption of death succeed to the blooming cheek of life; I saw how the worm inherited the wonders of the eye and brain. I paused, examining and analysing all the minutiae of causation, as exemplified in the change from life to death, and death to life, until from the midst of this darkness a sudden light broke in upon me—a light so brilliant and wondrous, yet so simple, that while I became dizzy with the immensity of the prospect which it illustrated, I was surprised that among so many men of genius, who had directed their inquiries towards the same science, that I alone should be reserved to discover so astonishing a secret.

There are an almost endless number of potentially interesting moments in *Frankenstein*, and we could have decided to work on any one of them. (This is true, in fact, of most book-length texts: Longer pieces of writing have more material to work with.) Here's how we chose this one.

- It was a place we had made a lot of notes on in our initial reading, especially about how life and death were related.

- In our wrap-up, we'd noted a weird set of issues about how Victor talked about himself.
- When we reread the passage to see if we were still interested in these ideas, we saw something new and interesting—this thing where Victor says both that he's a genius and that he was forced to do the work that led to his moment of genius.

When we started working with the moment, it proved to be productive. That's because:

- **THE MOMENT RAISED A LOT OF QUESTIONS.**
  - How does the relationship between life and death work here? What does he mean when he says that "to examine life we must first have recourse to death"?
  - How exactly does Victor see himself in this passage? He says he was "forced" to do all kinds of things, but he also compares himself to "men of genius."

- **THE MOMENT ISN'T TRANSPARENT.** It's full of contradictions and confusion—which gives us a lot to work with.

- **YES OR NO QUESTIONS WON'T SUFFICE.** For instance, if you asked, "Does Victor think he's a genius?" your first response might be yes—he more or less says so—but if you look closely, you'll notice many words and phrases that make that idea problematic.
  - For example, Victor says he's "forced" to do this work; he's "animated by an almost supernatural enthusiasm," which sounds like it might be a force outside himself; he says he "was led to examine" how life and death worked through corpses.
  - And he says, "A sudden light broke upon me," which sounds like he didn't do anything to earn his breakthrough—it happened to him.

- **THE MOMENT IS SHORT ENOUGH TO HANDLE.** We can look closely at the language of the passage without getting overwhelmed. A short passage gives you the opportunity to work in depth, really exploring language, syntax, and grammar to figure out what makes the moment tick.

- **THE MOMENT IS LONG ENOUGH TO OFFER SOMETHING TO WORK WITH.**

All of this indicates that this passage is a good one to work with. It's confusing and contradictory—and that's great.

Pitfalls and Problems: Choosing a Moment

Not every moment is equally productive; here are some things to watch out for.

There Is No Perfect Passage—Just the Passage That Interests You

Don't agonize endlessly over your choice, trying to find the perfect passage that unlocks the whole text. Texts aren't puzzles that click together when you find the one single right answer. When you work on a text, your task is not to "solve" it but to explore it and think through what that exploration reveals. Remember, this is just the beginning of the process. To figure out what you really think, to test your ideas, and to ultimately communicate them to others, you need to keep moving forward. Be careful with your time!

There Is No "Most Important" Passage

Don't choose a moment because it's "important." Often people try to choose the moment that's talked about the most in class or in the criticism or (ahem) online. But since a text is made up of many component parts that add up to a whole, any part that interests you and fits the criteria we've talked about is probably as valuable and as available for analysis as any other part. In fact, if you've discussed a moment extensively in class or you've found a lot of writing on it in your research, you may actually find it more difficult to say something about it. Focusing on a moment you've read or heard a lot about can also lead you into inadvertent plagiarism since it can be hard to sort out which ideas are yours and which come from somewhere else.

For instance, if you set out to choose the most "important" part of the King speech, you'd probably end up with the section in which he talks about his "dream" for his children. But since this part has been discussed for so long that it is practically a cliché, it'll be tough to find something interesting to say about it.

Don't Decide Ahead of Time What Your Passage Shows

It's never a good idea to choose a passage to use as an example of something you already "know." Your interests should come into play when you choose a passage, but that's very different from starting with an issue and using it as the lens through which you read the text. Doing this will limit your reading; you'll end up turning your passage into an example of your idea instead of making it the real subject of your discussion.

Let's say, for example, that you decide you're arguing that "Mary Shelley's *Frankenstein* is a cautionary tale about the uses of science and technology." This means, almost inevitably, that you'll end up talking about how, in *Frankenstein*, science and technology lead to destruction—and you'll ignore questions, issues, and complications that the moment might have offered if you hadn't already decided what you thought. It can be useful to have a preliminary hunch that grows out of your initial questions and summaries, but in order to engage in meaningful analysis, you have to be willing to go where the text takes you.

READING CLOSELY: PART I

Once you've chosen your moment, you'll need to go back and read it closely. This process involves many of the steps we talked about in chapters one and two, but now you'll also need to look closely at every word. As we've said before, close reading lets you slow down enough to think about things that seem clear on first reading but that turn out to be odd when you're reading with the goal of asking questions. It's the close reading of specific moments that will eventually allow you to say something about a particular issue in a particular text.

To start the process of close reading in your passage:

1. Reread your moment, slowly and carefully, in different ways.
   - Read it silently, in your head.
   - Read it aloud (or have a friend read it aloud, record yourself and then listen to it, or listen to an audiobook of the text).
   - Read it one sentence at a time.
   - Read it in larger sections.

2. Give yourself space to work.

- Create more space for note taking by typing or writing out your moment. Retyping your passage can help you read it more clearly because when it's separated from the larger text, you can see it as a whole. You also understand your passage in a different way through the act of typing it out. (Be careful to make sure your retyping is completely accurate! You don't want to end up with an essay based on a typo.)
- Create more room to work by double- or triple-spacing between lines.
- Retype the passage in a large font to make it easier to read.

3. Make the text more visual using a variety of colored pens or highlighters.
- Mark language that seems strange or odd or interesting to you.
- Mark any places where the syntax seems strange or interesting.
- Mark repetition.

4. Mark and annotate the text more.
- Make lots of notes in the margins, delineating what you find interesting and why, now that you've come back to the passage with a new level of interest.
- Use different types of annotation—definitions, summaries, tags, rearranging, questions—as you need them.
- Note what the context of your moment is: who is speaking to whom, what just happened before the moment, what happens next. You're focusing on a moment, but that moment is part of a larger text, and you need to know where it fits into that text.

Pitfalls and Problems: Avoiding Analysis by Leaving the Text Behind

It's important to follow these steps because effective analysis requires you to stay with your moment and to look at it as if it were under a microscope. It's easy—and very tempting—to leave your moment behind or to use it as a jumping-off point to talk about big ideas. If you aren't used to working analytically, you might find yourself falling back on habits that move you away from the text. Here are some habits to watch out for.

Leaving the Text

In analytic work, a basic rule of thumb is to draw your questions directly from the text. While it may be tempting to ask questions that assume connections between the text and your experience, between the text and other texts, or between the text and a movie you've seen or something you've read in another course, these can't replace questions that are grounded in the text. To put it another way, just because there's no right answer doesn't mean you can make stuff up or talk about whatever crosses your mind.

Because interrogating the text is difficult and time-consuming, it's tempting to try to avoid it by:

- looking at the "big picture" and skipping over the specifics of the text.
- glossing over the parts of the text you don't understand.
- explaining a passage you understand fully, which, since it doesn't raise any real questions for you, leaves you nothing to talk about.
- making statements instead of asking questions.

All of these approaches lead to dead ends and problems. Here are some examples.

> When King says "that America has defaulted on this promissory note," it reminds me of the huge problem of student debt. Pretty much everyone I know has gone into debt to pay for school, which is a sign that America has defaulted on its promise of education and opportunity.

While it's true that your experience will inevitably influence your reading of a text, it shouldn't *replace* that reading. Here the reader's experience and the link she's made between King's concerns and her own become the heart of the paper, replacing the text, which should be at the center.

> When Berger says that painting a naked person turns him or her into a nude, an object, it sounds like the way people treat animals—as if they didn't have feelings, as if they were just there for someone else's pleasure. Could you read this as also being about people and their pets?

Here the reader's mind leaps from a concept in the text to another concept that he thinks is related. While this concept may serve as the springboard for a different paper (on whether humans objectify their pets and ignore the pets' true nature, for example), that paper would only be tangentially related to Berger's piece. The actual text would disappear, and the student would be writing instead about something he already thinks rather than staying with the text and thinking through something new.

> King talks about how the constitution promised "the unalienable rights of life, liberty, and the pursuit of happiness" to "black men" and "white men." Didn't he care about women's oppression? When he gave that speech in 1963, women (white and black) couldn't open a bank account or get a mortgage in their own name.

The issue with this argument is what critics call *a-historicism*; in other words, it doesn't take the historical moment in which King gave his speech into account. The modern women's movement had barely begun, and we can't expect King to know about things that hadn't yet happened. More broadly, picking an argument with King about something he's not talking about is actually a way to avoid looking at what King is talking about and how he goes about it.

> "next to of course god america i" was written in 1926. What does it show about American attitudes toward patriotism in the years after World War I?

This question turns the text into an example of a historical event or trend. To take it up, you'd have to leave the text and look for information elsewhere, and then you'd have to talk about a huge issue (attitudes toward patriotism), an entire period (the decade of the 1920s), and a whole lot of people. You'd end up generalizing, and generalizations are the opposite of analysis. Plus, they lead to boring and ungrounded writing. Most important, you'd be making the text into nothing more than an example of something else, instead of putting it at the center of your analysis.

> Why can't human beings understand once and for all that everyone, regardless of race, creed, or color, is equal? And why do the people like Dr. King who try to make everyone see this end up getting killed so often?

The questions here are huge, and though they're triggered by reading King's speech, they aren't really about the speech. If you tried to answer them, you'd end up speaking in very general terms, and what you'd say wouldn't be connected to the text. The texts you read in college often raise big questions, but **your task is to deal with those questions within the scope and context of the text itself**:

If you turn a text into a jumping-off point or an example of something else, it's a sure sign you're not working with its specifics.

> Why did Mary Shelley make Victor Frankenstein so obsessed with death?

This question requires the student to read the mind of the author. To answer this question, you might go to the book's introduction and read about Shelley's life. You might notice that she had a baby who died, and you might decide that's your answer. Or maybe you'd get stuck on the fact that Shelley's mother died when she was born or that there was a woman who committed suicide when she fell in love with Mary Shelley's husband. But now you've left the text behind, and you're writing an essay on *Frankenstein* as a map of Shelley's life—which is a different thing than writing about it as a text.

It's not very interesting or productive to spend your time searching for parallels between the author's life and the book. Knowing facts about the author's life and the period she was writing in can enrich your understanding of the text, but this doesn't necessarily mean that there are one-to-one correspondences between biographical details you find interesting and the moment you're analyzing. This form of "looking for a right answer" turns you into a would-be channeler of the writer and erases your voice.

> What's the message of *Let the Great World Spin*? Is McCann talking about cross-cultural understanding after 9/11?

This question has a similar issue: It asks you to read the mind of the author in order to find a single "message" or meaning in the text. When you read the text this way, you also risk falling into what literary critics call "the intentional fallacy." Named by the critics W.K. Wimsatt, Jr. and Monroe C. Beardsley, the intentional fallacy is the mistake—the fallacy—of believing that the author's intentions can be found in the text. (This is particularly tempting when the story is written in first person and the protagonist can be mistaken for the author.)

Here's the problem: A text is not a map of a writer's intentions or of his or her mind, and a novel is not a history or an autobiography. Shelley's not alive, so we can't ask her what she meant by any of the choices she made in her book. We could ask McCann—but if we asked him, who knows if he would tell us the truth—or if he would even know or remember what he intended when he was writing? In any case, looking for the message or the biographical link or the author's intention is just another way of shutting the text down and looking for a right answer. To return to Barthes's metaphor, when you turn to biography or look for a single message in the text, you're only consuming the text, not playing it.

Even when you're talking about a text like King's speech, you still want to focus on the speech rather than its author. Of course King is speaking from personal experience; as a black man living in America in the 1960s, he had experienced discrimination firsthand. But stating that fact doesn't take you very far—whereas staying focused on the text and looking at its structure and the strategies it uses to get that message across allows you to say something interesting.

FROM QUESTIONS TO ESSAYS

Once you've chosen your moment and have started asking questions about the specific language and syntax, you're in the territory of analysis. But before we plunge even more deeply into that work (and show you the wide range of tools and approaches that will help you do it), we need to take a step back and talk about what a college-level essay is—and isn't.

CHAPTER FOUR

WHAT IS AN ESSAY?

People tend to throw around the term *essay* as if its meaning were obvious—but no one's born knowing what an essay is or how to write one. So in this chapter, we're going to spend some time demystifying the most common type of college essay: the analytical essay, in which the author creates a narrative to explain her ideas about a subject to a reader.

Many students think of the essay as an alien form of writing, utterly unlike any other writing they've done. And understandably, people find it hard to think in an alien form. So sometimes students find themselves unable to write anything at all; more often, they fall back on formulas that promise to make essay writing fast and simple. When they arrive at college, many of these students are surprised to learn that the formulas they've relied on don't yield work that impresses their instructors. The problem is that most formulas don't give you the chance to say anything, which means your work is nowhere near as good as it could be. But it doesn't have to be that way. Essays aren't really an alien form, and formulas don't constitute the only approach to writing them. In this chapter, we'll show you some ways of understanding the essay as a much more familiar kind of writing—one that you can both understand and produce.

FORMULA VS. STORY

The most common essay-writing formula most students learn is known as "the five-paragraph essay." Typically that essay has:

- an introduction, in which the author previews what he'll be talking about (the importance of the theme of death in *Frankenstein*, for example).
- three paragraphs in which the author gives examples of the point he's already made (i.e., there's a lot of death in *Frankenstein*).
- a conclusion that reiterates his one idea (death is a central theme in *Frankenstein*).

Here's what that kind of essay looks like.

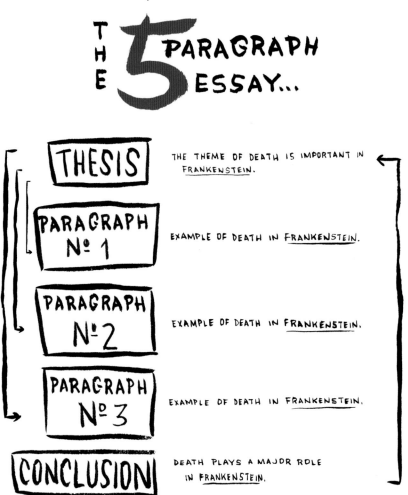

THE 5 PARAGRAPH ESSAY...

THESIS — THE THEME OF DEATH IS IMPORTANT IN FRANKENSTEIN.

PARAGRAPH Nº 1 — EXAMPLE OF DEATH IN FRANKENSTEIN.

PARAGRAPH Nº 2 — EXAMPLE OF DEATH IN FRANKENSTEIN.

PARAGRAPH Nº 3 — EXAMPLE OF DEATH IN FRANKENSTEIN.

CONCLUSION — DEATH PLAYS A MAJOR ROLE IN FRANKENSTEIN.

Sometimes this essay has more than five paragraphs, but the basic structure is always the same. If you think of an essay as having a shape, a five-paragraph essay would be a circle: It ends where it began.

In contrast, an analytical essay starts in one place and ends in another. As we said in the introduction, essay writing actually bears a strong resemblance to a type of writing you know well—storytelling. A good story:

- invites the reader or listener in with a compelling opening.
- sets the stage effectively through description of the person, place, or thing the story is about.
- carries the reader or listener along while the author/teller investigates her subject.
- shows the implications of the events it details (we call this the "so what?").
- winds up somewhere that makes sense for the story but that couldn't be anticipated from the beginning.

In other words, a story doesn't end in the same place it began. Instead it develops. If you were to sketch out the trajectory of a story, its shape would be more like an arrow or a flow chart than a circle.

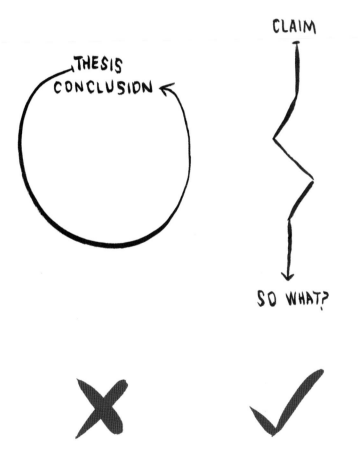

All of this is true of essay writing. An effective essay may not have characters or a plot in the same way a story does, but it should:

- introduce the reader to the subject of the story: that is, the topic of the essay.
- introduce a moment in the text in which this topic comes up and a specific phenomenon in that moment.
- investigate that phenomenon in a way that's interesting and compelling.
- discuss the implications of this investigation.
- come to a conclusion about the topic that builds on these implications.

But an essay is a very particular kind of storytelling. One way to understand it is to think about it as a kind of travel writing: the act of telling the story of a journey.

THE JOURNEY

The process of writing an essay is a lot like taking a trip to a place you've never been. Before you leave on your trip, you may have some idea of where you're going, but when you actually start traveling, your trip (like any interesting journey) will almost certainly include misdirection, unexpected delays and pathways, fortuitous discoveries, detours, and complications. All this unpredictability is what makes travel exciting. But when you tell a friend about your trip after you return, you're likely to skip a lot of that messiness: You make decisions that allow you to craft a coherent and interesting narrative. Nobody wants to hear every detail of your trip. When people are listening to a story, they expect it to have a beginning, a middle, and an end. And they want it to get somewhere, not just circle around endlessly.

The trip itself—the actual crazy, messy, fun, frustrating, exciting journey you take—is a pretty good metaphor for the process of figuring out what you're saying in an essay. But that messy journey is not the same as the thing you hand in—because, just like your friend, your reader will be bored if you make her follow every detour and train delay. The story you tell your friend about your trip is a lot like the final, polished essay you hand in—the product. We've talked plenty about process already, and we'll continue to do that throughout this book, but here we're focusing on the product.

Here's how the metaphor works: Let's say you were lucky enough to go to Italy for summer break. When you get back, you sit down to tell a friend about your trip. You could decide to start at the beginning and relive every detail—but that's not going to be too interesting to somebody who wasn't there. Instead you probably want to start by giving her a sense of what was amazing about your trip. If you discovered that you think Italian food is the best food in the world, for instance, and you spent your summer exploring why it's so good, you'll want to let her know that. You don't want to tell her all the details up front, of course—not only will you lose your friend's attention, but you'll probably end up repeating yourself. You just want to give her some sense of what this story is focusing on.

To apply the metaphor to the essay, this stage constitutes your introduction. You don't want to start out by encapsulating your whole essay—if you tell your reader everything up front, why should she read the rest of the paper? Instead you interest her by establishing your topic and offering a claim that sets a direction for your narrative. In this illustration, the introduction is the tall bump at the beginning from which you can look out, in a general way, over the trip you're about to take.

LOOKING OUT

MIDWAY

THE END!

Returning to our metaphor, let's say you began your trip by taking an overnight flight to Rome. You're pretty exhausted by the time you get to your hostel, so you set out in search of a cup of coffee. You find a little place down the street, full of Italians standing at the counter drinking tiny cups of espresso. You're not sure how to order, so you just point to the closest Italian and ask to have what he's having. A moment later, a perfect little cup of foaming brown liquid appears on the marble bar in front of you. It's a revelation. How can a simple cup of coffee be so unbelievably good?

When you tell your listener about this, you'll want to let her see the moment as though she's in it with you—but what you show her is an edited version, one that skips over extraneous details. She doesn't need to know, for example, what it was like to check in to the hostel. And you're not going to restate what you've already told her: There's no point in re-introducing your thoughts about food in Italy here. Instead, use this moment to show her where you are. What's interesting to you? What's crazy? What do you not understand?

To go back to your essay, just as when you're telling a story, you want to set the scene. Where are you locating your readers in terms of the text under discussion, and what issue or phenomenon are you exploring? This is different than providing a topic and direction in the introduction: Here you're showing your reader the exact thing you're looking at. Then you want to make your specific question clear: What do you notice about that thing? What is it you're investigating?

Returning to the metaphor, let's say that on your actual trip, you were so overwhelmed by the strange goodness of that first cup of espresso that you found yourself setting out on a quest to understand why Roman coffee is so amazing. Of course, that's not all you did in Rome—you saw some ruins, met some people, and picked up some souvenirs—but when you tell the story, you don't need to give your friend all of those details. If you've decided to focus on coffee in this part of your story, you're going to skip over some of the other material, however interesting it might be, so that you don't lose the thread.

You'll want to show your friend how you explored your question about Roman coffee. Your search may have taken you in a lot of different directions. Perhaps you asked a million questions of every Italian you met; maybe you planted yourself in coffee bars all over the city to watch the baristas; possibly you consumed twenty cups of coffee a day in the interest of research. Whatever your approach, your goal was the same: You wanted to know more about *exactly* what makes Roman coffee so good. That meant leaving generalizations about "all Roman coffee" behind: To really understand this phenomenon, you needed to know exact information.

But even when it comes to these on-topic details, you'll want to pick and choose what you recount when you tell your story to your friend. You don't need to drag her into every coffee bar you stumbled upon; you just want to show her the stuff that matters to the story and moves your narrative along.

To return to your essay, you've set the scene and laid the groundwork; you've asked a question. Now you're exploring the phenomenon you're interested in by looking closely and specifically at it, from a lot of different angles. In your final draft, you'll take your reader through that exploration process, focusing on the directions that were fruitful and leaving out dead ends, misdirection, and even interesting but irrelevant points. Your exploration process will be messy, but in your final paper you want a clear narrative your reader can follow.

To go back to the story, once you've collected all of this material, you'll analyze it by asking more questions of it. For example, you might take what you've seen in all of your coffee bar time and come up with a list of questions to ask the baristas. Or you might compare one coffee technique to another to think through each path's possible implications for coffee superlativeness. When you take a look at what you have, you come to believe that you've actually figured out the secret to great Roman coffee. You're thinking it has to do with the specifics of the baristas' hands-on care as they take the coffee from bean to cup. (Keep in mind that this is *your* theory, based on *your* observations: Other people probably have their own ideas about this great mystery, so you'll want to provide evidence that your theory holds water.)

You'll want to tell your friend what you've figured out and how your discovery changes things for you. Does Rome look different to you now that you understand the secret of its coffee? Do you think you'll be able to export this great secret to America and make your fortune in the coffee business? In other words, what does this whole Roman coffee thing add up to?

In terms of the essay, this is the point where you put things together. You analyze what your close examination has revealed about the textual moment you've been looking at, and then you go on to explain the **implications** of your analysis. How does it change the way your reader understands something about the phenomenon or about a particular character or event or moment in the text? In a short essay, this might be where you stop: You've noticed something, raised a question about it, investigated that question, come to a conclusion, and explained its significance.

But what if the story of your trip isn't over and you want to tell your friend about the next place you visited? Let's say you decided to travel from Rome to Naples to check out the coffee there. When you tell your friend about this part of the trip, she'll need to know that—otherwise she could find herself in a Neapolitan café with no understanding of how she got there. It's possible that you took all kinds of detours and wrong turns in moving from one place to another, got caught up in a train strike, and were stuck on a siding in the middle of nowhere; maybe you even hopped off the train because some tiny town caught your eye. All of that may have been interesting to you, but if you didn't experience anything that matters to the particular story you're telling about your trip, including it will bore your friend and cause her to lose the story's thread.

In terms of the essay, you need to show how you moved from the idea you arrived at in your first section to the question you take up in your next section. Here's where the old formulas really fail: If you're writing a five-paragraph essay, all of your ideas relate to the "thesis" in your first paragraph, so there's no meaningful connection between ideas. That's why five-paragraph essays require "transition" terms like *thus, as you can see, therefore, moreover,* and *similarly.* There's nothing wrong with these terms, but in the five-paragraph essay, they're words that attempt to hide the problem by creating rhetorical links where logical ones are missing. Signposting a false transition is not the same as making a genuine connection between ideas: The failure to tell a story doesn't go away. To create meaningful links, you need to think about where you want to go next and why, and how it relates to where you've been.

Going back to our narrative, when you arrive in Naples, your task, so to speak, is **to be here now**. You don't want to tell your friend about Rome again—she was just there with you. And you can't tell her about Palermo, your next stop, because, in your telling, you haven't gotten there yet. Instead let her see the moment you're in by building on what came before. You don't want to repeat what it's like to drink Roman coffee; instead you might tell her about how you used what you learned about Roman coffee to explore what was going on with coffee in Naples. Or maybe you got more interested in applying your hands-on theory about Roman coffee goodness to the outstandingly good Neapolitan pizza.

To return to the essay, once again, you're setting the scene, finding another phenomenon that you're interested in and asking a question about it, looking closely to explore what's going on there, making an argument or claim about it, and thinking about the implications of what you've seen. The difference here is that you're not starting from scratch: The topic of your essay remains the same, and the question you ask about this new phenomenon should emerge from the work you've already done on the first phenomenon you looked at. You're applying what you've already figured out in order to explore something new.

These explorations are the building blocks of your essay. In a short paper of a page or two, you'll only have one such exploration (think of it as a weekend trip). In a longer paper, you may have three or four. It all depends on what you're looking at, how closely you're looking, what questions you're asking, and where those questions take you. There isn't a good or bad number here, just as there isn't a set number of paragraphs for each exploration. (This is another place where the five-paragraph-essay formula is inadequate: What's so magical about three examples and five paragraphs per essay?)

Let's return to the metaphor. In your storytelling, you've traveled through Italy and you've arrived at the end of your time there. At this point in your tale, you're in the train station in Milan, getting ready to leave the country. Do you need to describe your whole trip? Of course not: You've just done that. And though, in your story, you might be heading across the border to explore French food, you can't convincingly tell your friend about what you'll find there unless you tell her the whole story the same way you just told her about Italy. Instead tell her what your trip so far has added up to. What ideas or understandings about Italian food are you bringing home with you? What do you want her to take away from your story?

In other words, now that you've reached the end of the essay, you don't need to restate your introduction and you can't jump into an entirely new exploration. Instead **tell your readers how what you've shown them can change the way they understand the text**. How should they see the text differently now that they've followed your questions and ideas through your essay? By working out your specific questions about specific moments in the text, you've arrived at the place where you can say something significant about the whole text or about the phenomenon you were focusing on and how it relates to the topic of your paper. And you won't be generalizing or repeating yourself or falling back on what other people have said. Since you've tested your ideas by looking at them closely, your argument has real power. By building up your ideas step by step, you've let your readers see something they wouldn't have seen if you hadn't shown it to them.

Now that you understand how an essay works, let's look more closely at some of its key elements.

SEQUENCE AND STRUCTURE

As we've said, the act of figuring out what you think about a text may be messy; it almost certainly won't be linear. But a final essay needs to follow a clear narrative so the reader can understand the development of your idea and its implications. An effective analytical essay moves in a sequence, and different parts of the essay fulfill different functions in the storytelling process.

The Beginning

The first paragraph of a paper can be hard to get your head around. Students sometimes try to tell the whole story in the first paragraph (that's what the five-paragraph essay basically prescribes), but that inevitably leads to repetition and a desperate search for something else to say in the rest of the paper. Another common approach is to begin with very general statements—but as we've said, your essay isn't about generalities. Instead it's about your idea—your claim—about a particular text or phenomenon. So what should you do?

Remember, you're telling a story to a reader. What does your reader need to know in order to have a sense of where he is and what this story is about? In an analytical essay, he needs some basic information about the text you're writing about. Then he needs a one- or two-sentence overview of the issue that interests you in the text and a brief reference to its context. Once you've set the stage in this way, you can introduce your claim.

What Is a Claim?

We mentioned a "claim" at the beginning of our explanation of the "journey" metaphor. A claim is your idea about the phenomenon you're looking at. (Your professor may use the terms *argument*, *thesis*, or *reading*. These terms are interchangeable.) **When you make a claim, you're telling your reader, "Something interesting is going on here, and I'm going to show you what it is and why it matters."**

A claim is not the same as a statement of fact, just as an essay is not a collection of facts about the text or topic being discussed. For instance, if you were writing an essay about *Frankenstein* and you were looking for a five-paragraph-essay-style thesis, you might come up with this as a potential claim.

> The novel *Frankenstein* is about a man who decides to create life and then, when he succeeds, abandons his creation.

That's a perfectly good bare-bones summary of a key aspect of *Frankenstein*, which is about a scientist who creates a monster. But this statement is also obvious to just about anyone who's read the book because it's composed entirely of facts. An essay needs facts—but an essay that simply presents facts without using them as a jumping-off point for the exploration of ideas is boring because everything in it is obvious. In contrast, a claim is:

- an idea that you arrive at through close attention to and analysis of your phenomenon.
- an idea that reasonable people can disagree about.
- an idea that has to be demonstrated and proved using evidence from the text.

A claim is also not the same as a statement of opinion. A statement of opinion might be, for example, "I think this character is a jerk," or "I love this author and everything she writes." You may have strong opinions about the text, but while an opinion can draw your attention to what interests you, it's not sufficient grounds on which to base an essay. That's because while opinions can be based in facts, they don't *require* facts. And while opinions may come from analytical thinking, they may also be emotional responses or statements of conventional wisdom. **Claims, on the other hand, require both facts and analysis.**

Students sometimes panic when they hear that they're expected to make a claim about a text—especially when that text is complicated or well known. What makes them qualified to say anything about such a text, they wonder, and what's left to say? But as we've noted in earlier chapters, everybody sees the world a little bit differently, so every reader has something a little bit different to say about the text she's reading. And every writer is entitled to make a case for her point of view, as long as it's based in the facts of the text and arrived at through analysis. In other words, **what qualifies you to make a claim about a text is the work you do to read it closely, analyze it, and draw some conclusions about it.**

Stating a claim in the first paragraph can also make students nervous because they feel like they're announcing something without substantiating it. The truth is, that's exactly what they're doing. And that's okay. You can't tell the whole story in the first paragraph, and you shouldn't try. You're just setting up the pieces you need to situate your reader so that you can show him how you play the text. And remember that your claim statement shouldn't include all the details. In our "journey" example, you, the storyteller, told your friend that you'd discovered that Italian food was the best in the world, and you told her that during your time in Italy, you decided to find out why. But you didn't give her the whole story up front, and you certainly didn't start by telling her what you'd figured out by the end of the trip.

We've come up with some metaphors that may be helpful in terms of thinking about the special work the first paragraph does. All of them basically say the same thing, so go with the one that makes the most sense to you.

- **THE RECIPE METAPHOR:** If you cook, you know that virtually every recipe starts by giving you a brief description so you'll know what kind of dish it makes. If you're writing a recipe, you'll want your reader to understand what he'll have at the end of the process. If you're describing how to bake a cake, for instance, you'll want him to know whether it's vanilla or chocolate, whether its super complicated or good for beginners, and whether it's suitable for a kid's birthday party or an adult dinner. But you only have a few lines here, so you don't want to list all the ingredients and steps.

  In an essay, the introduction functions as this overview, and the claim statement or guiding question lets the reader know what story this essay is telling.

- **THE LAB REPORT METAPHOR:** If you do lab work, you know there are certain expectations when it comes to reports. You begin with your introduction of the experiment: a brief explanation of the phenomenon you're looking at, why and how you're looking at it, and your hypothesis about it. It's important that your reader understands what you're trying to find out, but you don't include your materials, method, observations, or conclusions here.

  Similarly, you want to introduce your essay by laying out the phenomenon you're investigating and what you want to know about it, without going over all the specifics at this point.

- **THE FILM METAPHOR:** A filmmaker uses an opening (or establishing) shot to set the terms for a film. What country are we in? What language is being spoken? What season is it? Is it the nineteenth century or the twenty-second? And who or what are we focusing on here? That opening shot explains to viewers what universe they're in and indicates the direction of what's coming.

  The opening paragraph of any essay does the work of the establishing shot. In an essay, you're setting up the text or phenomenon you're writing about and the initial presentation of your idea about it.

The Middle

This part of the essay (sometimes called the "body") is where you really explore something: You explain the particulars of the textual moment you're looking at, ask a question about it, and take up your question through close reading and analysis. In the "journey" metaphor, it's what happens in your story after you get to Italy and have that first amazing cup of coffee. As we said before, though you state a claim or ask your key question in the opening paragraph, you haven't yet gone through the process of proving your idea. That's what the middle of the paper is for. Given how much you're going to do, it stands to reason that the middle actually constitutes the bulk of your paper.

Let's go back to our metaphors.

- **THE RECIPE METAPHOR:** The middle of the essay is equivalent to the directions you provide for the process of baking the cake. If your recipe is going to work, your reader will need to understand how to move through it step by step—preheating the oven, combining ingredients, mixing the batter, and so forth. It's important that each step is done in order so that the cake turns out right: If you make the frosting first, for example, it may harden up while you wait for the cake to bake, and by the time you're ready to ice the cake, the frosting will be unusable. So the recipe needs to be written in a way that lets the reader take each step in the right order.

  Similarly, in the middle of your essay, you need to help your reader understand the development of your ideas by creating a logical sequence of events and moving step by step in your discussion. Otherwise your reader will be confused. And if your reader can't follow your ideas, you won't be able to convince her of anything.

- **THE LAB REPORT METAPHOR:** The middle of your lab report comprises your materials and methods. Since a good lab report lets a reader successfully repeat your experiment, you want to make sure that you explain things step by step: You need to combine Chemical 1 and Chemical 2 before you can use the resulting mixture to work with Chemical 3. If your steps aren't clear, your reader might find himself putting chemicals together in the wrong order, which means he won't be able to confirm your findings—and he might even blow things up.

- **THE FILM METAPHOR:** The middle of your movie (we're assuming in this case that you're making a crowd-pleasing story-based movie) is a series of scenes through which your narrative plays out. Each scene builds on the one before it; each scene takes up a particular problem or issue or event, spins it out, and sets up the next scene.

Of course, when you're developing a recipe or undertaking an experiment or actually shooting your film, the order won't be this clear. You might experience a baking failure here or there, set your lab notebook on fire, or realize you're missing a crucial scene. But as we said in the journey metaphor, this is all part of your process. When you're creating a final product for use by others—a recipe, a lab protocol, a movie—you'll have smoothed out all of those wrinkles so that they're invisible to the user.

The End

So what do you end up with? Your recipe should result in a delicious cake. Your lab report is successful if your results are replicable and your conclusions are the logical outcome of your experiment. Your movie will end, ideally, by wrapping up the loose ends and closing in a way that's satisfying to the person who just spent the last two hours watching it.

In the essay, this is your conclusion. This is another point where you might get nervous. If you aren't going to repeat your introduction (and thus your claim), what are you supposed to do? Well, by the time you get to the conclusion, if things have gone well, you've presented, explored, and substantiated your claim. And that means you don't need to do any of that again. **You can think of the conclusion as the place where the claim pays off**—the place where you show your reader why it's useful to think about the text in the way you're thinking about it. **We call this the "so what?" factor** because you're addressing the question you anticipate your reader asking: *How do I see your subject differently, now that I know all of this?*

PRODUCT VS. PROCESS

In this chapter, we've told you what an essay is. But we haven't addressed how you go about writing one, and that's an important distinction. **The finished essay is a**

product: the piece of work that's intended for public consumption. **The product isn't what you start with: It's a narration of what you've learned.** While your final draft reads as though it's a journey of discovery, by the time you've written it, you've figured things out. That's what process is for. Once you're at the product stage, the person doing the discovering is your reader.

In the rest of this book, we'll take you through the steps of writing an essay that's all about the process of discovery—first for you and then for your reader.

CHAPTER FIVE

ASKING QUESTIONS, GENERATING IDEAS

As we said in chapter four, the writing process is all about discovery. And the only way to discover something about a text is to ask questions. As we discussed in chapters two and three, looking closely at the language of a text allows you to start asking questions, and when you do that, you're acknowledging that something is going on in the text that isn't immediately obvious. As you'll see in this chapter and the next one, asking questions also generates ideas. In this chapter, we'll talk about recognizing opportunities to ask questions and about what those questions can do, and we'll give you some tools to help you ask productive questions.

Asking questions lets you:

- move beyond the assumption that the text is always right and can't be investigated or questioned.
- look at anything that seems strange or contradictory or that doesn't make sense.
- think about gaps and problems.

OPPORTUNITIES FOR ASKING QUESTIONS

The kind of question-asking we're talking about might be best understood through a metaphor. It's as though the events of the text—the plot or central ideas—are the train, and the words of the text are the tracks that keep the train running along. On first read, it appears that the words—the track—are carrying the events along smoothly. But the places we're interested in are moments where, if you look closely, you notice that the train and the tracks actually diverge. The train is still moving, but when you look out the window of the train, you see that the tracks have gone off in a different direction.

This divergence happens in places where the text seems to be saying one thing, but when you read more carefully, you find that the words expressing the ideas of the text actually seem to be saying something else. Questions let you investigate what's going on with that divergence and generate meaningful material from what you see.

These moments of divergence are places where, if you don't pay attention to the tracks under the train, the text can mislead you. This kind of misleading can take many forms. Here are a few.

Sometimes the Text Contradicts Itself

On occasion, a text will suggest one idea and then take up another idea that seems to contradict the first one. Take, for instance, this section from Bram Stoker's novel *Dracula*, in which Jonathan Harker, one of the protagonists, prepares to search the vampire's body as it lies in its coffin in order to find a key and escape from Castle Dracula. Jonathan writes:

> I knew I must search the body for the key, so I raised the lid, and laid it back against the wall; and then I saw something which filled my very soul with horror. There lay the Count, but looking as if his youth had been half renewed, for the white hair and moustache were changed to dark iron-grey; the cheeks were fuller, and the white skin seemed ruby-red underneath, the mouth was redder than ever, for on the lips were gouts of fresh blood, which trickled from the corners of the mouth and ran over

the chin and neck. Even the deep, burning eyes seemed set amongst swollen flesh, for the lids and pouches underneath were bloated. It seemed as if the whole awful creature were simply gorged with blood; he lay like a filthy leech, exhausted with his repletion.

In this section, you'll note a clear contradiction: Dracula, lying in his coffin, is dead, and yet his "youth" is "half-renewed." You might reasonably ask, *How can he be both dead and made young again?* Students who work on this moment often find themselves stymied by the idea that Dracula exists in two categories: He is, at one and the same time, alive and dead. It's tempting to try to resolve this problem by placing the character in one category or another: Either he's dead or he's alive. But if you do so, you're rewriting the text. In fact, this moment is a real opportunity to think about a problem in the text. Instead of asking, *Is he alive or dead?* it's more productive to ask, *What does the fact that he is described as both alive and dead do?* These types of questions allow you to start doing real analysis.

Sometimes the Text Has an Agenda

In fiction, the text often wants us to take what a character or the narrator says at face value, even when doing so doesn't make sense. These are moments to pay attention to.

For example, in *Frankenstein*, Victor describes his work process as if it's completely straightforward and obvious.

> To examine the causes of life, we must first have recourse to death. I became acquainted with the science of anatomy: but this was not sufficient; I must also observe the natural decay and corruption of the human body.

But what if we ask why he "must" go about it this way? As soon as we do, several things happen: We can see that there is no "must"—that it's just what Victor's decided—and we can ask more questions. And that lets us think about what's at stake for this character in telling the story this way.

Nonfiction writing also often has an agenda—but in nonfiction, that agenda is usually linked to the author instead of to a character. A nonfiction piece may use rhetorical strategies aimed at minimizing possible objections and maximizing readers' buy-in. These are moments in which you can ask questions about how the piece builds its arguments.

Atul Gawande's article "The Checklist" begins by talking about the extreme bodily harm that humans can now survive, thanks to the scientific advances that are now commonplace in hospital intensive care units. As we mentioned in chapter one, Gawande tells, in some detail, the story of a three-year-old Austrian girl who falls into an icy pond and is not discovered for thirty minutes. The little girl is technically dead. Gawande takes us through the process of this child returning from the dead, thanks to medical technology.

Because Gawande starts out with this very emotional story, by the time readers learn that the little girl is saved, we're strongly in favor of extreme medical intervention. And Gawande's matter-of-fact language suggests that what happened to the little girl was no miracle: It's simply what modern medicine can do.

Once we're invested, Gawande turns the tables. *What if that doesn't happen?* he asks. *Whose fault is it?* He writes:

> For every drowned and pulseless child rescued by intensive care, there are many more who don't make it—and not just because their bodies are too far gone. Machines break down; a team can't get moving fast enough; a simple step is forgotten. Such cases don't get written up in *The Annals of Thoracic Surgery*, but they are the norm. Intensive-care medicine has become the art of managing extreme complexity—and a test of whether such complexity can, in fact, be humanly mastered.
>
> On any given day in the United States, some ninety thousand people are in intensive care. Over a year, an estimated five million Americans will be, and over a normal lifetime nearly all of us will come to know the glassed bay of an I.C.U. from the inside.

The turn that Gawande makes here is extremely effective, and his agenda in this meandering piece begins to become clear. Now that he's shown us what medicine can do—now that he's asked us to identify with the child's parents and to become emotionally engaged in her recovery—he's going to show us why and how that kind of response often doesn't happen. He's setting out to demonstrate how important it is that human error can derail the possibilities technology offers, since, just like that little girl, most of us will have to rely on extreme medical measures at some point in our lives.

The effect of Gawande's storytelling suddenly becomes clear. We, the medicine-requiring public, are often deprived of the possibility of miraculous recovery because of the complexity of ICU medicine. Like the little girl in the pond, we want our hearts restarted and our lungs taught to pump air again. It may not be the doctors' fault that ICU care is so complex—but if doctors can't live up to the engineering, they must be reengineered themselves. The story of doctors using checklists in the hospital could be told in a page or two, but the author uses lengthy asides like the story of the little girl to help his readers feel that this story is their own story.

You might ask why this matters. The answer to this depends, in part, on why you're reading and writing about this essay. If, for example, you're taking a medical engineering class and your task is to critique the list, you'll need to be able to recognize the co-opting work the little narratives do before you can move past them to look at the list objectively. But even if you're reading this essay for a composition course, it's important to see how the piece creates emotional engagement and to think about what that emotional engagement does. For example, it gives the reader the illusion of expertise on a subject she most likely knows nothing about. When you get carried along by the emotional vignettes in Gawande's essay, you suddenly feel qualified to weigh in on technology, ICU protocols, and human error. Knowing that this new "authority" on the subject comes at least as much from an emotional response as from the facts lets you assess Gawande's claims and create a more nuanced argument.

Sometimes the Text Takes You for a Ride

It's often pleasurable to sit back and let the text take you somewhere—after all, that's why we call it leisure reading. But when you're reading for analytical purposes, you have to be able to see past what our old friend Roland Barthes calls "the pleasure of the text" in order to decipher how that text is operating.

For instance, if we look again at "next to of course god america i," the e.e. cummings poem we talked about earlier, there's a moment near the end when the speaker, who until now has been talking mainly about America, suddenly mentions the "heroic happy dead."

> what could be more beaut-
> iful than these heroic happy dead
> who rushed like lions to the roaring slaughter

The line "rushed like lions to the roaring slaughter" makes use of alliteration (the use of the same sounds at the beginnings of words or in the stressed syllables), with the *r* in *rushed* and *roaring* (and to some degree at the end of *slaughter*) and the *l* in *like* and *lions* and *slaughter*. And *roaring* is onomatopoetic—that is, it's a word that sounds like what it's describing. Read the line out loud: It's fun to say.

Those great sound effects can blind you to the words' actual meaning, but if you slow down and ask a few questions, interesting things pop up. For instance, the men are described as lions, so you might assume, on a first read, that they're the ones who are roaring. But when you look closely, you can see that what's actually roaring here isn't the men but the slaughter. Then you might ask, *What does it mean for a slaughter to roar?* Once your attention has been drawn to "roaring slaughter," you might notice that these lion-like men are "heroic." Heroes usually fight battles, but, you might ask, *Is a slaughter the same as a battle?* This might lead you to look up *slaughter*, and suddenly all kinds of ideas about war and heroism are bubbling up in your brain.

When you slow down enough to notice what's speeding you along in the poem, you can start to see that what seemed like a fun little set of word games is actually a complicated discussion about patriotism. And once you see that, you can explore the tension between the word games and the complex ideas that lie beneath them. If you think about the metaphor of the train and tracks that we talked about earlier, cummings's poem can easily carry you along: The speed and rhythm make you want to take the ride. But your job as reader is to pull the brake.

Nonfiction texts can also take you for a ride. As we said before, these pieces often try to make a case—to convince you of something. Let's look, for instance, at Martin Luther King, Jr.'s speech at the March on Washington.

We talked in chapter two about paying attention to all the ways King talks about money and obligation. But if you look closely, there's a moment where the metaphor switches from a financial one to a religious one. King starts by saying that the marchers have "come to cash a check," a "promissory note" contained in the Declaration of Independence that says all men are created equal. Later in the speech, King says that America "has defaulted on this promissory note." And then comes this sentence: "Instead of honoring this sacred obligation, America has given its colored people a bad check, a check that has come back marked 'insufficient funds.'" If you're just reading quickly, you're probably thinking, *Yup, more financial language*—bad check, insufficient funds, *even* defaulted *sounds kind of financial*. But one word in that sentence is from a different kind of language. The obligation America has failed to honor isn't just any obligation. It's "sacred."

It's easy to overlook *sacred* among all the financial references; since religious and financial language makes for an odd pairing, you might be tempted to read right past it and focus on the financial language. But if you slow down, you can ask a lot of productive questions. What does *sacred* actually mean? What does *sacred* add to what King is saying here and what he's already said, and how does it change your understanding of the speech?

TESTING A WORD'S SIGNIFICANCE

If you're not sure whether a word is significant, you can test it by swapping it out with a similar word. You could rewrite the phrase this way, for instance.

"instead of honoring this **fundamental obligation** ..."

What's the difference between a "fundamental obligation" and a "sacred obligation"? According to *Merriam-Webster*, something that is sacred is "worthy of religious veneration," "entitled to respect," and "holy." *Sacred* also means "highly valued and important." Is this the same as *fundamental*? Which sounds worse, failing to honor a "fundamental" obligation or a "sacred" one?

You could also figure out what role sacred plays by taking the word out of the sentence and seeing how or if that changes it. Without sacred, King would be saying, "Instead of honoring this obligation ..." And that means that the obligation you're not fulfilling is just an everyday thing, not a sacred one, so it's not that big a deal. Without sacred, the stakes of King's argument go way down.

SPOTTING OPPORTUNITIES

How do you go about spotting places where the language diverges from the events of the text? Here are two simple but effective habits that will help tremendously.

1. Looking for Patterns and Repetition

If the text keeps doing something, it's worth paying attention to. This is true in both fiction and nonfiction texts: Repetition—of words, phrases, or ideas—is a sign that something interesting is going on. And if a pattern emerges in a text, that's worth looking at, too. Repetition is a type of pattern, of course, but this category also includes patterns formed by repeated syntax, line breaks or other kinds of spacing choices, and the way a text switches back and forth between speakers or between topics.

If we look again at "next to of course god america i," we can see an example of what happens when you look at a pattern of repeated syntax.

> thy sons acclaim your glorious name by gorry
> by jingo by gee by gosh by gum

It would be easy to see the line "by jingo by gee by gosh by gum" as just a lot of nonsense syllables. But when you're reading a text closely, you should assume that every word—even those that seem purposeless—is doing work of some kind. In fact, we find several forms of repetition and patterning in this phrase. For example, **alliteration** appears again, in all the *g* sounds. And there's the **repeated syntax** of *by* gee, *by* gosh, *by* … etc., which brings up what seems like a contradiction: The fact that each expression is set up in the same way makes the expressions essentially interchangeable, but since there are so many of these phrases, each slightly different, we can ask what each one adds. The repeated syntax here functions as a call to attention.

When you start paying attention to these phrases, you might decide to look them up to see if they really are nonsense. If you did, you'd find out that *by gorry*, *by gosh*, and *by gum* are all ways of saying "by God," with *God* replaced by something that sounds similar to avoid using his name casually. The four different phrases are actually **variations on a theme**. Even *by gee*, which is defined as an expression of surprise or enthusiasm, is also a euphemistic version of "by Jesus." So now cummings's speaker is saying that the sons of America acclaim America's glory, emphasizing it by adding **four different forms** of *by God* to the end of his statement. Now that you know this, you may want to pause and ask whether saying something four different times makes the speaker more convincing or less so? More confident or less so? Why or how? In thinking through these questions, you may find you've come to some new ideas about what's going on with the speaker and hence with the poem.

When you've noticed a pattern, it's also useful to notice **if and when the pattern breaks**. Here, for instance, there are five phrases in cummings's rhythmic, alliterative list. We looked at four. It would be very easy to assume that "by jingo" is just another version of the same thing. And it is. But as a quick dictionary check will tell you, it's also something else: *by jingo* relates to a kind of nationalism in which people support their country out of nationalistic fervor, the sense of "my country, right or wrong." When cummings puts *by jingo* in the list with all the forms of *by God*, he adds another layer of meaning, one you can use to help you think through what's going on with patriotism in the poem.

We saw another example of the importance of pattern breaks in our discussion earlier of Dr. King's use of *sacred*. This word, after all, is an interloper in the very clear pattern King established of financial language—*sacred* is a word from a different set of values.

You can see another form of patterning in Gawande's article, which shifts between reportage and analysis on the use of checklists in the ICU and emotionally engaged narratives about particular patients. This pattern allows Gawande to transform what could be a dry argument about checklists into an emotionally charged argument from experience that allows for only one conclusion. The pattern keeps readers engaged and draws them into the story so they're invested in its outcome—and are on Gawande's side throughout. There could be good reasons for doctors to avoid using checklists—but we don't know because Gawande doesn't address this question. Instead he uses storytelling techniques to craft a piece that allows room for only one point of view.

2. Looking at Strange Grammar or Syntax

Syntax refers to the way a sentence is put together—that is, the way the words are arranged. For example, look at these two sentences.

> I'm comfortable here.
> I'm not uncomfortable here.

Although they mean the same thing, the effect of each sentence is very different. In the second one, phrased as a double negative, what do you find yourself thinking about—comfort or discomfort?

To apply this concept, check out this sentence. Victor Frankenstein is talking here about his construction of the Creature.

> Unless I had been animated by an almost supernatural enthusiasm, my application to this study would have been irksome, and almost intolerable.

The odd syntax is a red flag. The sentence seems to be saying one thing, but when you look closely, its meaning becomes less clear. Does Victor find his work "irksome and almost intolerable," or doesn't he? It's interesting that he's avoiding a direct statement precisely when he's talking about what he's done and how he feels about it.

Moments like this one, where the **syntax makes the sentence difficult to understand**, are worth exploring. Double negatives, sentences that seem to move in two directions at once, sentences with many subordinate clauses, and sentences that coil back on themselves can all indicate places where the text is fighting with itself or saying more than one thing at once. These moments of syntactical confusion constitute another example of the train and the tracks diverging. If you read through them quickly, your brain neatens them up, causing you to miss some of what's going on. For example, here's that weird sentence from *Frankenstein* again.

> Unless I had been animated by an almost supernatural enthusiasm, my application to this study would have been irksome, and almost intolerable.

And here are two paraphrases that simplify that weird sentence in ways that remove the opportunity for asking questions.

> If I hadn't been motivated by something greater than myself, it would have been almost impossible to do this.

In this example, when the student simplifies "animated by an almost supernatural enthusiasm" to "motivated by something greater than myself," two interesting opportunities for asking questions disappear. First, the student has lost the idea of "animated by," which suggests more than just *motivated*; it has the sense of almost being literally picked up and put to work by an outside force. And second, the simplification of "almost supernatural" to "something greater than myself" obscures Victor's point that whatever is animating him is *almost* a force not from this world but not quite.

> If I hadn't been so totally into it, working on this project would have been way too hard and gross.

In this example, the student has overlooked key words again. By turning "animated by an almost supernatural enthusiasm" into "been so totally into it," she's skipped over some of the most interesting—and confusing—language of the passage; in the student's reading, Victor drives himself to do the work instead of being driven by some other force. And by turning "irksome, and almost intolerable" into "way too hard and gross," she loses the idea that *irksome*—that is, bothersome—and *intolerable* are not similar terms at all.

On the other hand, if you pay attention to the grammar and syntax in this moment, many questions arise. For example, you might notice that Victor uses passive voice rather than the more common active voice. He says, "I had been animated by an almost supernatural enthusiasm." Passive voice makes it hard to tell who's actually doing the action. (The classic example is "the ball was thrown." But who threw it?) Once we've noticed Victor's language, which implies that he's not in charge of his own actions, we can ask what effect Victor achieves by using passive voice.

Now that we've explored a number of ways that the train can diverge from the tracks in your chosen moment, let's look at some tools that can help you explore those places of divergence.

TOOLS FOR GENERATING QUESTIONS

Dialogic Journals

The first and perhaps most useful tool for generating questions about a specific moment is the *dialogic journal*.

The dialogic journal is a chart that helps you track what's interesting to you in a particular moment and what you're asking about it. It is not intended to produce answers: It's a starting point, a way of generating questions which in turn will help you generate more material.

The idea behind the dialogic journal is very simple. *Dialogic* means to be in dialogue or conversation with something or someone. In this case, the goal is to put you—or your ideas and questions—in conversation with the language of the text you're analyzing. It's a great tool for **getting your ideas out of your head** (so you can work with them more effectively), **generating ideas and questions** (so you have something to talk about), and **making choices about what you want to pay attention to** (so you can organize your thinking instead of drowning in too many ideas).

Another reason the dialogic journal is effective is that it's a **focusing device**. This is especially useful for students who find that they always go too big, either by talking about huge issues ("this is about death") or by looking at a whole story or text at once ("this book is all about death"). As we've said, it's almost impossible to support these kinds of blanket statements; instead you generally end up making lists of examples that "prove" your blanket statement, which lands you back in five-paragraph-essay mode. The dialogic journal's format is a way to ensure that you're working with smaller chunks of text that you can look at super closely and really investigate. Think of this process as holding a magnifying glass to the text. When you look this closely, you can see details and nuances that would have otherwise gone unnoticed. That gives you more to work with. The close-looking process that is required for dialogic journaling allows you to generate the material you need for a focused analytical essay.

To find the material for your dialogic journal, you'll want to go back to a moment you've chosen in the text and read through it once again, highlighting **every word or phrase** you find strange or noteworthy or weird. Remember, this is about your choices. Your goal here is not to find the material everyone agrees is "important" or to figure out what other people might find interesting about this passage—instead your aim is to discover what *you* find interesting so you can ask questions about it.

Once you've highlighted this material, you can begin building your dialogic journal. Remember that the journal is a dialogue between you and your moment, written out on the page. To create these two "speakers," divide your page lengthwise with a line down the middle. On the left half of the page, the text "speaks": This is where you transfer the language you've highlighted. You'll want to include quotes and page references; avoid paraphrases since they leave the specifics of language behind.

The right half of the page is for your part in the conversation. This is where your questions, thoughts, and comments go. Each time you add a quote to the left half of the page, use the right half of the page to talk to yourself about why you're noting this particular quote. You might:

- ask yourself a question about what's going on in this piece of language.
- look up and write down a dictionary definition.
- note how this piece of language resonates with something else you've noticed elsewhere in the text.

Try to avoid coming up with all-encompassing ideas about your quotes in the dialogic journal. It's also a good idea to **frame your thoughts in the dialogic journal as questions whenever possible**. The dialogic journal isn't the place to finalize your ideas or to figure it all out. The purpose of the exercise is to generate possibilities for writing, not to outline the paper. You're not ready to do that yet; if you force it, you're likely to limit your possibilities (which can lead you to run out of things to say).

An important note: Don't just fill out the left half and leave the right half for later! You want to make sure that you have a reason for adding each piece of language to your dialogic journal. This is a good way of sorting out what's interesting to you and what's not: If you don't have anything to add on the right half of the page, you probably don't need to spend much attention on a given quote. When you add the material on the left half all at once, you're not actually thinking about what's grabbing your attention in the text; you're making a list, and then you'll need to justify that list instead of trusting your ideas and questions.

Here's an example of a dialogic journal on a section of *Frankenstein*. Here Victor Frankenstein talks about the beginning of his project, which is finding the principle of life.

TEXT	QUESTIONS AND NOTES
"Unless I had been animated by an almost supernatural enthusiasm,"	He says he was *animated by*, like he's a cartoon character being drawn by someone else. Is he in charge, or is someone/something in charge of him?
"almost supernatural enthusiasm"	According to *Merriam-Webster*, *supernatural* means "beyond the regular universe," so is Victor saying he's being forced to do this by some godly force? But what about "almost"? Does he believe in it, or doesn't he? And *enthusiasm* doesn't just mean something you're excited about; it also means "an absorbing or controlling possession of the mind by any interest or pursuit." So, is this what's controlling him? And is it part of him or outside of him?
"Unless I had been animated by an almost supernatural enthusiasm, my application to this study would have been irksome, and almost intolerable."	This sentence is really confusing: *irksome* means "irritating, annoying, and tedious," and *intolerable* means "unbearable," something you can't tolerate. So is he enthusiastic about this task, or is it awful? He kind of says both at once, and in this weird backwards and confusing way. What's going on there?
"To examine the causes of life, we must first have recourse to death."	Why? He states this like it's a fact, but why should that be so? How does death produce life? Isn't this backwards? *Recourse* means "access or resort to a person or thing for help or protection: to have recourse to the courts for justice" and "a person or thing resorted to for help or protection." So death is helping him in some way? That's weird.

"Darkness had no effect upon my fancy; and a churchyard was to me merely the receptacle of bodies deprived of life, which, from being the seat of beauty and strength, had become food for the worm."	Does Victor think that all people are strong and beautiful when alive? He says he's not afraid of the dark or of ghosts, but dead bodies aren't either of those, so what's the point of telling us what he isn't afraid of? Is he secretly saying he *is* afraid?
"I must also observe the natural decay and corruption of the human body."	Why? How does that help to understand where life comes from? Why *must*? Again, he states it like it's a fact, but is it?
"I was led to examine the cause and progress of this decay, and forced to spend days and nights in vaults and charnel-houses."	Why *led*? Why *forced*? Who's forcing or leading him? A charnel house is defined as "burial chambers and places where dead bodies or bones are deposited." So he's hanging around graves looking at dead bodies. Yuck!
"My attention was fixed upon every object the most insupportable to the delicacy of the human feelings."	*Fixed*: Same thing. By what or whom? Also, *insupportable* means "unbearable" (like *intolerable*, before): He can bear things that a human can't? He's not a human? Or he's not as delicate as a human? Or he's so enthusiastic about this project that he can bear anything? Very weird.
"I saw how the fine form of man was degraded and wasted; I beheld the corruption of death; I saw how the worm inherited the wonders of the eye and brain."	… so death degrades, wastes, corrupts. This is definitely different than ghosts. He's definitely creeped out by death, which again raises the question of why he's so sure it holds the answer to understanding life. This is the second time he's mentioned worms (dead are "food for the worm," earlier). Obviously worms eat dead bodies, but he's in there messing around with those bodies, almost like he's trying to inherit their wonders, that is, the wonder of life. Does that make Victor almost like a worm?

At first glance, some of the questions in this dialogic journal might seem weak or silly. That's okay: Later on, you can winnow out the ones you don't want to keep. When you're creating a dialogic journal, though, **it's important to write down all of your questions**. At this stage, there's no such thing as a stupid question. And sometimes the weakest-seeming question can actually open up some interesting ideas.

For instance, remember that moment we discussed earlier, where Victor declares, "To examine the causes of life, we must first have recourse to death," as if it's an accepted fact? You might ask, "Why?" That's not a stupid question, though it may seem that way because of how Victor presents this idea: The rhetorical strategy he uses makes it easy to be carried along by his view of things. Asking *why* allows you to create a new relationship with the text. You're thinking critically about what the protagonist says instead of simply being co-opted by it. Asking questions about things the text presents as "obvious" or "natural" is important: Don't let the text bully you.

The dialogic journal above has two columns, but if you're working with a difficult text (a Shakespearean play, for example), you might want to use a three-column format. In a three-column version, the first column is for material from the text, the second for your paraphrase into ordinary English, and the third for your comments and questions. The three-column journal can also be very useful even for texts that seem to be written in straightforward English. It's easy to mistake paraphrase for analysis; this method lets you clearly distinguish between the two. The "paraphrase" column also stops you from saying that a passage "basically" means X or Y, and helps you see places where close reading will be useful.

Let's take a look at an example of a three-column dialogic journal, based on a passage a student paraphrased from Shakespeare's play *Macbeth*.

> Cure her of that.
> Canst thou not minister to a mind diseased,
> Pluck from the memory a rooted sorrow,
> Raze out the written troubles of the brain
> And with some sweet oblivious antidote
> Cleanse the stuff'd bosom of that perilous stuff
> Which weighs upon the heart? (V:iii:40-46)

And here's the journal.

QUOTE	PARAPHRASE	QUESTIONS AND THOUGHTS
"canst thou not minister to a mind diseased"	can't you attend to a sick mind?	The word *minister* is funny here—it means "attend to," but it also has a religious sense, right? And how do you attend to a mind?
"pluck from the memory a rooted sorrow"	tear out a deep sadness from the brain	*Pluck* seems like you're just lightly pulling something out, like a hair, but if the sorrow is "rooted," doesn't that mean it's deep? So it can't be plucked? What does this contradiction do?
"Raze out the written troubles of the brain"	erase/carve in the written woes of the mind	Okay, that's weird. Which is it—erase the problems she's got or carve them into her head? If it can mean both, what's that about?
"the brain"	[Lady Macbeth's mind]	Why "the brain" and not "her brain"? Why generalize it? Is he still talking about Lady Macbeth here?
"some sweet oblivious antidote"	some medicine causing forgetfulness OR some medicine that isn't aware of or has forgotten something (see OED definitions for *oblivious*)	The double meaning here is really strange: Does Macbeth want her to forget, or does he want the medicine to not know what she's forgetting, or ... ???
"the stuff'd bosom"	the stuffed (taxidermied? full? dead?) heart (OED)	Is her heart full, or is it dead? That's pretty different .... What does this ambiguity mean? Does it relate to this issue about the "oblivious antidote"?
"Which weighs upon the heart?"	that is a burden to the heart	How did Macbeth get from talking about the brain to talking about the heart?

Once again, in this journal we've made choices about what to include and what to skip. For example, the first line looked pretty straightforward to us, and we didn't think it was all that interesting, so we left it out. Another writer, however, might look at that line and have some questions about its imperious tone. For example, she might ask, "Why is Macbeth ordering the doctor around like this?"

Pitfalls and Problems: Dialogic Journals

The most common difficulty students face in working with dialogic journals is keeping their observations and questions directly connected to the language of the text. Sometimes, despite your best efforts, there's a gap between the words you put on the left half of the page and the questions you ask of them on the right—and this can cause you to leave the text behind as you move forward. Here are some forms that can take.

Disconnection

"canst thou not minister to a mind diseased?"	Can't you fix a sick mind?	What's going on with how he thinks about Lady Macbeth as a person?

The question about how Macbeth thinks about Lady Macbeth, his wife, is an interesting question to pursue. The problem with raising it now, however, is that it has no actual tie to the specific language in the left column. This means that nothing in the current moment actually led you to come up with that question. Because you don't have anything to ground your thinking in, you're likely to leave your moment or spin off into general statements. If you come up with questions like this, you can put them in a fourth column (or in your notes) labeled "Questions to Think About Later," i.e., when you know more about this moment and have specific ideas about Macbeth's take on his wife.

Misreading

"canst thou not minister to a mind diseased?"		Why is Macbeth talking to a minister about a "mind diseased"? He probably thinks a minister can heal her, especially if she's sick in her spirit in some way.

The student assumes she knows what *minister* means—it's a familiar word—so she skips the looking-up and paraphrasing step. (*Minister* here is a verb meaning "fix" or "help.") This leads her to misread the line, and that misreading carries through into the rest of her work as she tries to reconcile her understanding of *minister* with the text she's reading.

Answering Your Own Questions Prematurely

"Which weighs upon the heart?"	that is a burden to the heart	How did Macbeth get from talking about the brain to talking about the heart? By talking about her heart, he's saying she's bad to her core.

The first question in the right column, about the shift from *brain* to *heart*, is something that's worth noticing and thinking about. However, the student sets out to answer the question prematurely—and, as we've said before, dialogic journals at this stage are about opening things up, not closing them off. By answering his question at this stage, the student shuts down his exploration process because he's reached an "answer." Because he hasn't looked closely enough at the actual language of the text, he's jumping to a basic and generic response.

Forgetting What You Know

Another common pitfall in dialogic journaling is forgetting what you know. For example, look at a moment in *Macbeth*. Macbeth is now king, but he's also responsible for the murder of his friend Banquo. When Banquo's ghost appears at the table, Macbeth tries to explain what he's seeing to Lady Macbeth.

"But now they rise again,/With twenty mortal murders on their crowns,/And push us from our stools."	But now dead people come up from the grave with twenty fatal blows on their head and push us off our chairs	What's going on with Macbeth's seat? Does this mean that Banquo is trying to steal Macbeth's throne?

This question might seem interesting, but it ignores a crucial point: Banquo is a ghost. The student here is approaching this moment as though she doesn't know what a ghost is—as though a ghost is the same as a person. If you acknowledge the thing that seems obvious, you can use what you know about it to look at the passage more productively—for instance, you can now think about the significance of Macbeth seeing a ghost.

The dialogic journaling process we've shown generated lots of questions. But sometimes you get stuck: You look at your moment in the text and, though you know you're interested in it, you can't come up with a single question. And for some people, the dialogic journal seems too restrictive: They want a freer-flowing form. While we think it's a really useful tool and an important technique for you to try, the dialogic journal is not for everyone in every situation. Don't despair. There are lots of techniques for generating questions.

Quote-Question-Response-Question

The most straightforward technique is the *quote-question-response-question* approach (a bit like the one we worked with in chapter two with the John Berger excerpt). For instance, after reading this line:

"Unless I had been animated by an almost supernatural enthusiasm"
[quote]

… you might ask yourself:

→ Why is this interesting? [**question**]

… then you might write down something like:

> → Because it's only "*almost* supernatural," which shouldn't be able to make him do anything—it's not like an actual supernatural force. [**response**]

> → So what does saying "almost supernatural" do? [**question**]

> → Well, he's a scientist, so maybe he doesn't want to say that something actually supernatural was making him do it. [**response**]

> → So why raise this idea of the supernatural animating him at all? [**question**]

… and so on. The idea is to elicit questions by beginning with the text and talking to yourself about it. It's worth noting that each question comes directly out of the statement or idea that precedes it. There's no jumping, no moving three steps ahead and just writing down the "result" of your thinking.

This technique can be useful if you're worried about jumping from idea to idea without thinking about the intermediate steps, or, conversely, if everything about the moment you're working with seems obvious to you. In order for this technique to work, though, you have to give yourself permission to ask questions that may seem stupid or obvious. Remember, some of your questions here are just a means to an end, getting you to more useful and better questions. Don't edit yourself, and don't put pressure on yourself to come up with a brilliant question or response at every turn.

PRACTICING: QUOTE-QUESTION-RESPONSE-QUESTION

1. Choose a short quote from your moment, and write it at the top of a blank page.
2. Generate a question about the quote.
3. Write down a response.
4. Question that response.
5. Write down another response.
6. Keep going until you run out of questions. Then take a break; when you come back to your work, mark the questions that seem worth pursuing.

Wheel-and-Spoke Diagram

Another, more visual, way of generating questions is a technique called the *wheel-and-spoke diagram*. Here you write a word or phrase that seems central to your moment at the center of the page. For instance, if you're writing about the passage in *Frankenstein* we talked about earlier where Victor works on figuring out the secret of life, you might put "recourse to death" at the center. Draw a circle around that phrase, and draw a number of "spokes" that radiate from there. At the end of each spoke, ask a question. It's a good idea to have lots of spokes—at least six or seven—so you have time to "warm up" and get into your questions. Just as with quote-question-response-question, you'll probably find yourself asking some pretty straightforward questions at the beginning; instead of judging or erasing these, keep going. If you self-edit as you go, you're not likely to follow your chain of thinking to more productive questions.

Here's what a wheel-and-spoke diagram might look like.

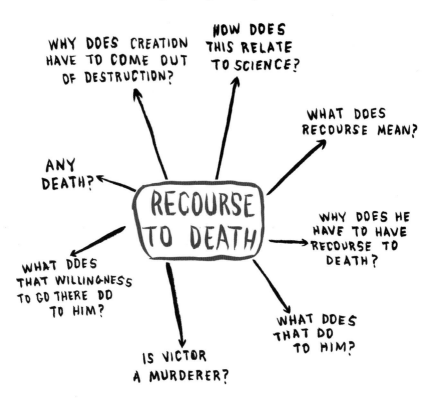

Once you've created a wheel-and-spoke diagram, you can use it to make choices and to generate more material and more questions. It's a good idea to look back at your wheel-and-spoke sketch and decide which questions seem most useful to you (and cross out those that seem less useful). Remember what you're looking for: questions that go beyond yes or no answers, questions that are about the text but move beyond plot summary, and questions that look at strangeness in the language instead of speculating or leaving the text behind. Then see if any of your questions are related: Is one, for instance, a subset of another? Indicate these connections on your drawing as well, perhaps with arrows or highlighted lines.

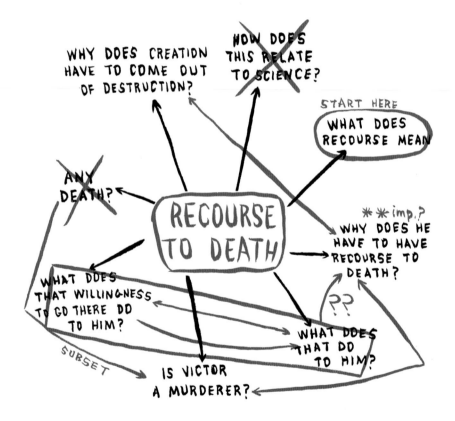

Once you've focused on the questions you find most potentially productive, you can generate more questions by responding to your first questions right beneath them on the same page. You can create lists of sub-questions that go with your questions; you can also choose a question that seems particularly productive or interesting, put it at the center of a new wheel-and-spoke diagram, and ask questions of it.

The wheel-and-spoke technique is effective in part because it gets you away from the formal writing process, which can free you up to work more productively. This is useful if you have trouble getting words on the page. It can also be great for writers who are paralyzed by having too many ideas: Getting everything out of your head and putting it down on the page in this way lets you see what you have so you can decide what to focus on.

PRACTICING: WHEEL-AND-SPOKE DIAGRAM

1. Choose a word or phrase that you think is important in your passage.
2. Write it in the center of the page, and draw a circle around it. That's your wheel.
3. Now draw a number of spokes radiating out from your wheel.
4. At the end of each spoke, write a question that relates to the word or phrase in the wheel.
5. Take a break. Then return to the diagram and cross out any questions that now seem boring, irrelevant, or unproductive.
6. Draw connections between any questions that seem to be linked.
7. Beneath each question that seems interesting, jot down any immediate responses or sub-questions that strike you.

Free-Association Drawing

Sometimes you believe you have nothing to say about the text at all: You can't think of any questions, everything seems self-evident and clear, and there's nothing for you to investigate. When that happens, a *free-association drawing* can be a useful tool. This is a form of brainstorming on the page. It's less formal than a dialogic journal or even a wheel-and-spoke drawing because it involves single words, not full phrases or sentences. Free-associating is pure process. It lets you see that you actually *do* have some ideas: They're just not on the tip of your tongue, or perhaps you don't yet trust them. After all, if you've read the material and thought about it, you are likely to have *something* to say about it—even if it doesn't initially seem that way.

Here's how it works: Write a key word from your moment in the middle of a page. Draw a circle around it, and keep tracing this circle until you come up with the next word that the first word makes you think of. Then draw a line from the first circle, write down the new word at the end of the line, and trace a circle around the new word until you come to another new word. Continue this process until you run out of space or words.

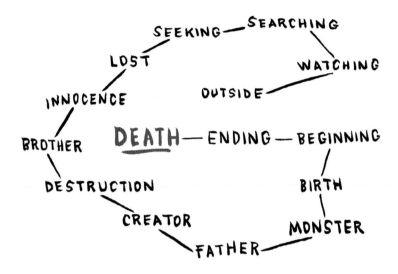

Free-associating carries some dangers, of course: It's easy to leave the text behind by following the trail of your associations (i.e., blood in *Dracula* makes you think of the color red, which makes you think of Christmas, which makes you think of presents …). If this happens, you'll need to assess and make choices about what's on the page, getting rid of anything that seems irrelevant. Then you can take a look at what's left. Is there one issue or topic that seems to come up over and over? Do you have a cluster of issues or ideas? Maybe a word in the top right corner actually connects to one in the middle and the words in between aren't useful; maybe the most important word is over there at the bottom and other words are subsets of it. Mark these connections with a pen or highlighter. Then transfer the words or cluster of words you're interested in to another page. For each word or cluster, create a question. You can do it in this form.

DEATH Why does Victor think he has to look at death to make life? Isn't that backward?

… or you might do a wheel-and-spoke drawing for each word you want to focus on. You might even decide to move your material into a dialogic journal at this point.

Mind Map

Another even more wide-ranging approach is a *mind map.* In a mind map, you leave out the lines between words that characterize free association: You're throwing words at the page, seeing where they stick, and then figuring out the connections later.

Start with a key word or phrase from the text, and write it in the middle of your page. Then just toss out any word or phrase that occurs to you about that key word or phrase as it appears in the text. Once you've run out of steam or your page is full, you can come back to your mind map and draw connections. If you find that you've left the text behind, cross out the stuff that's irrelevant to the text. Then turn the key words or phrases into questions.

It's a very good idea to work by hand as you engage in these exercises; you might also try working on oversized paper or a whiteboard. Moving away from the computer can break down formality and offer you a chance to engage more closely with your ideas. And using big spaces to work on can often open things up for you: As the spatial limitations recede, so do some of the limitations you place on your own thinking. Give it a try.

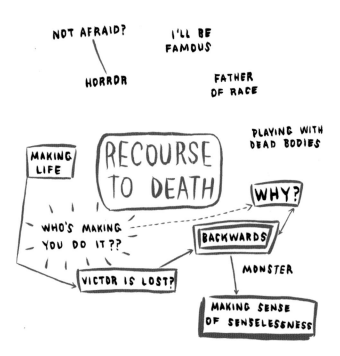

Hearing Your Ideas

Another option that works for some students is *recording yourself*. Talk to yourself about what's going on in your passage. Some people work best while they're pacing around, for instance, talking into their phones; then they can play back what they've just said and transcribe what seems most useful. *Working with a friend* can also be helpful here: Talking to another person who takes notes and asks questions can help you explore your ideas.

At this point, you've started engaging actively with the text and you've produced a lot questions. You're ready to organize and categorize your questions so that you can start focusing on your ideas and recognizing throughlines in your thinking.

CHAPTER SIX
IDEA THREADS

In the last chapter, we moved through the process of generating questions in a variety of ways. But once you've generated those questions, what are you supposed to do with them? It's tempting to think that the next move is to head right into drafting: You could, you might think, pick a question, answer it, and start turning that into your paper. But that's not the most productive way to proceed: You haven't yet made the decisions that will let you generate material for a strong, coherent paper with a clear focus.

Before you start responding to your questions, you need to take stock of them. What general territory do your questions cover? What do they focus on? What interests do they reveal to you? Which questions seem most important, and which are you less invested in? To make these decisions, it's helpful to use a visual structure to reorganize your questions, grouping those that relate to one another. We call these question groupings *idea threads*. By creating idea threads, you'll be able to see your own interests in the text more clearly, and this in turn will help you make some preliminary choices about the direction you want to pursue in your paper.

CREATING IDEA THREADS

Creating idea threads is a fairly straightforward process, though it requires you to think hard about what your questions have in common. Here's how to do it.

- Go back to your preliminary work (dialogic journals, mind maps, free-writes, etc.), and mark ideas and questions that relate to each other. You might highlight all the questions that address the same issue in one color, for example, and all the questions that address another issue in a different color.

- Group each set of related ideas on a new page, and give each group a name that basically conveys what it's about. This will help you see what you currently have and let you begin the process of finding a focus for the paper.
- Use what you've seen to come up with more questions. This lets you delve more deeply into your material. The more specifically your questions address the language of your moment, the more thorough and convincing your essay will be. And once again, you're not obliged to take up all the questions you generate: You'll make choices as you go.

We'll start with the dialogic journal we did on *Frankenstein*, now with related questions categorized by color. We made the text red for "Victor's Responsibility," purple for "Supernatural Stuff," blue for "Death and Life," and green for "How Victor Sees Himself."

You may find that some questions or moments belong to more than one thread. That's okay: Create a system to indicate this so that later you can think about the questions these overlaps generate. We've done that here by making the text one color and underlining it in a different color. Do what works best for you.

TEXT	QUESTIONS AND NOTES
"Unless I had been animated by an almost supernatural enthusiasm,"	He says he was *animated by*, like he's a cartoon character being drawn by someone else. Is he in charge, or is someone/something in charge of him?
"almost supernatural enthusiasm"	According to *Merriam-Webster*, *supernatural* means "beyond the regular universe," so is Victor saying he's being forced to do this by some godly force? But what about *almost*? Does he believe in it, or doesn't he?
	And *enthusiasm* doesn't just mean something you're excited about; it also means "an absorbing or controlling possession of the mind by any interest or pursuit." So is this what's controlling him? And is it part of him or outside of him?

"Unless I had been animated by an almost supernatural enthusiasm, my application to this study would have been irksome, and almost intolerable."	This sentence is really confusing: *irksome* means "irritating, annoying, and tedious," and *intolerable* means "unbearable," something you can't tolerate. So is he enthusiastic about this task, or is it awful? He kind of says both at once, and in this weird backwards and confusing way. What's going on there?
"To examine the causes of life, we must first have recourse to death."	Why? He states this like it's a fact, but why should that be so?
	How does death produce life? Isn't this backwards?
	Recourse means "access or resort to a person or thing for help or protection: to have recourse to the courts for justice" and "a person or thing resorted to for help or protection."
	So death is helping him in some way? That's weird.
"Darkness had no effect upon my fancy; and a churchyard was to me merely the receptacle of bodies deprived of life, which, from being the seat of beauty and strength, had become food for the worm."	Does Victor think that all people are strong and beautiful when alive?
	He says he's not afraid of the dark or of ghosts, but dead bodies aren't either of those, so what's the point of telling us what he isn't afraid of? Is he secretly saying he is afraid?
"I must also observe the natural decay and corruption of the human body."	Why? How does that help to understand where life comes from? Why *must*? Again, he states it like it's a fact, but is it?
"I was led to examine the cause and progress of this decay, and forced to spend days and nights in vaults and charnel-houses."	Why *led*? Why *forced*? Who's forcing or leading him?
	A charnel house is defined as "burial chambers and places where dead bodies or bones are deposited." So he's hanging around graves looking at dead bodies. Yuck!

"My attention was fixed upon every object the most insupportable to the delicacy of the human feelings."	*Fixed*: Same thing. By what or whom? Also, *insupportable* means "unbearable" (like *intolerable*, before): He can bear things that a human can't? He's not a human? Or he's not as delicate as a human? Or he's so enthusiastic about this project that he can bear anything? Very weird.
"I saw how the fine form of man was degraded and wasted; I beheld the corruption of death; I saw how the worm inherited the wonders of the eye and brain."	... so death degrades, wastes, corrupts. This is definitely different than ghosts. He's definitely creeped out by death, which again raises the question of why he's so sure it holds the answer to understanding life. This is the second time he's mentioned worms (dead are "food for the worm" earlier). Obviously worms eat dead bodies, but he's in there messing around with those bodies, almost like he's trying to inherit their wonders, that is, the wonder of life. Does that make Victor almost like a worm?

If you used some other question-generating method instead of a dialogic journal, you can still employ this process. Use the same color-coding strategy we show above on your list of questions. It may be helpful at this stage to move your questions into dialogic journal form so that you can see which language from your moment generated which questions. Since you're just charting at this stage and not generating material, it's a pretty simple step. If the dialogic journal isn't working for you, that's okay, but you'll need to find a format that allows you to connect your questions with the language they come from. Otherwise you'll lose track of the actual language, and you'll likely leave the text behind as you move forward. If you skipped the question-generating step entirely after you created your mind map or free-association drawing, it's time to go back to chapter five and generate some questions!

Here are the four categories of related questions from the dialogic journal. We've labeled each one with the topic or idea that ties the questions together.

Victor's Responsibility

- He says he was *animated by*, like he's a cartoon character being drawn by someone else. Is he in charge, or is someone/something in charge of him?
- And *enthusiasm* doesn't just mean something you're excited about; it also means "an absorbing or controlling possession of the mind by any interest or pursuit." So is this what's controlling him? And is it part of him or outside of him?
- Why *led*? Why *forced*? Who's forcing or leading him?
- *Fixed*: Same thing. By what or whom?

Supernatural Stuff

- According to *Merriam-Webster*, *supernatural* means "beyond the regular universe," so is Victor saying he's being forced to do this by some godly force? But what about *almost*? Does he believe in it, or doesn't he?
- He says he's not afraid of the dark or of ghosts, but dead bodies aren't either of those, so what's the point of telling us what he isn't afraid of? Is he secretly saying he *is* afraid?
- … so death degrades, wastes, corrupts. This is definitely different than ghosts. He's definitely creeped out by death, which again raises the question of why he's so sure it holds the answer to understanding life.

Death and Life

- According to *Merriam-Webster*, *supernatural* means "beyond the regular universe," so is Victor saying he's being forced to do this by some godly force? But what about *almost*? Does he believe in it, or doesn't he?
- Why? He states this like it's a fact, but why should that be so? How does death produce life? Isn't this backwards?
- *Recourse* means "access or resort to a person or thing for help or protection: to have recourse to the courts for justice" and "a person or thing resorted to for help or protection." So death is helping him in some way? That's weird.
- Why? How does that help to understand where life comes from? Why "must"? Again, he states it like it's a fact, but is it?

- A charnel house is defined as "burial chambers and places where dead bodies or bones are deposited." So he's hanging around graves looking at dead bodies. Yuck!
- … so death degrades, wastes, corrupts. This is definitely different than ghosts. He's definitely creeped out by death, which again raises the question of why he's so sure it holds the answer to understanding life.
- This is the second time he's mentioned worms (dead are food for the worm earlier). Obviously worms eat dead bodies, but he's in there messing around with those bodies, almost like he's trying to inherit their wonders, that is, the wonder of life. Does that make Victor almost like a worm?

How Victor Sees Himself

- Also, *insupportable* means "unbearable" (like *intolerable*, before): He can bear things that a human can't? He's not a human? Or he's not as delicate as a human? Or he's so enthusiastic about this project that he can bear anything? Very weird.
- This is the second time he's mentioned worms (dead are "food for the worm" earlier). Obviously worms eat dead bodies, but he's in there messing around with those bodies, almost like he's trying to inherit their wonders, that is, the wonder of life. Does that make Victor almost like a worm?

Labeling your idea threads might seem pretty straightforward, but it's actually an important step. **Giving each topic a heading or name will help you see how the questions are connected, and that's important because if you don't have a focus, you won't have anywhere to start.** You need to know what you're looking at. The labels we have for our four categories are broad enough to encompass a range of questions but also specific enough to give us a focus. **If your categories are too broad, you haven't made any decisions**: You're still looking at everything. For example, if you named a category "Victor," that category would include all of your work. **If your categories are too narrow, on the other hand, you're going to miss connections** and you won't be able to generate enough material to write your paper. For example, if you made "worms" a category, it would only have one item in it and you wouldn't see how it connected to other ideas. If you end up with fifteen categories or just one, start over.

PITFALLS AND PROBLEMS: QUESTIONS AND IDEAS THAT AREN'T WORTH PURSUING

We've said more than once that when you're generating material, you should turn off the editing function of your brain. That's because this early work is about opening things up, seeing where your mind goes, making connections, and sometimes even stating the obvious or asking questions that seem dumb. But because you've stopped editing, when you start mining your dialogic journal for idea threads, you may find questions and ideas that aren't worth pursuing. It's useful to learn how to recognize these dead ends—not so you'll never jot them down again but so you won't waste time with them as you move along in the writing process. Here are some examples.

Changing the Text

| "Darkness had no effect upon my fancy; and a churchyard was to me merely the receptacle of bodies deprived of life, which, from being the seat of beauty and strength, had become food for the worm." | It's weird that he says "deprived of life" and not just "dead." "Deprived" makes me think someone did that to them, like Victor's working with dead bodies that someone killed; could Victor actually be a murderer? Did he "deprive" the bodies of life? That might explain the whole weird thing where he keeps saying he'll understand life by looking at death: It's because he would have seen the moment when life turned into death, because he was making it happen. And he is kind of creepy; I could believe he could be a murderer. |

Here the student has moved from an idea that came from the text—"deprived of life" *is* **an odd way to say "dead"—to creating a whole new narrative that leaves the facts of the book behind**. Then he uses that narrative (which only exists in his mind) to start to answer other questions he's raised in his dialogic journal. To avoid getting caught up in a version of the story that isn't actually in the book, make sure your ideas are congruent with the facts of the book when you read your dialogic journal. As we said in chapter two, knowing the plot isn't enough to write a good paper, but you can't ignore it, either: You need to know what actually happens in the book, not in an alternative version that might be more interesting. Your job here isn't to make stuff up; it's to work with what's already there.

Cherry Picking

| "I became acquainted with the science of anatomy: but this was not sufficient;" | It's interesting that he calls it a science. In the early days of studying anatomy, doctors had to rob graves (which is kind of what Victor's doing, actually) to get bodies to study because the church forbade cutting up people because people needed to be intact when they got to heaven. This is just one way the church stood against science (Galileo!), and it makes me think that he's pointing to the split between science and religion. |

We call this "cherry picking" because here the student has picked one word (*science*) and started free-associating about it. Here's the chain of ideas, generalizations, and examples: *Science of anatomy at one time faced obstacles from the church → the church is always opposed to science → look what happened to Galileo → by using the word* science, *Victor is definitely setting up a division between science and religion.* Though it may look like she's thinking about the passage, she's actually using the passage as a pogo stick to jump out of the text.

Asking Questions That Contain Assumptions

| "I became acquainted with the science of anatomy: but this was not sufficient;" | It's interesting that he calls it a science. In the early days of studying anatomy, doctors had to rob graves (which is kind of what Victor's doing, actually) to get bodies to study because the church forbade cutting up people because people needed to be intact when they got to heaven. This is just one way the church stood against science (Galileo!), and it makes me think that he's pointing to the split between science and religion. **What does it mean that he's setting up an opposition between science and religion?** |

Here's that same dialogic journal entry but with a question added to the right half. If the student adds this question to her idea threads, she'd be extending her discussion of an "idea" that has very little to do with the book. But she'd run into another problem as well: When you look at the structure of the question, "What does it mean that he's setting up an opposition between science and religion?" you'll see that **something that is not yet proven (that Victor is setting up an opposition between science and religion) is stated as a fact.** The student then goes on to question the potential ramifications of this "fact." Because she's phrased it as a question, it's harder to notice that she's actually setting an assumption in stone. Instead of doing real questioning work, she's working from an assumption or presupposition, which will create what scientists call *confirmation bias*: Since she's assumed it's there, she'll inevitably find it, whether or not it's present at all.

WORKING WITH IDEA THREADS

Once you've organized your idea threads, you can read them over and decide which topic you're most interested in working with. If you're equally interested in a number of threads, a good way to make the decision is to choose the thread that has the most questions. Be sure to take your assignment prompt into account: If one thread fits best with the prompt, go with that one.

At this stage, you may be tempted to start summing things up: After all, you have a topic and a set of questions, so it would be easy to plug in answers. Don't give in to that temptation! If you do, you'll quickly find that you don't have much of interest to say because you haven't generated enough material yet. In our example, for instance, you could easily sum up the question of Victor Frankenstein's responsibility by declaring, "Victor doesn't take responsibility." But that's not a particularly interesting statement, and there's not much you can say about it, so you'll likely fall back on the old five-paragraph-essay method of providing examples of places where this is the case. This is not the path to a productive paper.

Instead of closing your process down, use the idea thread you choose to generate more material. The most productive way to do this is by **using the focus of your idea thread as a lens.** You'll remember that in chapter five we used the metaphor of the magnifying glass to talk about looking closely at a moment in the text. The magnifying glass continues to be useful as you explore and re-explore your moment:

Imagine you've figured out something about your moment. Now, in order to generate more material and connections, you can load the lens of that magnifying glass with the thing you've figured out. When you go back and look at your moment again with this focus, you'll see more. You can implement that concept at this point in the process by using the focus of your idea thread as a magnifying lens to look at your moment.

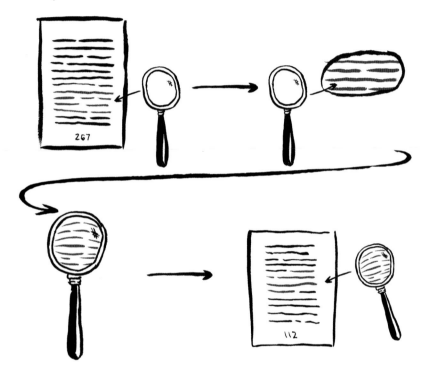

Once you have this lens, you can go back and ask questions about words and phrases in the passage that didn't interest you in your first pass. After all, what if you've skipped over something that, read through your lens, contradicts what you're saying? Or, on the other hand, what if you've skipped over something that could draw everything you're saying together? **You're responsible for the entirety of your passage, so you need to make sure you've asked questions about everything in it, even though you're not likely to use every single word in your final essay.**

Let's look at how this lens idea might work. If, for instance, you've chosen the "Victor's Responsibility" thread, you can start by looking at the work you've already done. For example:

"I was led to examine the cause and progress of this decay, and forced to spend days and nights in vaults and charnel-houses."	Why *led*? Why *forced*? Who's forcing or leading him?

In this moment in the dialogic journal, you've already done an important piece of work: You've identified a place where Victor isn't taking responsibility. The next step is to go back to the text on the left half of this section of the dialogic journal and ask more questions. You've looked at *forced*, so a logical follow-up question might be: *What is Victor forced to do?* As the text tells you, he's forced to go back and hang around dead bodies. This is a factual question, but that's okay: You're refreshing yourself on the basics of what's going on, and that can be really useful in generating more substantive questions. Remember, you don't want to edit yourself at this point. Once you've asked this question, you can use freewriting, a wheel-and-spoke drawing, a mind map, or a question-and-response setup to generate more questions. Here's what a question-and-response structure on this idea thread might look like.

What's Victor "forced" to do?

→ Hang out with dead bodies.

→ Well, wait, who "forced" him?

→ This was all his idea in the first place. Nobody else even knew about it.

→ So, is he trying to get sympathy by saying this? From who? Why? What does that do for him?

→ It makes it sound like he should be pitied.

→ How does that go with other parts in this passage where he's showing off, like when he says this would be "insupportable" to everybody else? He seems to be saying he's the toughest, so how does that work with wanting pity?

You'll note we haven't addressed every question we've raised here. It's better to let your mind keep moving so you don't shut your ideas down. You can always come back later to the questions you've left hanging.

There are other reasons to go back and look at your passage as a whole. You might, for example, have read a particular word or phrase as part of another idea thread. When you look back at the word or phrase through the lens of the idea thread, you may find that it also connects to *this* idea thread. You might even find that you can ask more questions about language you've already included in your idea thread. To really generate material, make sure you've raised as many questions as possible about your moment.

For example, when we looked at the phrase "I must also observe the natural decay and corruption of the human body," we originally asked questions about life and death.

"I must also observe the natural decay and corruption of the human body."	Why? How does that help to understand where life comes from? Why *must*? Again, he states it like it's a fact, but is it?

But now you've decided to focus on the idea thread about Victor's responsibility. When you look back at the passage and reread the phrase through this lens, you notice that *must* operates kind of like *forced*. Now you can ask some questions about this. For example:

What's the effect of him saying *must*? What does it do for him?

This time, let's see what happens if you approach this question with a freewrite.

Hmm … him saying *must* makes it sound like it's a fact, like it's inarguable. But it's not. And him saying he was *animated* and *forced* and *led*, and all those words where he isn't taking responsibility, are kind of doing the same thing, like, if he didn't decide to do it this way because he was kind of forced to do it like that, you can't blame him or even question him or say, wait, wasn't that your idea, Victor? So the "it's a fact" and "I didn't do it" both do this weird thing where everything Victor does is right and obvious. What does this do for him? Well, I guess it makes him look better. Maybe it makes him feel better? Does he need to feel better? What about?

As you can see, the student has generated a number of new questions about this piece of text by looking at it through this lens. And once you've generated all these questions, you'll need to go through the same process of choosing: Assess what you have, highlight the questions that seem useful, and add them to your idea thread. If you find that your questions are leading you to a new idea thread, you'll need to make new decisions about your focus.

This process of deepening your idea threads and making sure you've looked at the whole passage—instead of relying on your pass through a dialogic journal—may seem slow, especially when you feel like you need to be moving forward. But moving back and forth—in what's called a *recursive* process—is actually what keeps your thoughts from dead-ending. By asking yourself, *What did I say? What else can I say? What else is in the text? What can I say with what I've found there?* you keep moving forward. Cutting corners now won't save you time because without sufficient ideas you won't be able to draft something that looks like a real paper. And if you skimp now, you're more likely to face a blank screen later.

LOOKING AT YOUR PASSAGE WITH NEW EYES

If you're having trouble looking at your passage afresh, try this: Retype or handwrite your passage in its entirety, leaving lots of space between lines and in the margins to write. Then reread the passage through your lens, making notes on anything you notice now that you might have missed before.

> To examine the causes of life, we must first have recourse to death. I became acquainted with the science of anatomy: but this was not sufficient; I must also observe the natural decay and corruption of the human body. In my education my father had taken the greatest precautions that my mind should be impressed with no supernatural horrors. I do not ever remember to have trembled at a tale of superstition, or to have feared the apparition of a spirit. Darkness had no effect upon my fancy; and a churchyard was to me merely the receptacle of bodies deprived of life, which, from being the seat of beauty and strength, had become food for the worm. Now I was led to examine the cause and progress of this decay, and forced to spend days and nights in vaults and charnel houses. My attention was fixed upon every object the most insupportable to the delicacy of the human feelings. I saw how the fine form of man

was degraded and wasted; I beheld the corruption of death succeed to the blooming cheek of life; I saw how the worm inherited the wonders of the eye and brain.

Yellow: Existing stuff with Victor's responsibility

Blue: New stuff that maybe ties in with that … He says *must* 2 times here, kind of like *forced*, but now it's not just like someone is making him, it's like this is obvious, the only way to do it. He has no choice. So in a different way, this also sets up that there was no other option and in that way it's kind of not his fault or responsibility.

If you still don't see anything worth noting, take the time to do a three-part dialogic journal or to paraphrase each sentence in some form. Paraphrasing the material you're skipping over may allow you to see places that aren't as straightforward as you thought they were: When something is hard to paraphrase, that's because something strange is going on, and that strangeness may be worth investigating.

PRACTICING: CREATING IDEA THREADS, GENERATING NEW QUESTIONS

1. Go back to your dialogic journal (or your questions), and, using different colored highlighters, group the questions that seem to go together. If a question belongs in more than one group, indicate each color that it corresponds to.
2. Create a page for each idea thread. Add your questions to the idea threads they correspond to.
3. Reread each thread. Give each thread a title that encapsulates what it's about.
4. Choose the idea thread that seems most interesting or productive to you.
5. Now that you know what your focus is, ask more questions of the words and phrases you've already tied to this idea thread. To do this, you need to go back to your dialogic journal and look again at what you have. You also need to go back to the text and reread your passage in context to make sure you're not missing anything. Incorporate what you find into your idea thread.
6. Do the same with words and phrases you didn't originally think about with this topic or focus in mind. What do you see differently now? What questions can you now ask?

RECOGNIZING PRODUCTIVE QUESTIONS

The process of creating and expanding your idea threads is all about generating a lot of questions. That gives you real choices about what to focus on and write about. But not all of the questions you generate will be useful. That's okay—it's important to let yourself ask all the questions that occur to you, even if some of them turn out to be dead ends. But once you've produced all of these questions, you'll need to make some choices. So how do you know which questions are productive?

Productive questions:

- **open things up rather than shut them down.**
- are **specific** to the topic of your idea thread.
- **address a particular phenomenon**, "problem," or strangeness in the exact language of the moment you're looking at.
- are **analytical.**
- are **broad enough** to generate material and move forward.
- are **not so broad** that they'll lead to generalizations.
- **send you back to the text** to see what you can figure out.

For example, in our dialogic journal, we looked at the phrase "My attention was fixed upon every object the most insupportable to the delicacy of the human feelings." We noted that *insupportable* means "unbearable," which suggests that Victor can bear things that a human can't. This led us to ask:

He's not a human?

This is a pretty good question, even though at first it might seem straightforward. Here's why.

- It emerges from the specifics of the language of the text: that is, the phrase "insupportable to the delicacy of human feelings."
- It's directly related to an idea thread we're interested in—how Victor sees himself.
- It's broad enough to really generate material and move forward but not so broad that you'll find yourself writing a dissertation or generalizing.
- It's analytical: While it's clear on the surface that Victor is a human, the question of what "human" really means here is not so obvious. To figure

that out, you'll need to look closely at the language of the text and you'll have to think about the specifics of the moment.

So our initial, seemingly simple question is actually quite rich. That means it can potentially lead to some complex, closely read explorations—which means we might be able to come up with a lot to say about it.

When you're assessing your questions to see if they're productive, keep an eye out for questions that begin with *why*. Even though we tend to talk about all the question words together—*who, what, where, why, when,* and *how*—not all question words are equally useful. Be wary of *why*. Questions in the form of "Why does X do Y?" often lead to problematic responses and dead ends. Look at what happens when the student wants to know more about the moment when Victor, having just brought his creation to life, turns from it and flees. Specifically he asks why Victor abandons his new creation. Here's what his dialogic journal looks like.

"I had worked hard for nearly two years, for the sole purpose of infusing life into an inanimate body. For this I had deprived myself of rest and health. I had desired it with an ardour that far exceeded moderation; but now that I had finished, the beauty of the dream vanished, and breathless horror and disgust filled my heart. Unable to endure the aspect of the being I had created, I rushed out of the room"	He just leaves his creation? He calls it a dream, but now that it's real he just walks away from it? Why?

Here are some of the things that could happen when this student tries to respond to his *why* question.

- **THE ANSWER'S IN THE TEXT.** To respond to this, the student could go back to the text and find an answer. He might say, *Victor fled because when he saw the Creature, his heart was "filled with breathless horror and disgust."* This is factually correct, but that won't take him very far since he's just restating what's in the text. It's a surface answer, not an analytical one.
- **THE ANSWER IS REALLY A LABEL.** The student could respond to the question of why Victor flees by judging and labeling him. *Victor's a baby,* the student says. *He's a bad scientist; he's selfish.* All of this may be the case, but what work do these opinions do for the student's analysis? Lik-

ing the characters isn't a prerequisite for writing about the text they're in, and opinion-based labels halt analysis rather than moving it forward.

- **THE ANSWER IS A GENERAL "RULE."** The student might propose a response like this: *Victor runs away because he realizes that creating life is trespassing against God and he was wrong to have begun the experiment in the first place.* But there's no evidence of this in the text itself; it's just another way for the student to state his opinion. On top of that, he's set up that opinion as if it's a baseline rule that everyone knows (creating life equals playing God, which is wrong).

- **THE ANSWER REQUIRES MIND READING.** Another way to find an answer to the question of why Victor flees is to assume the role of Victor's therapist. This can lead to something like this: *Victor abandons the Creature because when Victor's mother died, he experienced it as abandonment, so he can't connect to his creation.* While this looks like it's based in the text—it makes use of an event that does occur in the story—it's still a way of jumping out of the specific moment and rewriting the text. And once again, it provides a seemingly definitive answer that stops the conversation instead of moving it forward.

You may have noticed that we've used the word *answer* here, when we generally say *response*. That's because *why* questions often lead to responses that *feel* like answers—they *seem* as if they're true. But as you saw in the examples above, if they are true, it's usually because they're coming straight from the text, and if they feel true, it's because they are opinions rather than explorations. That's not analysis.

Instead of *why*, it's more productive to form questions using *what*. What sets up a field of inquiry that won't lead you toward labeling or trying to read a character's mind. For instance, if you change the question about Victor abandoning his creation from *why* to *what*, you could phrase it in a very straightforward way: *What causes Victor to flee his creation?* Responding to that would require you to go back to the moment and read it closely to see exactly what Victor says. What words seem off? How does he justify or explain himself? These kinds of questions move you right into analysis based on specifics. So when you're reading your threads, **keep in mind that all question words are not created equal. If there's a question that uses *why*, reframe it using *what* or another question word.**

1. Go back to your idea threads.
2. Evaluate your questions according to the guidelines for productive questions.
3. Highlight the questions that meet these guidelines.
4. Cross out any questions that seem unproductive.
5. Look for questions that start with *why*, and try reframing them as *what* questions.

If you end up with more questions crossed out than highlighted, don't despair. You should:

- go back to your idea threads and ask more questions about what's there.
- go back to your dialogic journal to look for more questions.
- return to your passage and create a new dialogic journal.
- do a new wheel-and-spoke diagram to help you come up with more questions.
- look back at your crossed-out questions to see if you can salvage any of them by rewording the question.

By the time you've worked through your idea threads, you've amassed a lot of material. But your paper can't be composed entirely of questions and preliminary responses. In the next chapter, we'll show you how to start taking up those questions.

CHAPTER SEVEN
DISCOVERY DRAFTS

In this chapter, we'll talk about the stage that many people find to be the most difficult step in essay writing: moving from note taking, dialogic journaling, idea threads, and other preliminary work to producing a first draft. This is the point at which a lot of writers freeze up. Faced with the blank page, they have no idea where or how to begin. **The good news is that since you've done all of this preliminary work, you don't have a blank page.** You've already produced a lot of material for your first draft, and—because you've chosen your idea thread—you have at least a general idea of what the story of your essay will be. In this chapter, we'll explain what discovery drafts are all about. We'll show you how to generate some more material and give you some methods for organizing what you already have and creating a draft you can work with.

ABOUT DISCOVERY DRAFTS

We call this stage the *discovery draft* because the aim is to *discover*, through writing, what you have to say. *Discovery* **also emphasizes that this is still process work.** As we've said, process writing is all about taking risks, generating material, and not editing too much; if you start censoring yourself now, you could shut down some really interesting ideas and end up with surface-level work that doesn't take you very far.

There is, of course, a critical difference between discovery drafts and other process work: **In a discovery draft, you begin to create the narrative of your essay.** This draft is where you really think about, investigate, and explore what the questions you've raised suggest or offer, and it's where you begin to tell a story. For this reason, students often mistake a discovery draft for a final product. But this draft isn't a repository of final answers. It's true that you come to the discovery draft having already figured out some ideas, but those ideas will likely change and deepen as you keep working, and new questions will likely emerge from this process.

Students also try to polish their work at this stage—they mistakenly think that the first draft is really the same thing as the last draft, and they want their writing to be clean, complete, and perfect. So they treat every word as the final word—making it hard to get any words down on the page at all.

The discovery draft is still a *form* of process writing. And **process writing is useful precisely because it's not neat and clean**. It's not ready for prime time. Process writing requires you to make a mess as you try things out, travel down pathways that may or may not prove useful, test ideas, float questions, talk to yourself on the page, sketch out your thinking … . It's the place where you can take risks. And **strong essays depend on risk taking**: If you don't ask real questions or try out ideas, you simply won't have anything interesting to say. It can be frightening to launch into the unknown without a map, to start writing without knowing where you're going, or to explore a complicated idea without knowing where (or if) you'll come out. But letting go of the final product and doing process writing is crucial.

It's important to remember that you're not writing to a formula. While we're taking you through a series of steps as we explain methods and approaches, we know that every writer works (and thinks!) a little bit differently. You may, for example, be a writer who is most comfortable just sitting down and drafting new material early on in your process; you may be a writer who needs multiple outlines; you may work best cutting and pasting together the work you've already done and filling in the gaps. Whatever method works best is the one you should use—and if you combine these methods or use a variation, that's great, as long as you're moving forward productively. In this chapter, we'll give you some options and show you what a discovery draft looks like.

The choices that you make at the discovery draft stage aren't set in stone; you can always revisit earlier work to pick up ideas that didn't make it into the draft. And there's a really important distinction between a discovery draft and later drafts that will help you avoid getting locked into one set of ideas too early in the process: **A discovery draft starts by asking a question, not by stating a claim.**

Questions, Not Claims

Back in chapter four, when we discussed what an analytical essay looks like, we talked about having a *claim*; i.e., a big idea your paper is going to show your reader. Students often think that paper writing begins with coming up with a claim: After all, it's the idea that underpins your essay. But **in order for a discovery draft to actually discover something, it can't yet have a claim**. That's because any claim you could make in this draft would be general or vague or self-evident: You haven't yet done the work that would result in a claim. Instead a discovery draft is based on a series of questions that let you explore what interests you about a specific phenomenon in the text. Notice that we said *explore*, not *answer*. That's because you're still in the process of discovering what you think.

But here's the thing about asking questions: It's a risk-taking act, which means it's hard. In a classroom setting, students often feel that asking questions means starting from a position of weakness ("I don't know"), and naturally they'd rather start from a position of strength ("Here's what I know"). This is equally true of essay writing, but that kind of safety-first attitude, though understandable, isn't helpful, either in class or on the page. The challenge here is being okay with questions, which means being okay with starting with what you don't know. It might help if you **think about questions not as a sign of ignorance but as a sign of intent: "Here's what I want to understand."**

This is exactly how questions function in many disciplines: An artist, for instance, might ask what would happen if he uses two different kinds of media in the same work. A scientist might ask herself what could happen if two chemicals were combined or how a plant might grow differently if it wasn't subject to gravity. Asking a question like this is really about stating an agenda: You're saying to yourself, *Here's what I'm going to explore*. When you're writing a discovery draft, you're still in the early stages of exploration and you don't yet know what you're going to find out. That's a good thing because if you had no discoveries left to make at this stage, you'd bore yourself and your readers.

WHAT HAPPENS IN A DISCOVERY DRAFT

As we've said, discovery drafts are still considered process work. This isn't the place to worry about typos or grammar or effective connections or making sure you have all the pieces of an essay that we talked about in chapter four. But, as we also said, discovery drafts require you to make choices and think about order. This means that, even though every draft will look different, a strong and effective discovery draft does have a basic shape or sequence.

A strong discovery draft:

- starts with an opening paragraph that introduces an overall question.
- is made up of a series of modular pieces.

Each module of the draft:

- introduces and contextualizes a specific phenomenon you find interesting in a moment in the text.
- asks a question about that phenomenon.
- explores that question by looking at the specific language of the moment. moves toward thinking about the implications of your exploration.

In a discovery draft, you might engage in this process once, or three times, or five, depending on the scope of your assignment and where your work takes you. You might have several questions emerging from one moment in the text, or you might work with a series of moments from across the text (or even, depending on the assignment, with more than one text). Don't get too hung up on the connections between the moments: Just keep going, and see where your ideas take you. Once you've written your discovery draft, you'll have plenty of opportunities to evaluate, restructure, revise, and really think through the significance of what you've discovered.

Tackling the Blank Page

As any writer can tell you, the hardest part of writing is tackling that blank page. When we ask student writers about what they do when they start writing, they often tell us that they'll sit down at the computer and just look at the screen for a while, unsure of what to do next. We get that. Beginning to write is hard. But as we said earlier, you've already generated a lot of material through your notes, dialogic journaling, freewrites, wheel-and-spoke drawings, and so forth. **If you've done all of this work, there is no blank page.**

Getting started can be especially difficult for writers who don't trust themselves: *Who am I*, such a writer might think, *to say anything about this?* And that anxiety, coupled with the fear of the blank page, can lead you back to the five-paragraph essay. The old model had one thing going for it: a set of rules. But as we've said, reverting to that old, boring structure won't pay off for you in college writing. So what to do?

This is a good time to remember something we've said earlier: While student writers tend to think of writing as a product—the thing that you hand in—the fact is that most of the writing you do on a given product is better thought of as *process*. What we mean by this is that **writing is a form of thinking.** That doesn't mean that you work everything out in your head and then put it on the page. **But you also don't need to wait until you've figured it all out to start writing**. Working ideas out in your head before you sit down and put ideas on the page feels safer than beginning to write when you don't yet know what to say—but it's not the most productive way to go.

When you think on the page, ideas happen, connections occur to you, and confused ideas or half-formed thoughts become clearer. If you try to work everything out in your head beforehand, you're likely to self-edit, rejecting ideas that seem incomplete or not totally worked through or searching for complete answers. When you do that, you tend to shut down possibilities and lose the opportunity for exploration—which means that you have less material to work with and what you do have is impoverished. So it's always best to start by writing.

Remember that what you're writing is just a draft. You're thinking on the page, not creating a product. So you're free to take risks, follow random ideas, change your mind, write in a stream of consciousness, ignore the rules of grammar and spelling, and, most important, play with ideas. After all, you're the only reader of what you produce at this stage. Nobody is grading you on it or criticizing your choices. The freer you can be in these early written responses, the more material you'll have to work with later.

It's also worth noting that the process of writing often shows you that you have more ideas than you think. Many students who are accustomed to working through their ideas only in their heads come to the conclusion that they have nothing to say. That's because they're subconsciously rejecting ideas they come up with. Getting your thoughts out of your head and onto the page short-circuits this type of self-critical editing. The physical act of writing (or typing) lets you move through your thoughts with less self-censorship. When you just start writing—without waiting to figure everything out—you'll find that the act of writing helps you discover and create responses.

And as you write, you can also dig down into ideas in a way that isn't possible when you're thinking them through in your head. By writing stuff down, you give yourself space to choose one idea, open it up, think about it from different directions, and drill down into its implications—usually by asking more questions as you go.

Freedom Through Freewriting

One way to begin writing your draft is to use your idea threads to generate a free-write. The point of freewriting is to get your ideas out of your head and onto the page, to see what you're thinking and to work through connections. That's easier said than done, but fear not: This is still process writing. What you're really doing here is **talking to yourself on the page,** and it's that conversation that lets you figure out what you're thinking. Freewriting really comes in handy here. As we've said before, freewriting involves sitting down with your notebook or computer (or a big piece of paper or a whiteboard or whatever you're comfortable with) and writing as freely and continuously as possible.

Try this process.

- Go back to your idea thread to remind yourself what you wanted to explore.
- Choose one question to begin.
- Don't feel you have to begin with your first passage. Start with the phenomenon and question you have the most to say about.
- Ignore the rules of formal writing. This isn't formal writing.
- When you get stuck, ask yourself another question or go back to your idea threads to pick up a question there.

The prospect of freewriting at this stage may still seem pretty daunting to you because it's so closely connected to actual draft writing. You may feel as though you have nothing to say or that you have so many things to say that it's impossible to get started. And plenty of students have a hard time freewriting because they see it as just as formal and demanding as the essay itself.

To free yourself up, here are some tricks and ideas.

- Begin by asking yourself a question. Your question might come from your idea threads; if that doesn't seem useful, a more general question will do. "What am I talking about here?" is perfectly okay if it gets you started. Your question will give you something to respond to and help you start that conversation with yourself.

- If prose writing seems overly formal, write a list of phrases or words. Free-writing should be exactly what it sounds like: free. Breaking down the formality of the sentence and the paragraph can be really helpful.
- Start with the piece or question that interests you most, or the one you can wrap your head around most readily, instead of the one that comes first in your passage or the one you think is most "important."
- Instead of giving yourself a page limit or forcing yourself to work through an idea until it's done, give yourself a time limit. Set an alarm for five minutes, or ten or twenty, and keep writing for that period of time. If you run out of things to say, it's okay to write, "I have no idea," or something like that until the next thought comes to you. Or you can ask yourself another question. The idea is to keep thinking on the page, no matter what.
- When you're stuck, going back to the text will almost always be helpful. That's because the text is the source: Everything you're trying to think about is there, and as you develop your ideas, you'll see more and more in the text and be able to make more connections between the things you notice. **The more you look, the more you'll find.**

It's inevitable that some of your writing will look like garbage. Don't worry—it's part of the process. All writers come up with a fair bit of garbage as they figure things out. That's necessary: How can you figure out what's important if you don't let yourself throw everything on the page where you can see it? Sometimes the most unlikely directions turn out to be the richest ones. So don't dismiss any of your ideas before they make it onto the page. We've seen plenty of students say, "Well, what about … no, never mind. That's stupid." But you don't have anything to lose by writing everything down. You'll have plenty of time to assess what you've got, make decisions, cut things out, or add things in.

Here's what an initial freewrite might look like. As you'll recall, we've been working with e.e. cummings's "next to god of course america i." A student in the process of moving from idea threads into a discovery draft starts by choosing her thread and reading it over. In this case, the thread the student is working on is "silence." Here's the thread.

Silence

Deafanddumb, the way he's using it, is a way of saying the language that people who can't hear or speak use, which is signs. So in that way, it's like

Italian or whatever. And I guess the idea of "even deafanddumb" shows that everyone, whether they can talk or not, is still acclaiming (what? must be America ... it's like he's talking directly to America). But he doesn't say *sign*, he says *deafanddumb*, so even though he's saying it as an example of a language, what really sticks out is the idea of NOT being able to speak, being dumb. So in every language, even silence, people affirm your (america's?) glorious name, but if you're doing it silently, it can't be heard. And if it can't be heard, maybe you're not doing it at all. So in one phrase is the idea of speaking to affirm glory and NOT speaking or not being able to speak. Is that happening in the poem, too? I mean, is it affirming or not affirming?

"then shall the voice of liberty be mute?" Now the thing that can't speak or be heard is liberty. Connects to the dead soldiers?

What about the speaker? He talks and talks, and then he stops talking and someone else says, "he spoke. And drank rapidly a glass of water" Past tense of *speak*, so he's not speaking anymore. And then he drinks "a glass of water," so he can't be talking. What's going on? Speaker has nothing left to say? (he's mute now?) What he's said has kind of shut him up? Why also drinking water? What's important about that? Does it matter that it's rapidly? Why's he thirsty? Has he been talking that long?

When the student looks back at the first entry, she's reminded that it was the word *deafanddumb* that got her interested in this topic in the first place. She likes what she's written so far, but she wonders if there's anything else in that part of the poem that she needs to look at. The whole line is "in every language even deafanddumb/thy sons acclaim thy glorious name." She writes:

> *Thy* is America (I know because *thy* is "your" and the name that's being acclaimed here is definitely America because he praises it in the first line and the patriotic songs he's quoting from are all about how great America is). So in a way, since he's talking, he's acclaiming her: he's like "one of her sons," which is cool ... he's doing the thing he's talking about, the thing that even people who can't speak or hear do. Don't know if this is useful ...

As you can see, the student is definitely talking to herself in this freewrite. She isn't concerned about whether her language is paper ready—she's just trying to get her ideas on the page as they occur to her.

As she keeps reading, she sees that she was interested in the idea of *liberty* being *mute*. She starts to look more closely at that section of the poem by asking, "What would silence liberty?" Since the poem is more or less one long sentence, it's hard to know exactly where to start, but when she looks for the words closest to "then shall the voice of liberty be mute?" the nearest complete idea is this.

> what could be more beaut-
> iful than these heroic happy dead
> who rushed like lions to the roaring slaughter
> they did not stop to think they died instead

She starts her freewrite by asking, "If liberty is mute, what silenced it?"

> Okay: liberty being mute connects to the dead people? Liberty is sad that they died? But the dead are heroes and beautiful, so liberty might not be sad if they died for her. Except that even if they're heroes, how heroic can they be if they didn't stop to think about what they were dying for? … and if they'd thought, they might not have died? What does this have to do with liberty? Maybe it's their NOT thinking that silences liberty? Does not thinking connect somehow to not being able to speak/being mute?
>
> Liberty might be silent, but the slaughter is roaring. What should roar is the dead because they're "lions," but they don't say anything (they're dead). Slaughter means the killing of animals for food or the killing of a lot of people, like in a massacre. Putting *roaring* next to that makes it sound like the people being killed are crying and yelling: it's horrible. Is that what might make liberty silent? Like liberty can't bear what's going on? That's sad.

The process of deepening and expanding your idea thread is really about seeing what's there and what's not there. Sometimes that's obvious: In the cummings example above, for instance, it was easy for the student to see that she hadn't done much with the connection between liberty and muteness. But sometimes it's more difficult to see what you do and don't have, so you may need to make things clearer for yourself by organizing the thread material.

When the student goes back again to her "silence" idea threads, she sees that her initial ideas about the speaker have a lot of questions and not a lot of responses. She uses different colors to highlight what she knows and what she's asking.

> What about the speaker? He talks and talks, and then he stops talking and someone else says, "he spoke. And drank rapidly a glass of water" Past tense of *speak*, so he's not speaking anymore. And then he drinks "a glass of water," so he can't be talking. What's going on? Speaker has nothing left to say? (he's mute now?) What he's said has kind of shut him up? Why also drinking water? What's important about that? Does it matter that it's rapidly? Why's he thirsty? Has he been talking that long?

The highlighting makes it clear that there's a lot here for her to think about. What she knows (in blue) summarizes what the poem told her: There was a speaker, he stopped talking, and then he drank some water. She has lots of questions here (in yellow), and she's not yet sure what to do with them. To start sorting out what she thinks and what she's most interested in, she may go back to a question/response series or she may do some more freewriting or create a wheel-and-spoke diagram.

Sketching Out Your Ideas

Another more visual way to deepen the ideas in your thread is to sketch them out, labeling and making notes as you go, and seeing what occurs to you. This is a way of thinking on the page through a combination of images and words. This process can then be generative because as you sketch and write, you're building connections between parts of the text and generating ideas about them.

As you draw or write by hand, you're likely to notice ideas or questions emerging from what you've already figured out. For example, in the sketch below, the student uses a drawing to visualize the difference between talking about liberty in any "language" versus in "deafanddumb." Similarly, as she draws the "heroic happy dead," she starts thinking about what they would look like if they had died in battle. And that suddenly makes her question why the speaker describes them as "beautiful," which is something she hadn't thought about before.

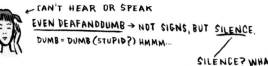

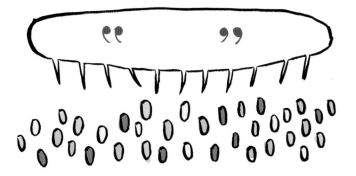

TAKING BREAKS

It's a good idea to build periodic breaks into your writing process. An excellent time for a break is anytime you're about to assess, edit, or otherwise work with what you've already done. Stepping away lets you come back to the project with fresh eyes. It gives you the perspective you need to look at what you have and to interrogate your own ideas. So work on something else, go for a walk, watch a movie, go to the gym, eat, or hang out with a friend. When you come back to your project, you'll have a much better perspective on the material you've generated. And remember—you can't take a break if you've left all the work of writing the essay to the last minute!

ORGANIZING, CATEGORIZING, DELINEATING

You've collected the material you generated earlier, come up with some new material, and started making choices about what you want to keep. What's the next step? That decision might depend on what kind of writer you are.

When we talk about types of writers, we usually divide people into two big camps.

Associative writers tend to jump from idea to idea, going from one thought to the next in a free-associative way that's not necessarily linear. Associative writers often have no trouble generating lots of writing—but they don't always have a lot of control over where they're going. An associative writer might begin, for example, by writing about religion in *Frankenstein*, might move through a discussion of Zen Buddhist beliefs, and might end up talking about traveling in Tibet. A connection might exist between all of these focal points, but the thread of the original discussion—about religion in *Frankenstein*—may be lost.

Associative writers are lucky because they tend to have a lot of ideas—but they have difficulty creating hierarchies of ideas that let them decide which ideas are more important and which are less so, and they often struggle to figure out what's central and what's extraneous or unrelated. Associative writers tend to create a great deal of process work, but they may have difficulty getting to claims or conclusions or final drafts. And sometimes they have so many ideas that they become paralyzed and can't produce anything at all.

Self-critical writers, on the other hand, are very concerned with product. A self-critical writer will often write only one draft of a paper—but that one draft, highly polished when it's done, can take a very long time and be very painful to write. Self-critical writers tend to have a hard time getting started, since they're working on the final draft from the beginning. The typical self-critical writer may delete just about every phrase he puts on the page—or may not put any phrases on the page at all for a very long time because he's composing and editing in his head. Self-critical writers are likely to work with clearly defined outlines and plans and often have an excellent sense of the structure and direction of an essay. But they also shut down ideas and questions that threaten this structure, and they don't give themselves space to take risks and try things out, so their papers can be very short, very direct, and sometimes lacking in ideas. (Non-native speakers may also have these difficulties because they're so focused on getting the words right, understandably, that they lose track of the ideas.)

It's important to remember that these general types aren't absolute: There's lots of crossover. Some writers who are generally associative, for example, can become self-critical if they get overwhelmed by their own ideas—or if they don't trust their own thinking. Some writers who are generally self-critical can find themselves generating endless prewriting work as a method of figuring every last thing out (and avoiding the dreaded draft). But it's still useful to think about your approach to writing in terms of these categories: Being aware of your own practices can help you avoid trouble by choosing techniques and approaches that are right for you.

If you tend to write and write and write but can't organize your ideas, for example, you may find wheel-and-spoke graphs or grouping particularly useful. On the other hand, if you find yourself paralyzed when you sit down to write, you may want to draw a mind map or give brainstorming or free-associating a try. The idea is to turn your approach to writing into a strength, not a weakness, by addressing the areas where you get stuck in a way that makes sense to you.

So how do these writing "types" relate to how you work on your discovery draft? If you understand what's comfortable and what's scary to you in your writing process, you can make decisions that keep you moving forward.

A self-critical writer may find that it's really helpful to create an outline before she starts drafting. Self-critical writers like to have a lot of control over their writing, which is one reason it can be tough for them to get started. After all, where do you begin if every word has to be perfect? If you create an outline, you'll have a starting point. That takes some of the pressure off, and the structure may help you keep moving forward, giving you something to go back to when you get stuck.

If you're an associative writer, outlining and other highly formal organizing structures may not make a lot of sense to you. If that's the case (and it isn't the case for *all* associative writers; remember that these are broad categories), don't feel obligated to outline. We'll talk later in this chapter about some other methods that can be helpful in getting your discovery draft going.

Outlining

To create an outline, go back to the material you've generated from your freewrite. Highlight the material that looks useful, and then group it as you did with idea threads earlier, putting similar pieces together. (It can also be useful at this point to go back to your questions, dialogic journals, and other process work to see if there's anything useful that you can move into these groupings.)

Once you've done this, take a look at what you have and create a rough order. As we said, the discovery draft is basically a series of modular pieces. In each one, you:

- **summarize** what's going on in a given moment or describe a given exhibit. Remember that an *exhibit* is anything that you're looking at and analyzing that isn't a passage in a text. Set the scene for your moment, giving enough context so that your reader knows what's going on (and so that you remember to take it into account).
- **identify the phenomenon** you're interested in. What's the strange or weird or interesting or anomalous thing you've noticed?
- **ask a question** about it.
- **take up that question and explore it**, using the text or exhibit itself as **the basis** for that exploration.

Putting your material in a rough order that follows this progression may be enough of an outline for you. On the other hand, you may prefer to create something more formal. If that's the case, it's worth thinking carefully about the format of your outline. In high school, most students learn to make an outline that involves a lot of letters and numbers. It might look something like this outline, which builds on the dialogic journal on *Frankenstein* we showed you earlier.

Thesis: In *Frankenstein* science is bad, and religion is good.

A. page 30: Victor blames science for what he's doing
  i. says he was motivated by almost supernatural enthusiasm
  ii. seems to say somebody else made him do it
  iii. takes credit for being a genius but says it's science's fault

B. page 32: scientific process in making the Creature
  i. "pursued nature to her hiding places"
  ii. "unnatural stimulus": science vs. nature
  iii. "profane fingers": science vs. God

C. pages 149-50 speech to crew, 152 final words
  i. still think glory is a good idea?

ii. tells Walton it's okay to follow science

iii. fatal flaw

Conclusion: Victor never learns, still thinks science will let him be like God

This outline format is very attractive to a lot of writers. It looks neat, complete, and very clear; its structure, with all those numbered categories and subcategories, seems to scream, "I know where I'm going!" But if you look closely, you'll see that this outline form gives you no direction: It's essentially a list with no real questions. And a list doesn't do the crucial work of connecting your ideas. If the student follows this format, her essay will likely be a list, too, connected by "transition words" that take the place of actual connection.

Another problem with this outline is that it begins with a foregone conclusion—*Frankenstein* is about science versus religion—and then offers a list of quotes and moments in the text that serve as examples of that conclusion. Since each idea in the essay is really just a broken-out part of the big idea, it's not surprising that the writer's ideas don't connect well to one another—or that her conclusion more or less restates her big idea. This means that, basically, she's set herself up to produce a five-paragraph essay. In fact, her whole outline really boils down to this.

Thesis
Example A
Example B
Example C
Conclusion

So how do you avoid these problems and still create a useful structure for yourself? Try working with a form that's familiar to anyone who's done a science experiment in high school: a flow chart.

first passage: page 26: summarize what's going on: Victor working with death to understand life

⬇

phenomenon: "almost supernatural enthusiasm"

⬇

Victor doesn't seem like he's taking responsibility for what he's doing: almost like he's blaming God (this is what I'm noticing)

... but if you look closely he's actually blaming science: it's "ALMOST supernatural" → magic of science

so what? so science becomes the thing that makes everything go wrong

second main passage: when the Creature is born

phenomenon: Victor calls on "Great God" and says the Creature is demoniacal (from Hell)

suddenly he's talking about God and the devil in terms of him and the Creature (this is what I'm noticing)

calling on God—correcting his idea of "beautiful" through repetition: once he's finished the experiment he can see clearly because science isn't possessing him anymore (this is my close read)

so what? science is a force of evil that possesses him and means he can't see clearly, but when he's done with it he's back to being a regular human again below God

passage 3: final words: "seek happiness in tranquility" etc. to Walton

phenomenon: "seek happiness in tranquility" but "Yet why do I say this? I have myself been blasted in these hopes, yet another may succeed" → why contradict himself?

↓

seems like he's learned his lesson, but he still thinks glory and science are a good idea: his very last words, "Yet why do I say this? I have myself been blasted in these hopes, yet another may succeed" totally undermine his generic, preach-y "Seek happiness in tranquility, and avoid ambition" (this is my close read)

↓

Victor never learns, still thinks ambition is good, humans should want to be God-like. (implications)

You'll notice that in this outline, the student's ideas connect to one another. She's not creating a list: She's outlining a story, a narrative of her ideas. And she's not front-loading the essay with her big idea and then repeating it over and over. Instead she's asking questions and sometimes leaving the work of responding to them for later in her drafting process.

It's completely okay for a first outline to have some holes in it. After all, this outline is for a discovery draft—you should be making discoveries as you go. And it's also okay if you begin moving in a direction that leaves your carefully planned outline behind. If you find yourself in this situation, just keep writing! See where your questions and ideas take you. As you'll see, you'll have plenty of opportunities to assess what you have, to make some choices about directions, and to work on structure. Whatever else you do, don't self-edit at this point!

If you're an associative writer, you may find this kind of outlining in advance of writing to be too restrictive. Outlines may feel like they box you in too much. If that's the case, you'll want to think about a looser "grouping" technique. This will give you enough direction to help you overcome the terror of the blank page, but it won't make you feel like you're locked in.

Grouping

Grouping is a useful technique because it lets you get everything in one place. Since associative writers can generate a lot of ideas, it's easy for them to lose track of what they've done. **Stepping back to reread and then do this kind of grouping helps them corral their ideas.**

You might, for instance, reread what you have, looking for patterns, repetition, and ideas that come up a lot and connect to each other. On another page or document or on a whiteboard, group the points you're noticing in a way that makes sense to you. If you're a particularly visual writer, you might include images or symbols or both so that your groupings are a combination of words and pictures.

Going back to what she has and grouping connected ideas lets the student writing on cummings see that she has a bunch of stuff scattered across her notes that relates to the poem's tone. She first groups these pieces so that she can see the connections between them more clearly. Then she highlights the specific lines in her writing that address tone directly.

> So in every language, even silence, people affirm your (america's?) glorious name, but if you're doing it silently, it can't be heard. And if it can't be heard, maybe you're not doing it at all. So in one phrase is the idea of speaking to affirm glory and NOT speaking or not being able to speak. Is that happening in the poem, too? I mean, is it affirming or not affirming?
>
> Putting *roaring* next to *slaughter* makes it sound like the people being killed are crying and yelling: it's horrible. Is that what makes liberty silent? Like liberty can't bear what's going on? That's sad.
>
> He wants to get the taste out of his mouth—not literally, but that idea? So does that mean the poem is sad/upset? Because it kind of sounded happy in the beginning, all those patriotic songs and the rhythm of "by god by gorry by gum." Hmm. Don't know.

Storyboarding

If you don't find either of these approaches useful and you're having trouble working your ideas through in words, you might want to create a storyboard. A storyboard can be a solution for people who hate outlines.

Storyboarding is a method borrowed from the movies. Earlier we showed how a student used sketches to figure out what she was thinking and to deepen her ideas. Here we're using a storyboard in the way a director does when she's getting ready to shoot a film. By creating a series of drawings accompanied by some directions and dialogue, the director can work out her sequencing; later, when she's shooting, the storyboard serves as a reference and reminder of the key pieces in the story she wants to tell. In the same way, a writer can use a storyboard to guide her drafting process.

HEROIC, HAPPY DEAD

ROAR

RAWR

ROAR

ROAR

HOW ARE THE DEAD BEAUTIFUL ??

BEAUTIFUL DEAD ≠ ROARING SLAUGHTER

Just as with a text outline, you may find yourself leaving your plan behind as you write. That's fine—as long as the map helps you get going, it's served its purpose. The storyboard is a way to think about sequence and the story you're telling without having to get tangled up in sentences and paragraphs.

GETTING READY TO DRAFT

Once you've generated some form of outline based on all the productive work you've done so far, you're ready to face the draft. Even though you've done a lot of work, you may still be nervous about launching into your discovery draft. So how do you start to draft?

The most important thing to keep in mind at this stage: **You've already started. You have all this stuff that you've already figured out. Now you just have to put it together and build on it.**

Start by putting a copy of your outline or storyboard or groupings somewhere you can see it: beside your computer or perhaps taped to the wall above your workspace. Print out your notes, questions, idea threads, and so forth so that you have all your material in one place—and make sure you have your text or exhibit on hand. If you're the type of writer who works best by just sitting down and producing at this point, feel free to start writing.

If you want a little more structure to help you get started, work directly on your outline (perhaps on poster paper with lots of space between points), or copy it into a new document on your screen. If you start this way, you've already mapped out the draft, so there's no need to panic. You just need to write through the gaps.

Some people find that even with an outline, there's still too much blank page left. If you fall into this category, don't despair. Remember that you've already generated a great deal of material in your freewrite and you've highlighted and organized that material. Now go back and incorporate that material into your document, below your outline headings. Once you've done this, you should find it much easier to turn your notes and ideas into full sentences and paragraphs, narrating what you've already figured out. And that process may in turn help you feel comfortable enough to ask new questions and make new discoveries.

(You might want to do this cutting-and-pasting process on poster paper and then turn to the computer and write through your sections, using your poster paper filled-in outline as a guide. If you're working on the computer, you may want to print out your filled-in outline so you can see it more clearly: People tend to read printed material more closely than they read material on a screen. Experiment to see what works best for you.)

It's worth asking yourself where in your outline you want to start writing. The answer to this question may not be as obvious as you think. Most students are taught to start writing their essay at the beginning and to move straight through to the end. For some people, this is the most natural way to proceed. If that works for you, great. (Though please note: You should never start with an introduction in a discovery draft. You'll write that last, once you've figured out your overall question by writing through all the pieces of the essay.) But if the beginning feels like a tough place to start, it's fine to start somewhere else.

You can begin by writing through any one of your ideas, regardless of where it falls in your order. That's because writing an essay is really a series of encounters with questions: **Every piece of your essay emerges from a question you're asking about a phenomenon. You might ask any number of questions about any issue in the text that interests you, but we use the term *module* to mean a piece of the essay in which you point out the phenomenon you want to explore, raise a question about that phenomenon, and come to some understanding of what you think is going on there.** Each time you do this, you're creating a module. And that's why you can start with the question that feels most generative or that you've done the most work with.

DRAFTING

The material that you've moved into your working document helps you start the draft, and lots of this material will likely show up in your modules. But it's not enough to simply connect these pieces: You won't yet be telling a story, and that's what a draft tries to do. To turn what you have into modules, you have to know what a module is and what it should do.

A good discovery module does four things.

1. It introduces and contextualizes a specific phenomenon you find interesting in a moment in the text.
2. It asks a question about that phenomenon.
3. It explores that question by looking at the specific language of the moment.
4. If you're ready, it addresses the significance of what you've figured out.

When you look at these bullet points, you'll see that they build on each other: Each module takes up a question about a phenomenon in your moment and develops your ideas about it.

Sometimes a module is a paragraph, but often it takes more than one paragraph to do all this work. Let's look at a couple of modules on the cummings poem. These sections are based on the preliminary work that we showed you earlier. As you'll see, this student isn't worrying about a formal introduction; instead she's working her way through the pieces that interest her.

> After going through a number of quotations from patriotic American songs like "My Country Tis of Thee," the speaker says that "in every

language even deafanddumb/thy sons acclaim thy glorious name." The "thy" is referring to America, and in a way, he's one of the "sons" that "acclaim" America since all the songs he quotes praise her.[1] He says that America's sons acclaim her "in every language," but the one example he gives is "deafanddumb."[2] It's strange that of all the possible languages he could have mentioned, he chose one that isn't actually spoken.[3] At first glance, it just seems like the speaker wants to emphasize that even people who can't physically speak and have to use sign language to do it are praising America. But what happens when you look at "deafanddumb" more closely?[4]

The way cummings writes it, with the three words stuck together, makes it stand out, and when you read it, even though you know he means sign language, what you see is deaf *and* dumb, the language of people who can't hear or speak. They are dumb, which means silent.[5] So what does it mean to praise a country in a way that can't be heard? Is unspoken, unheard praise even praise? It feels here like something has changed: the speaker started out sounding confident and excited about America, declaring his love for it, indirectly calling himself her son, but now there's a silence where it seemed before that wherever you went, in whatever language people were talking, they would be singing America's praises. "deafanddumb" changes the poem's mood: before, you could almost hear a stadium full of people singing patriotic songs and now, just nothing—silence.

---

[1] This is something the student noticed in a freewrite, so she threw it in. And as you'll see in the second paragraph, as she writes she ends up building on this idea and using it to help her figure out the implications of what she's noticed. But if this idea hadn't proved to be useful, that would be okay, too. A discovery draft generally includes lots of ideas that get cut later in the process. It's important to let yourself try out ideas here.

[2] Here the student is identifying the exact issue she's looking at. This is important: If you quote a whole phrase, you need to be sure to tell your reader exactly what you're holding your magnifying glass up to.

[3] Having pinpointed the phrase, the student goes on to say what she finds interesting about it.

[4] Now the student asks a question. Notice that it's a pretty straightforward one. That's fine.

[5] The question the student asks allows her to start exploring exactly what's interesting about this phrase.

Here's the second module she worked on. She's not thinking too much about connecting the different modules yet; for one thing, they may not end up in the order they're in now.

Later on, the speaker asks "what could be more beaut-/iful than those heroic happy dead/who rushed like lions to the roaring slaughter." At first it sounds like he's complimenting the dead men since he calls them "heroic" and "happy" and says they are like lions (lions are always portrayed as brave, the kings of the jungle). But then comes an odd phrase, the "roaring slaughter." What does it mean that the slaughter is roaring?[6] What should be roaring are the lions, but instead it's the slaughter. *Slaughter* means the killing of animals for food or the killing of a lot of people, like in a massacre, so if it's roaring, it makes you think about all those animals or people moaning and screaming and crying. And it feels even louder because a little bit ago in the poem, the speaker put the idea of silence in our minds.[7] The "roaring slaughter" changes the tone: Before everything seemed patriotic and glory-filled, but now the speaker's language makes you pay attention to how noisy and awful war is.[8]

But wait a minute: the heroes are dead, so they could be the victims of the slaughter, which would be sad, but they're also the lions, which means they could easily slaughter a whole bunch of gazelle or whatever. Did they rush heroically to battle and then get slaughtered? That's depressing.[9] Or did they rush into a crowd of people or animals to slaughter them? That's awful. Are they the victims or the killers? Should we feel sorry for them, or are they guilty? What does this do to the question about liberty being mute? Before I thought liberty was mute because it was sad

---

[6] Again, the student clearly shows what she's looking at and what she wants to know.

[7] Here the student is exploring what she thinks is happening with the odd phenomenon of the "roaring slaughter."

[8] At this point the student incorporates an idea from her freewrite that lets her say why this whole question of the roaring slaughter is significant.

[9] Here, the process of writing about the lions and the slaughter gave the student more ideas and opened up another question for her: Who is slaughtering whom? As we've said, when you write and focus on something specific, the act of writing often catalyzes your thinking and takes it somewhere that you didn't know you were going when you started. That means that this discovery draft module turned into something much more like a freewrite. Don't fight new ideas when you're writing; you can neaten them up later.

because people had died for it. But now I think maybe liberty is mute because it's so upset that people killed. Were they killing for America? In a war, soldiers on both sides kill and then could be killed. Okay, this is getting weird and all over the place. But not stopping to think does kind of make them seem like animals, acting on instinct, not like people who could think. And that kind of ties in with silence, too, because if they aren't human, they can't talk.

And here's the third module she wrote, based on the third chunk in her idea thread.

At the end of the poem, right after asking if "the voice of liberty" shall "be mute" the speaker stops talking, which cummings emphasizes in several ways. First, he closes the quotation marks around the speaker's words. Second, the narrator of the poem suddenly comes in and says, "He spoke" so in case someone missed the quotation marks, they would still know that he's done talking. And then on top of that, he drinks a glass of water, so obviously he can't be speaking any longer. What's the effect of so much emphasis on the sudden silence? What's the function of having the speaker drink the water? By having the speaker drink the water, cummings reminds readers that there is a speaker, a person, not just some anonymous, all-knowing poem talking. It kind of humanizes it, and that makes me think about the feelings of the speaker more than I did before. And what that does is make me think about him drinking, and drinking "rapidly." He needs a drink badly, to clear his throat maybe, but more, it seems, when you consider what he's just said about liberty maybe being mute and the terrible slaughter and even the possibility of the "heroic" dead maybe also being savage, he needs a drink to get the taste of all that he's said out of his mouth. It continues this sense of the poem moving from celebration to mourning or maybe even anger. And maybe this connects to the way the poem emphasizes his new silence: like he's run out of words to say.

The student can keep writing, checking back with her outline or storyboard as needed, until she runs out of things to say. She's not editing herself as she goes: It's too early to figure out what she needs and what she doesn't. That will happen in the next stage. Creating a discovery draft is all about getting words on the page.

FRAMING THE DISCOVERY DRAFT

Though your discovery draft has a modular structure, it's likely still a loose and messy document. When you've written through your ideas, you may end up with a draft that's full of specific questions and your responses to them or maybe something less structured. What you definitely don't yet have is the framing structure that will turn this draft into something you would want to hand in. For one thing, it's missing an opening paragraph that establishes the overall context of what you're looking at and presents the overall question you're asking. It's also missing a conclusion—even a discovery draft needs some form of ending. And you'll need to think about sequence and order, which also means thinking in a preliminary way about connections. While all of these considerations seem like they move your discovery draft firmly into the realm of product rather than process, don't be daunted—they're still preliminary. Creating this basic infrastructure is part of the process of figuring out what your paper is about.

Begin by assessing what you've written so far. (Just a reminder: You'll want to step away from your work before assessing it so that you can clear your mind and have the necessary distance to really see what you have.)

Print out your draft. This is super important. You can't see your whole paper at once on a computer screen, and it's harder to engage with text on a screen. (There are lots of reasons for this, but one is simply that your eye skips around more and you don't focus as well.) And you can't intervene as effectively with screen text.

Then arm yourself with some highlighters.

- For each module, mark the phenomenon that you're talking about (i.e., *deafanddumb* in our first module example or *roaring slaughter* in our second example).
- Then, in another color, mark the question that you're asking about that phenomenon.
- In a third color, highlight your exploration.
- In a fourth color, mark what, if anything, you've figured out about the question you've asked concerning your phenomenon.

Depending on your working style, you may want to move your questions to a separate page so you can see them more clearly, or you may just want to work with them in the draft. If you haven't shown the exact phenomenon (word, phrase, or syntax) you're looking at, that's a cue to go back and add that information. Similarly, if you find that you don't yet have questions in your discovery draft, now is a good time to go back and try to figure out what you're asking in each module. A freewrite or a wheel-and-spoke drawing might help you do this.

Figuring Out Your Topic

Once you've identified your phenomena, your questions, and your explorations, you're ready to figure out the topic for each module. **By *topic*, we mean what each module is really about: the concept or idea that your module takes up.** For example, if you're working on the cummings poem, when you look back over your work, you might find that what you're really talking about in the first module is praising in silence (or praising without speaking). This is not a concrete concept that the text makes obvious: It's an abstract idea that the student sees as a preoccupation in the text and wants to explore. In the second module, the student sees that her topic is really the noise of war. In the third, she sees that her topic is the speaker ceasing to speak. To figure out her topics, the student has looked back at her modules and asked herself, *What am I talking about here?* The topic may be apparent to her when she rereads. If you have a hard time figuring out what your topic is, talk to yourself about it: Create a mind map or do a freewrite or brainstorm or talk things through with a friend. It might be useful to jot down all the possible topics you can think of and then test each one to find the best fit.

Adding It Up Part I: Overall Topic

Once you've identified your questions and your topics for each module, you can use these pieces to build the framework for your draft. Begin by doing some math: Add up the topics you've come up with for each module, as you would for a math equation, and see what you get. (You might list the topics on a separate page or a whiteboard, if this is useful to you.)

For example, when the student adds up her topics, she finds that what she's talking about, overall, is silence in "next to god of course america i." Here's how she got there.

praising in silence (module 1)

+

war is so noisy; that's all you hear (module 2)

+

the speaker is out of words/drinks water instead of speaking (module 3)

=

silence (overall topic)

You may find, of course, that you have more modules in your draft. No problem. Put all the pieces in, and see what you come up with.

Adding It Up Part II: Overall Question

Every discovery draft needs an overall question: a question that synthesizes the questions you ask in each module. To create your overall question, do the same sort of math you did for the topic: Add up your specific questions, and see what overall question this leads you to. In the case of our example, here's how this might look.

What does it mean to praise a country in a way that can't be heard? (module 1)

+

What does it mean that the slaughter is roaring? (module 2)

+

What's the effect of the speaker drinking the water? What's the effect of emphasizing the sudden silence? (module 3)

=

What is the relationship between silence and patriotism in the poem? (overall paragraph)

As with the topic, this process may not be quick or easy. You may find that none of your questions seem exactly right and you need to tweak them; you may find that you need to freewrite or create a mind map in order to figure out what your overall question is. You'll note that the third module we showed you has two questions. You may need to decide later whether to keep both or focus on one, but right now, we're just adding everything up.

Writing the First Paragraph

Once you know your topic and overall question, you're ready to write the first paragraph. The job of the first paragraph is to introduce your reader to the material you're going to address in your paper. In a discovery draft, this means you'll need to:

- show your reader where you are. What text or exhibit are you looking at?
- identify your topic.
- ask your overall question.

For the student working on the cummings poem, a draft version of an introductory paragraph might look something like this.

> In "next to of course god america i," e.e. cummings[10] starts his poem by quoting broken off pieces of American patriotic songs. The poem also contains patriotic language about acclaiming America's "glorious name," and so it seems at first as if it is a tribute to America.[11] But as the speaker of the poem continues talking, questions come up about his point of view. Even though he says all these patriotic things, and even though he uses language associated with patriotism and pride in country, the speaker and poem bring up silence and not being able to speak in a number of ways that start to take away from that feeling.[12] What is the relationship in the poem between patriotism and silence?[13]

---

[10] It's important to mention the title of the work and the author in the first paragraph. This tells the reader exactly what you're talking about, and it also signals to the professor (who, of course, will probably be the one reading the paper) that you're thinking of your readers and giving them the information they need.

[11] Here the student gives some basic context of what the poem seems to be about, broadly speaking. This is important because it's laying the foundation for her to introduce her topic. If she started talking about silence and patriotism without first establishing that patriotism is a big subject in the poem, her topic and question would seem to come out of nowhere.

[12] The sentences starting with "But" and continuing to "that feeling" highlight the issue she's interested in. And she's providing evidence for her topic by establishing that it comes from moves the poem makes.

[13] Now that she's established all of this (what her text is, what it's about, what she's particularly interested in), she can ask her overall question. As we said, in a discovery draft, you end your introductory paragraph with a question, not a claim.

Writing the Conclusion

Once you've framed the beginning of your discovery draft, the next step is to frame the ending. In a discovery draft, as we've said, your task is to figure out what you have to say. That means that a conclusion in a discovery draft is just an opportunity to synthesize your ideas, think about how they build on each other, and see where you end up. A conclusion, even a preliminary one, isn't just an act of restating: **It's a chance to think about what you can see that you couldn't see before, now that you've done all of this work.**

In a discovery draft, a conclusion is basically another math equation—but in this case, you're adding up what you've figured out. To do this, print out your draft and read it. (Don't worry about editing or changing anything at this point.) On a separate page, jot down what you've discovered in each module. Then jot down where all of these discoveries take you. This tells you what your conclusion is. Bring these notes back to your draft, making sure you explain your thinking fully enough for your reader to follow you.

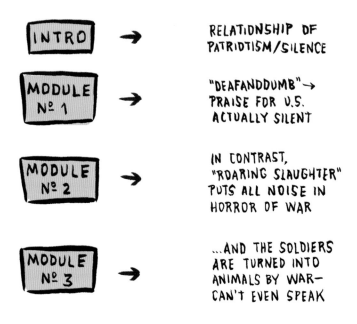

MODULE Nº 4	→	SPEAKER STOPS; DRINKS WATER: HAS TO GET BAD TASTE OF WAR OUT OF MOUTH. HE, HIMSELF, LIKE "VOICE OF LIBERTY" SILENT.
ADDS UP TO	→	PATRIOTISM TRIES TO SPEAK OF THE GLORY OF WAR, BUT WAR ITSELF IS SO LOUD THAT PATRIOTISM, WHICH IS WHAT THE VOICE OF LIBERTY IS, GETS SILENCED BY THE THING IT'S TRYING TO SPEAK ABOUT.
SO WHAT?	→	SO WAR CREATES PATRIOTISM, BUT AS A RESULT, ALL WE ARE LEFT WITH IS SILENCE.

When you finish writing your discovery draft, it will probably feel like a big deal—and it should. After all, you've gone from generating disconnected ideas to making choices about which of these ideas you want to keep exploring to actually writing them through in narrative form. That's huge: You've done a lot of work and made real progress; you now have the beginnings of a paper.

At this stage, students sometimes think their next task is to clean things up, add more quotes and page citations, and get the thing done. But you still have some distance to travel before you reach the final product. The first step in moving from a discovery draft toward a final product is assessing what you currently have. That's where you can assume control over the baggy monster that is the discovery draft. In the next chapter, we'll show you how.

CHAPTER EIGHT

WORKING WITH YOUR DISCOVERY DRAFT

In order to move forward from the discovery draft, you first need to assess what you have. That's because when you're writing, you're immersed in the process, so you don't have a lot of perspective. Whether you write quickly without worrying too much about being perfect or you write slowly and with agonizing precision, you're likely to get lost in your ideas, concentrate on individual words to the exclusion of larger concepts, make leaps, repeat yourself, leave out evidence, forget to ask questions, and so on. In this chapter, we'll show you how to assess what you have, make decisions, and move forward productively to a second draft.

ASSESSING YOUR DRAFT

The first step in working with your discovery draft is to read it to see what's there. This is a pretty basic move, but students are often hesitant to go back and read their work. They might be short on time, or they might be reluctant to know what's there—or not there. If you take stock of what you have, so the thinking goes, you'll have to do something about it. We like to think of it in a different way: If you know what's there, you *can* do something about it. And if you don't, it's tough to find and develop your most interesting ideas. We think the Danish philosopher Søren Kierkegaard puts it pretty well: "Life can only be understood *backwards*; but it must be lived *forwards*." In other words, *to get started* you have to work your ideas out on the page—as you do in your discovery draft—but to move forward, you need to understand what you've done and what you have, and that means you need to *look back*.

When you're looking back, try to treat your paper as though it's somebody else's work so you can respond to its contents without judgment. Avoid criticizing yourself; everyone who writes will inevitably write some garbage, as we've said, and certainly everyone has some garbage in their discovery drafts. That's not a failure—it's just part of the process. And **yelling at yourself for having garbage in your discovery draft not only wastes time; it undermines the confidence you need to keep writing.**

It's always easier to read your work and see it clearly if you've taken some time between writing and reading. If you read your draft immediately after you've written it, either it will look great ("I'm a genius!") or, more likely, it will look terrible ("I'm an idiot!"). The truth is, you probably don't fall into either category: Your discovery draft will likely have some good stuff, some half-baked stuff you can improve on, and some stuff you can ditch.

Taking an Inventory

When you take an inventory of your work, you're checking to see what you have in stock and making a record of what you find so you can assess it, just as you would if you were working in retail. And, as in retail, you need to be honest about what you see. If all the soup cans are dented, you probably won't be able to sell them. Be sure to note both what's working and what needs some attention.

Begin by printing the essay with an extra-wide right margin (so you can write in it). Read it through once, keeping an eye out for key markers of the different sections of the essay. Remember what you're looking for.

- a first paragraph that includes:
  - context
  - the topic of the paper
  - the overall question

- for each module:
  - the context of the moment you're discussing
  - identification of your phenomenon
  - a question about the phenomenon
  - an exploration with evidence from the text
  - preliminary implications

Circle or highlight each of these instances right on your essay. Each time you do, use the margin to note what you've found. This helps you see the essay's overall structure and main moves without getting caught up in looking at specific phrases or word choices and missing the big picture. As you move through the paper, avoid the temptation to cross things out or to start rewriting right away; you'll have a much better sense of what you want to do if you get an idea of the whole paper first.

Once you've done this, go back to the beginning and read paragraph by paragraph, doing a "says/does" inventory: Each time you get to the end of a paragraph, make some notes in the margin—just a few words—about what the paragraph *says*. What's the main idea here? If the paragraph has more than one idea, mark down each one; if it just carries on an idea from the previous paragraph, mark that down as well. If you left stuff out in your discovery draft, as sometimes happens (i.e., "I need an introduction" or "conclusion goes here" or "needs more"), circle or highlight the note to make sure you remember.

Each time you write down what you're saying in a paragraph, make a note about what the point you're making *does* for your paper. Is there a reason to include that point, or are you just following a tangent? In a discovery draft, you can often find yourself going in a lot of different directions; noting what each piece of the draft is doing will help you see what you have and give you a head start on figuring out the story you really want to tell.

Here, for example, is a discovery draft of a student paper on Virginia Woolf's 1931 essay "Professions for Women," with a "says/does" inventory in the margins.

INTRO:
SAYS: question is about relationship of Angel to real women—do I still think this?
DOES: establishes overall question—is this the right question?

In her essay, "Professions for Women," Virginia Woolf talks to an audience of young women about being a professional woman writer, how she became one, and the challenges that she has faced. In telling this story, she talks about a "phantom" called "the Angel in the House," and how she had to "kill" it in order to write. But what is the relationship between this "Angel" and a real woman?

INTRO MOMENT: Angel
SAYS: this is what the Angel is
DOES: shows what she's talking about, which I need to do to read it closely

Woolf describes the Angel because the "younger and happier" women in her audience "may not have heard of her—you may not know what I mean by the Angel in the House." She writes,

She was intensely sympathetic. She was intensely charming. She was utterly unselfish. She excelled in the difficult arts of family life. She sacrificed herself daily. If there was chicken, she took the leg; if there was a draught she sat in it—in short she was so constituted that she never had a mind or a wish of her own, but preferred to sympathize always with the minds and wishes of others. Above all—I need not say it—she was pure. Her purity was her chief beauty—her blushes, her graces. In those days—the last of Queen Victoria—every house had its Angel. And when I came to write I encountered her with the very first words. The shadow of her wings fell on my page; I heard the rustling of skirts in the room.

SAYS: Phenom: "sympathize." Is this a mind-meld? In which direction? Not the same as putting other people first.

DOES: Looks at this phenomenon "sympathize" (but it's only one of two and maybe not the important one? Does it belong here? Do I need it to explain the next one?)

The phenomenon that interests me is a strange contradiction right in the middle of this passage. Here Woolf says that the Angel "was so constituted that she never had a mind or wish of her own, but preferred to sympathize always with the minds and wishes of others." According to *Merriam-Webster College Dictionary Online*, one definition of *sympathize* is "to be in keeping, accord, or harmony." So on the surface, it seems like what Woolf is saying is just more of what she has just said: the Angel is supposed to always put other people first. But there are a couple of strange things here. First, if this definition of *sympathize* is right, then what she's supposed to be doing is not just putting other people first ("sacrific[ing] herself"), but in fact making herself be in "harmony" with other people. Is this getting along with them, or is she supposed to sort of mind-meld with them, so that what they want is what she wants? Or what she wants is what they want?

SAYS: Phenom #2: "prefer to sympathize" → so HAS a mind?
DOES: actually explores a useful phenomenon because this one seems more interesting to me

SAYS: if so: earlier descript made fun of
DOES: explores the effects of the thing I saw: makes the Angel less serious

SAYS: about purity: means choosing to be mindless, put body over mind

What I find stranger and more interesting, though, is that she "preferred to sympathize." If she *prefers* to sympathize, doesn't that mean she's choosing or deciding? *Merriam-Webster* says *prefer* is "to like better or best" (it also says "to promote or advance to a rank or position," but this would do the same thing). If what she likes or promotes is to "sympathize always with the minds and wishes of others," then how is it possible that she *also* "never had a mind or wish of her own"? If she's deciding to sympathize, doesn't that require a mind? And if she actually does have a mind, what does that do to everything else she does?

If you go back with this question in mind and look at the beginning of the description of her, suddenly it looks a lot weirder. The text says she's "intensely sympathetic ... immensely charming ... utterly unselfish." These words seem very over-the-top. When you think about them in connection with this question of whether or not she had a mind of her own, they seem fake to me. And when you keep reading, these sentences get less serious. "She sacrificed herself daily" sounds a lot less bad when you see that she's really talking about taking the least meaty cut of chicken or sitting in a draughty spot. She sort of becomes a parody of a stereotypical good woman, and all that stuff at the top seems silly or empty.

So what happens when you keep that in mind and read forward to the idea that "purity" is "her chief beauty"? The same thing happens. Blushing is a physical reaction to anything that's shocking, and it's supposed to show that she's innocent when she blushes. Grace means gracefulness like a dancer, but it also means a Christian idea of a kind of forgiveness or gift from God. So if "her blushes" are "her chief grace," then you can say that blushing is her holiness. So her holiness is really just a physical reaction. So if purity is so important, and it's the same in the sentence as *blushes*, because they're paralleled, then purity seems to just mean this physical reaction, so then she seems pretty mindless. But if that's what she "prefers" instead of how she's "constituted" (made up or formed according to *Merriam-Webster*), then she's making her body more important than her mind on purpose. So it's not that she's self-sacrificing or without a mind of her own or pure because she's made that way, outside her own control: It's that she chooses to be like that.

It's important that Woolf says, "In those days ... every house had its Angel. And when I came to write I encountered her with the very first words." It seems like she's saying there's a different Angel in every house, so every woman has her own to deal with. This would mean that the Angel is personalized and that it was somehow part of what women are naturally, that all women had Angels to deal with that belonged to them. But when Woolf says, "I encountered her," she changes that: Instead of saying, "I encountered mine," she says "her," which seems to say that there's only one Angel. So she's saying that women shouldn't feel like they're each responsible for their Angel, because the Angel is actually one big thing that's the same for everybody, not your own personal experience. So that means the Angel isn't something unique to every house, special to every woman, but the same thing. And that means she's sort of an idea of a woman being somehow beamed into every house. So Woolf is saying that women can't write because they are stopped by this bigger idea (made by society) of what a woman is, that gets in their way.

This becomes clearer when the angel starts talking. A little further in the essay, Woolf talks about what the Angel tells her to do:

> "My dear, you are writing about a book that has been written by a man. Be sympathetic; be tender; flatter; deceive; use all the arts and wiles of our sex. Never let anybody guess that you have a mind of your own. Above all, be pure." And she made as if to guide my pen. I now record the one act for which I take some credit to myself, though the credit rightly belongs to some excellent ancestors of mine who left me a certain amount of money—shall we say five hundred pounds a year?—so that it was not necessary for me to depend solely on charm for my living. I turned upon her and caught her by the throat. I did my best to kill her.

SAYS: the Angel is a liar → purity from mind, not body. Phenomenon: *credit*: why this word?

DOES: shows how this passage makes it even clearer that the Angel wants women to behave in a fake way. Also shows phenomenon: the word *credit*. Maybe too many ideas??

The Angel here shows that she's faking it or at least being the way she is on purpose. Instead of using *is* words, like the ones Woolf used in her description of her in the first passage ("She *was* immensely sympathetic"), she tells Woolf what to do using *be* words. By saying "you should be this way," the Angel tells Woolf, and by extension women, how to behave. This shows that there is nothing about women that is always, no matter what, "sympathetic … tender," since they have to be told to be this way. She also says flat out that it's the woman writer's job to "deceive," telling her to "use all the arts and wiles of our sex," which means, basically, that she should lie. At the end of this list that begins with nice words and ends with lies and trickery, she says, "[a]bove all, be pure." When she says this, she makes purity into something that comes from your mind instead of your body (which also shows that she actually has a brain). But what seems strange to me is the way Woolf uses the word *credit* to talk about what she does to stop the Angel. She uses the word *credit* twice in two sentences next to each other, so that made me pay attention. Why does she do that?

One definition for *credit* is "recognition, acknowledgment" (*Merriam-Webster*), and that makes sense for how it's used here. But most of the definitions for this word are about money: "the balance in a person's favor in an account" or "an amount or sum placed at a person's disposal by a bank and so forth." Woolf does talk about money here: She says that the reason she's able to kill the Angel is that she has money. She says that because she has some money "it was not necessary for me to depend solely on charm for my living." That's why she can kill the Angel. This is where who the Angel is, if you look closely, gets very clear. The reason that the Angel tells women that they need to "deceive" is that they need to be nice to men so that they'll support them. That's why women have to pretend not to have any thoughts and have to "flatter" and "deceive," because they have to get men to want to support them (in marriage I guess) so they have to be attractive to men in every way. Which means that when the Angel's purity is supposed to be her great virtue, that has to be a big lie, because there's nothing pure about this. It's more pure to support yourself.

Therefore when Woolf says she "take[s] some credit to herself," she's also using another *Merriam-Webster* definition for *credit*: "the provision of money, goods, or services with the expectation of future payment." She's saying that she's owed by others. So who owes her? Maybe her audience, because she's killed the Angel so they won't have to.

It's fine if your notes are basically a personal form of shorthand: After all, nobody needs to understand them but you. But make sure that your notes will actually be useful to you when you come back to your essay: Writing just "introduction" or "body paragraph 1" in the margin isn't helpful. For instance, in our example, if the student wrote the following notes about the first paragraph, in which she defines her phenomenon, she'd still be doing useful work.

> **SAYS:** phe = sympathize
> meaning mind-meld?
> **DOES:** questions what Angel does (purpose?)

This is very brief, but she's made clear to herself what's going on in the paragraph. If she writes this, however:

> phenom
> what it means
> what it does

… she'll have to reread the paragraph to figure out what she's talking about. For the same reason, don't summarize quotes or explain what the text says. **Your inventory is all about *your ideas.***

Mapping Your Essay

Your "says/does" outline gives you a better sense of what's going on in your draft— and what you're really interested in. Now that you have a more focused idea of what your essay is about, you can make some preliminary decisions about what belongs in the essay, what needs development, and what needs to be moved. Mapping your essay will help you figure all of this out.

Print out a clean copy of your essay (so you're not overwhelmed by the number of marks and highlights on the page), but keep the "says/does" draft handy. Use a different colored highlighter to mark each of the following.

- material that's working for you
- material that could potentially be working but needs development in some way
- material that works but needs to move elsewhere
- material that isn't working and can be cut

Here's how the student working on the Woolf essay marked up part of her draft, using blue for material that's working for her, yellow for material that could work, and red for material that she'll definitely cut. She doesn't plan on moving any material, so that color isn't marked.

The phenomenon that interests me is a strange contradiction right in the middle of this passage. Here Woolf says that the Angel "was so constituted that she never had a mind or wish of her own, but preferred to sympathize always with the minds and wishes of others." According to *Merriam-Webster College Dictionary Online*, one definition of *sympathize* is "to be in keeping, accord, or harmony." So on the surface, it seems like what Woolf is saying is just more of what she has just said: the Angel is supposed to always put other people first. But there are a couple of strange things here. First, if this definition of *sympathize* is right, then what she's supposed to be doing is not just putting other people first ("sacrific[ing] herself"), but in fact making herself be in "harmony" with other people. Is this getting along with them, or is she supposed to sort of mind-meld with them so that what they want is what she wants? Or what she wants is what they want?

What I find stranger and more interesting, though, is that she "preferred to sympathize." If she *prefers* to sympathize, doesn't that mean she's choosing or deciding? *Merriam-Webster* says *prefer* is "to like better or best" (it also says "to promote or advance to a rank or position," but this would do the same thing). If what she likes or promotes is to "sympathize always with the minds and wishes of others," then how is it possible that she *also* "never had a mind or wish of her own"? If she's deciding to sympathize, doesn't that require a mind? And if she actually does have a mind, what does that do to everything else she does?

This method really lets you see what you have without falling into the trap of deleting everything and starting over ... or assuming it's all fine and reading past the issues. Marking up your paper like this puts some distance between you and the work—and gives you the beginnings of a plan for revision.

Cutting Material Out

It's useful to have a sense of the things that you can nearly always cut out.

Going Off on a Tangent

> In the opening of "next to of course god america i" by e.e. cummings, the speaker puts together a number of quotations from patriotic American songs, including "land of the pilgrims." By quoting that line from "My Country Tis of Thee," the speaker evokes the image of the pilgrims and the hardships the first Americans suffered. Many times in the early years, their crops failed.

In this example, the student has taken something in the poem (pilgrims) and let it carry her off topic. The discussion of the pilgrims may be interesting to the student, but it's not contributing anything to the analysis of the poem.

Praising the Author

> In e.e. cummings's poem "next to of course god america i" the speaker says that "in every language even deafanddumb/thy sons acclaim thy glorious name." It's strange that of all the possible languages he could have mentioned, he chose one that isn't actually spoken. But that's part of what makes him such a great poet; he does things you don't expect, which keeps it interesting.

Here, when the student notices something interesting, she praises the author instead of asking questions. That's not going to help her out, because she's avoiding the real work. Her job in this essay is not to write a review of the poem or to celebrate the genius of e.e. cummings—it's to say something about the poem itself.

Developing Your Ideas

Here are some signs that you could develop your ideas further.

Clustering Questions

> e.e. cummings's poem "next to of course god america i" raises a lot of questions. When he quotes patriotic songs ("My Country Tis of Thee" and "The Star Spangled Banner" and some others), why doesn't he complete them? What is the effect of cutting the songs off like that? Why doesn't he use capital letters? Why isn't there punctuation?

These are perfectly good questions—in fact, they could be very productive—but presenting a barrage of questions without exploring them isn't actually analysis. Questions are where you start but not where you stay.

Stopping at Noticing

> The speaker says that "in every language even deafanddumb/thy sons acclaim thy glorious name." It's strange that of all the possible languages he could have mentioned, he chose one that isn't actually spoken. He also seems to be one of these sons who is acclaiming America.

The student has certainly noticed something interesting going on with *deafanddumb* in the cummings poem—but she hasn't explored or asked questions about this phenomenon. If she stops there and goes on to another idea, she hasn't done anything with her phenomenon.

Leaving Out Evidence

> When Woolf says about the Angel, "I did my best to kill her," she is saying that having money makes women independent.

Here the student has noticed something strange in the text: What's going on with Woolf saying she "did her best to kill" the Angel? But the student moves immediately from pointing it out to drawing a conclusion about it, without showing the steps of her close reading. That means her reader gets left behind, and since he can't follow her logic, he has no way of assessing the validity of what she's asserting.

Squeezing Too Many Ideas into Too Small a Space

> When the speaker asks "what could be more beaut-/iful than those heroic happy dead/who rushed like lions to the roaring slaughter" he sounds like he's complimenting the dead men since he calls them "heroic" and "happy" and says they are like lions (lions are always portrayed as the brave kings of the jungle). But then comes an odd phrase, the "roaring slaughter." What should be roaring are the lions, but instead it's the slaughter itself. When he connects that sound to people he calls "the heroic happy dead," he indirectly brings up the subject of war. War is

terrifying, but that part of it is often overlooked because of the way that
war is seen as patriotic.

Here the student has three ideas (*heroic happy dead*, *the roaring slaughter*, and *the link to war and patriotism*) jammed into four lines. They may all be interesting and worth exploring, but she needs to slow down and think about what she wants to say about each idea. If she doesn't, her reader won't be able to follow her thinking.

THE TRAP OF ADDING MORE (AND MORE) PASSAGES

Students are often tempted at this point to avoid the whole issue of development by simply adding more moments. Sometimes this is because the student feels like he doesn't have anything else to say about the moments he's already looked at; sometimes it's because he's already worrying about hitting the page requirements for the final draft. But to build a paper that really has something to say, you need to develop each point you make—and to do that, you need to limit the number of moments you look at. Otherwise you'll find yourself skimming over the issues instead of delving into them. You're likely to end up with a paper that looks more like a list than a narrative.

Cutting and Developing

It's easiest to notice places where all you have to do is either cut or develop. But when you're working with your discovery draft, you often need to do *both* in the same place in the essay. Sometimes you have a great idea but you're not sure what to do with it, so you end up generalizing or repeating what you've already said or otherwise leaving close reading and analysis behind. When that happens, this useless material is standing in for analysis, and you need to cut it. When you do that, you open up space to develop the interesting idea that you started with. Here are some examples.

Making Logical Leaps

Woolf says, "In those days—the last of Queen Victoria—every house had its Angel." She's suggesting that every woman had to deal with her own version of this stereotype. This means that all Victorian men oppressed women.

Here the student begins by reading the text closely—but then she takes a large logical leap, from analyzing Woolf's statement to deciding something about all Victorian men, without evidence. The student is jumping to an answer, which offers her the security of something she already knows or thinks—but she's leaving the specifics of the text behind. When she cuts the generalization, she creates space to explore her interesting point about the way the stereotype works.

Repeating Yourself

> After going through a number of quotations from patriotic American songs like "My Country Tis of Thee," the speaker says that "in every language even deafanddumb/thy sons acclaim thy glorious name." He says that America's sons acclaim her "in every language," but the one example he gives is "deafanddumb." He could have listed all kinds of languages—Italian, German, French, Chinese—but instead he gives an unusual example. *Deafanddumb* isn't even a language: It's a description of people who can't speak or hear. The language those people use is called sign language, so it's interesting that in choosing an example of a language he uses one that isn't one.

Here the student makes an interesting point (that *deafanddumb* isn't itself a language), but she doesn't do anything with it. Instead she restates the idea in different words. This kind of repetition is often a sign that you don't yet know what to do with what you've noticed. The best thing to do if you find yourself in this situation is to ask yourself, *Why does this matter?* and then jot down some notes or do a freewrite.

Generalizing

> When Woolf talks about having an independent income and then says about the Angel, "I did my best to kill her," she's saying that people with money can get away with murder.

Here the student notices that the text is connecting money with killing the Angel, but she doesn't address that connection. Instead she moves into a generalization that has nothing to do with what Woolf is talking about. In doing this, she's left the text behind without explaining what's interesting to her about the quote. Even if she thinks the connection is obvious, she needs to get it on the page.

DON'T TRASH YOUR WORK!

Doing these inventories will inevitably reveal false starts and dead ends. But this is not the time to cross things out or start over: You're just marking down what you see so you can make decisions about it. If you keep trashing your work and beginning again, you'll waste a lot of time and hard work. And if you're always starting over, you'll never be able to develop your analysis. It's important to give your ideas a fighting chance.

PRACTICING: INVENTORYING YOUR DISCOVERY DRAFT

1. Print out your draft. (Be sure to set up your page with a wide margin.)
2. Read it through, highlighting these key moves as you come across them. In the first paragraph:
   a. context
   b. the topic of the paper
   c. the overall question

   For each module:
   d. the context of the moment you're discussing
   e. identification of your phenomenon
   f. a question about the phenomenon
   g. an exploration with evidence from the text
   h. preliminary implications

3. Do a "says/does" inventory of your draft. Be sure to reread each paragraph before you inventory it. You don't want to have to guess about what's there.
4. Print out another copy of your draft.
5. Arm yourself with four highlighters for the four operations you'll perform:
   - stuff you want to keep
   - stuff you want to cut
   - stuff you want to move
   - stuff you want to develop

   Keep an eye out for places that require *both* cutting *and* development. Mark these with both colors.

PLANNING FOR REVISION

Once you have a handle on what's going on in your paper, you're ready to make a revision plan. You can map this out in different ways, but the goal is always the same: For each place you note an issue, come up with an action to address that issue.

Planning your revision is important for a number of reasons.

- You're less likely to be overwhelmed if you can see a finite list of tasks.
- If you're a compulsive editor of your own spelling and grammar, sticking to your list will keep you on the straight and narrow. Remember that you're still dealing with ideas at this stage! Focusing on spelling and grammar will pull you off course and distract you.
- If you tend to wander around in your writing, the revision plan can help you stay on track so you don't end up writing an alternative essay.

Before you can make a revision plan, you need to get a clear look at where things stand. The best way to do this is to literally cut and paste your highlighted draft. Here's how to do that.

- Make sure you have a working space big enough so that you can physically move around all the pieces of your essay.
- Using your highlighting as a guide, literally cut out anything extraneous with scissors and put those pieces off to the side.
- Use your highlighting and your "says/does" outline to decide on the order of your paper. Cut out any pieces that need to move. Decide where they go, and arrange them in that order on your workspace.
- Leave space after any area you marked as needing development so that you can see where new pieces will go.
- Tape each piece of the essay onto a sheet of poster paper or a whiteboard in the order that makes sense to you, leaving space where you know you need to write through your ideas.

Once you've decided what to cut, make those preliminary changes on the computer. Save your draft under a new name so that you don't lose any work you may decide you want to retrieve later. Then, using your poster paper as a guide, cut out all the material in the draft you decided was extraneous. Triple space after each place you marked as needing development. This will make it easier to come back to the draft later.

Now that you've clearly seen the areas that need work, you're ready to make a revision plan. This is definitely a moment in the process where different kinds of writers have different preferences. Some people like to have a very detailed plan of attack, while others are more comfortable with a looser strategy. Whichever way you write, you need a plan. (It's a good idea to keep this plan close at hand. You might try taping it over your workspace, for example.)

DON'T STALL BY OVERPLANNING

Some people love making lists: They can make endless sublists, to-do lists, sub-to-do lists, and so on. But at a certain point, these activities cease to be organizational or generative and simply turn into a way to avoid writing the essay. If you find yourself falling into this trap, set yourself a time limit: By such-and-such a time, you'll move on to the next step. Then stick to it.

Your revision plan might consist of any of these.

- a list of what you want to accomplish, arranged by priority
- numbering or lettering on poster paper to indicate the order in which you'll address the blank spaces
- a three-column chart, with the piece of the essay that needs action in the first column, the issue or concern in the second column, and the action to be taken in the third column.

Para 1, page 3	Don't actually analyze what's going on with "who rushed like lions." What's up with comparing "heroic happy dead" to lions?	I think I have a freewrite on this. Find it, or do another. Lions = king of the jungle, but is this comparison actually positive?
Para 3, page 4	"then shall the voice of liberty be mute"—it's a question, but I don't deal with that.	Think about this ... why matters? shall = future tense? look it up.

When you're prioritizing your revision moves, remember that you don't have to start revising at the beginning of the paper, nor do you have to start with the biggest issue. Instead start with the moment where revision seems most productive to you. For instance, it may be helpful for the student working on the Woolf paper to start with her first module and then build on the changes she makes there. But she can also start with the module she's most interested in or at the spot that seems easiest to address or that needs the most work. It's up to her. **The most important thing about a revision plan is that you make one—and that you use it to keep moving forward.**

Filling In the Gaps

It's tempting to think that you can make your revision plan and then start rewriting your discovery draft immediately. But if you're going to make new discoveries, you'll need to go back and do more analytical work. To do that, you'll need to decide how to tackle each issue you've identified. In each case, you may need to:

- go back to your text and make more notes.
- go back to your dialogic journals and idea threads and ask more questions.
- freewrite, brainstorm, or make a mind map.

One way to characterize this work is to return to our metaphor of the lens: You use what you've seen as a way to see more. For instance, in the e.e. cummings example, the student realizes through her assessment process that she's focusing on the idea that the speaker is critiquing patriotism. Then she can reread the poem with that idea in mind. Here's what that might look like.

> Freewrite: If he's critiquing patriotism, what does that let me talk about that I haven't? Well, the chopped off stuff. What's going on there? He puts enough that you can recognize it, right "land of the pilgrims," "oh say can you see by the dawn's early light" and "my country tis" but then he doesn't finish any phrase. Does it matter that they are recognizable anyway? Does that say something about patriotism? But they aren't all the same length: the dawn's early light is the whole line, but pilgrims is cut off right in the middle of a linked idea … he cuts out pride. Does that matter? What does cutting the phrases off do to their patriotism?

By looking through the lens of her idea about patriotism in this short freewrite, the student has discovered a variety of possible ideas to pursue. For her next move, she can highlight all the questions she asked, choose the ones she's most interested in, and start responding to them.

Once you've produced new material, how do you integrate it into your essay? You may want to:

- write directly onto the poster paper. This will necessarily mean the work you're putting on the page is rough; you'll have to go back and turn it into real sentences when you move it all back to the computer.
- work through each piece in a separate document and then print out each piece and paste it onto the poster paper in the appropriate place.
- work through each piece in a separate document and then move these pieces directly into your draft on the computer.

Different methods will make sense to different writers. Whichever method you choose, be sure to integrate your new pieces into your map or your computer file along the way. Your revised discovery draft definitely won't be a polished piece at this point, but it should include all of your work in one place.

PRACTICING: MAKING A REVISION PLAN

Make a revision plan for your essay using one of these techniques.

- listing what you want to accomplish, arranged by priority
- numbering or lettering on the pieces of your draft on the poster paper to indicate the order in which you'll address the blank spaces
- making a three-column chart with the piece of the essay that needs action in the first column, the issue or concern in the second column, and the action to be taken in a third column

Follow through on your plan!

All of this revision work will help you generate more material—and will also give you much more control over your essay. That will make things easier when you move into the next draft, in which you'll focus on the story you're telling and the claim you're making about that story. In the next chapter we'll show you how to build a strong claim.

But wait a minute: the heroes are dead, so they could be the victims of the slaughter, which would be sad, but they're also the lions, which means they could easily slaughter a whole bunch of gazelle or whatever. Did they rush heroically to battle and then get slaughtered? That's depressing. Or did they rush into a crowd of people or animals to slaughter them? That's awful. Are they the victims or the killers? Should we feel sorry for them, or are they guilty? What does this do to the question about liberty being mute? Before I thought liberty was mute because it was sad because people had died for it. But now I think maybe liberty is mute because it's so upset that people killed? Were they killing for America? In a war soldiers on both sides kill and then could be killed. Okay, this is getting weird and all over the place. But not stopping to think does kind of make them seem like animals, acting on instinct, not like people who could think. Before I thought liberty was mute because it was sad because people had died for it. But now I think maybe liberty is mute because it's so upset that people killed? Were they killing for America? In a war soldiers on both sides kill and then could be killed. Okay, this is getting weird and all over the place.

actually, the line in the poem is "they did not stop to think, they died instead." "Instead" definitely makes it sound like there are two options: stopping to think OR dying. If they had thought, they might not have died. And this is kind of re-inforced by the way that phrase appears in the poem; a lot of ideas are broken up, either across a line, or they aren't fully there. But, this idea is complete and written on one entire line, so you can't miss it. The speaker seems very clear here: he doesn't say they should have stopped to think but it's certainly implied. And then comes "then shall the voice of liberty be mute?" and in a way that phrase is also clearer because of the punctuation, which means you can't miss the question mark. But how does that relate to the not thinking? That's what I need to figure out.

But not stopping to think does kind of make them seem like animals, acting on instinct, not like people who could think.

CHAPTER NINE

CLAIM DRAFTS

Once you've assessed and reworked your discovery draft, you're ready to move onto the stage we call the *claim draft*. This may be your second draft or your third or your sixth or somewhere in between—the number isn't what matters here. What's important is that you've done nearly all the heavy-duty discovery work for this paper (though you may certainly make more discoveries as you proceed) and you're ready to start shaping your material into a coherent story with a beginning, a middle, and an end. And as we've said before, in analytical academic writing, that story begins with a claim, not a question.

WHAT IS A CLAIM?

A claim is the point that your paper is making: If you boil it all down, it's the thing that you're trying to say. As we said in chapter four, this is different from the topic of your paper, which describes what your paper is about. For example, the cummings essay we looked at in the last few chapters might have as its topic, "Patriotism in cummings's 'next to of course god america i.'" That tells you what the student's paper is *about*—but it doesn't tell you anything about what the paper is *saying*. **The claim encapsulates what the paper is saying about the topic—that is, the argument the student is making, the thing he is trying to convince his reader of.**

In a claim draft, instead of using the drafting process to figure out what you're thinking, you're now moving toward turning your draft into a *product*: a narrative aimed at convincing your reader of something. Claims both offer argumentation and serve as signposts for your paper. They help your reader better understand *why* she's reading your paper.

Students are often taught to start their writing process by coming up with a claim. But that process is, unfortunately, backward. You can't come up with an effective claim until you've done all the work of figuring out what you're talking about in your essay. **If you start the process of writing your essay by stating a claim, you're always starting with something obvious and observable. When**

your claim comes out of a process of questioning and exploring, it takes up something you've figured out, not just something you've observed, so it will necessarily be more complex and more interesting.

Sharing what you think (as opposed to what you observe or what you can generalize about or what you think you're supposed to say) is an act of risk taking: You're putting your ideas out there to be assessed and judged. But it's a risk you need to take if you want to do worthwhile work. And if you've built your essay step by step using the methods we've taken you through, you'll be able to come up with a convincing and effective claim because your thinking will come out of your close reading and analysis of evidence, not out of supposition or speculation or generalization.

Overall Claims

We're going to use the word *claim* in a number of ways in this section. When an author is asked to summarize her paper, she often provides what we call the *overall claim*. The overall claim presents the point your paper is making and why it matters.

A good overall claim should:

- take up a question that has at least two sides and choose its side clearly. If nobody can argue with your claim, you're not really convincing anybody of anything; you're just stating something that's already agreed upon.
- offer a direction that goes beyond "yes," "no," or "because it says so on page 43." An overall claim that is really a yes-or-no answer doesn't give your essay anywhere to go. The same is true of an overall claim that bases itself on a clear event or piece of language in the text.
- set out an assertion about something in the text, not about a general idea concerning the text, its main idea, or the author.
- come out of a process of close reading.
- allow your reader to understand something meaningful about the text in a different way.

For example, a claim like this:

> In Virginia Woolf's "Professions for Women," she demonstrates not only that women are capable of work but also that the social forces that seek to prevent women from working turn women into commodities.

… does all of these things. You'll note that you don't see any close reading in the claim statement: The student isn't pointing to a specific phenomenon here, nor does she ask any questions or present any evidence or analysis. All of that comes in the body of the paper. The overall claim just gives you the overview.

Here's what an overall claim for a paper on the cummings poem "next to of course god america i" might look like.

> In cummings's poem, the use of fragments of patriotic sayings leads the reader to question the very idea of patriotism, and in this way the poem complicates the idea of Americanness as wholly positive.

This claim:

- **makes the overall topic clear** ("the use of fragments of patriotic sayings").
- **shows what's interesting or strange about this topic** in the poem and **offers a direction that the paper will pursue** in exploring this topic ("leads the reader to question the very idea of patriotism").
- **shows why it matters** ("in this way the poem complicates the idea of Americanness as wholly positive").

The overall claim is **the whole story of the paper.** It comes out of all the close reading and analysis the student has done. The overall claim offers the reader a chance to read the text in a new way, one that isn't obvious.

The overall claim, however, never appears in this form in the essay. Instead it's divided into two parts: the opening claim and the conclusion. That doesn't mean you can skip over the process of writing it. It's important to figure it out because it will help you pin down the story you're telling and **it will provide you with the scaffolding for your opening claim and your conclusion.** Writing the overall claim is also helpful in alleviating the panic students often feel about getting somewhere new in their conclusion because, as you'll see, it lays out the whole story, including its end.

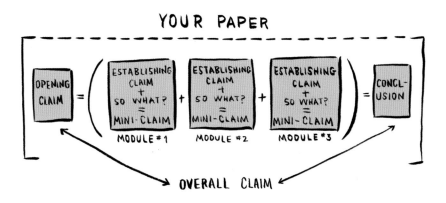

Opening Claims

In your opening paragraph, you offer an *opening claim*, which is a *portion* of your overall claim that introduces what you're talking about and sets the agenda for the paper. The reason you don't include the overall claim is that you don't want to give away the whole game in your first paragraph.

For example, an **opening claim** for the cummings essay might read something like this.

> In cummings's poem, the use of fragments of patriotic sayings leads
> the reader to question the very idea of patriotism, which in turn raises
> questions about Americanness.

This opening claim offers a topic and a direction for the paper, and it provides a teaser about what the student will say about the issue she's looking at in the text. The reader now knows that the paper will take up the question of patriotism and that it will do so by looking at fragments of patriotic sayings in the poem. He also knows that the student is interested in a problem she sees with patriotism in the poem. Finally, he can see that she's interested in exploring what the poem may be implying about the idea of Americanness. What the reader doesn't yet know, however, is what the student actually thinks *happens* to the idea of Americanness. That means she hasn't given everything away up front. You might think of the difference between an opening claim and an overall claim as the difference between telling someone the basic premise of a movie and spoiling the ending for them. We'll talk more about this and how to move from the overall claim to the opening claim later in the chapter.

BUILDING CLAIMS

Despite all the work you've done so far to figure out what you're talking about, you still can't get to a claim by simply surveying what you've written. If you approach the claim that way, you're likely to end up either with something way too specific (i.e., a claim about a specific phenomenon, which we call a mini-claim) or with something far too broad.

One way to think of building a claim is through a process of addition. As we've said, your essay is made up of a series of modules. In each module, you identify a phenomenon, ask a question of it, explore that question through close reading and analysis, and think through the implications of what you've seen. Once you've done that, you're ready to come up with a mini-claim about each module. And by adding up your mini-claims, you can figure out what you're claiming in your paper overall.

Mini-Claims and Establishing Claims

As you move through your discussion, each time you take up a new phenomenon, you'll need a *mini-claim* that consolidates your idea about that phenomenon and shows why it matters. **A mini-claim is an assertion of what you think about a particular phenomenon and why that idea is significant.** You'll remember that each module in the discovery draft asks a question about some specific language or issue in the text. **The mini-claim is the idea that your exploration of the phenomenon has led you to.**

A mini-claim is different from an overall claim because **it operates on a different scale**: It's limited to a specific phenomenon, while your overall claim covers more territory. In other ways, the mini-claim is similar to an overall claim: **Both encompass a whole idea**. The overall claim encompasses your whole idea about the paper. The mini-claim encompasses your whole idea about a specific phenomenon. And where your paper as a whole has an overall claim broken up into an opening claim and a conclusion, each module has a mini-claim broken up into an *establishing claim* and a set of consequences we're going to refer to as the *"so what?"*

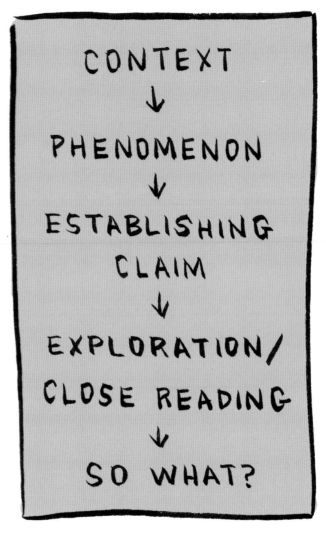

MODULE

Like the opening claim, the establishing claim is stated without the evidence that will prove it—the rest of your work on this phenomenon will show it. In the establishing claim, you boldly state your idea. The job of the rest of the module is to provide evidence for that idea. The "so what?" comes after you've shown the evidence for your ideas by presenting your close reading and analysis. It's the summing up of your exploration, an idea that you've earned the right to state because you've taken the reader with you through each point that the idea is built on.

Let's take a look at a student paper on *Frankenstein* to see how this works. The student's topic is the humanity or lack thereof of Frankenstein's creation. He's looking at how Victor Frankenstein describes his project, how he interacts with the creation when he first brings him to life, and finally, the Creature's view of himself.

The student's first module looks at what Victor thinks he's setting out to make by closely reading the language Victor uses to describe his project.

> After Victor Frankenstein is picked up by the explorer Walton in the middle of the ocean, he tells Walton how he came to have the power to generate life and how he went about the project that led to the birth of the Creature. He explains to Walton that, though at first he considered animating not a human but a being "of simpler organization," in the end he began the "creation of a human being."[1] But what's interesting is that a few lines later, he says that what allowed him to keep working even when the project was difficult was the idea that "A new species would bless me as its creator and source; many happy and excellent natures would owe their being to me. No father could claim the gratitude of his child so completely as I should deserve theirs."[2] But the idea that what

[1] This section, from the beginning of the paragraph through "'creation of a human being,'" does the work of introducing the phenomenon by setting up the context in which it occurs. Note that though the student includes some quoted language, there is no close reading. Using the occasional quote this way is fine, but don't mistake it for close reading.

[2] With this quote, the student is presenting the phenomenon, which is the fact that Victor just contradicted himself about a very basic part of his experiment—that is, what he thought exactly would result from it. This is why the student had to include Victor saying he "began the creation of a human being." That quote, on its own, is not a phenomenon. But he needs it so that he can show the weird contradiction in the second quote, about "a new species." To go back to our train metaphor in chapter five, the student was happily riding the train of the plot when he read the first quote. *Okay,* he thought, *this guy figured out a way to create life, and he decided to build a human.* It's not until he got to the second quote, a few lines down, that he felt the clatter and bump of the train veering off the track. He's worked through what he thinks is going on here, and now he's taking his reader through it, showing her the place where the train jumps off the tracks (the "new species" idea) and exploring what the contradiction between "human" and "new species" might mean.

he is making is a "new species" raises the question of what Victor actually thinks his experiment will produce.[3]

According to *Merriam-Webster*, "a species is a group of animals or plants that are similar and can produce young animals or plants." Scientifically speaking, humans belong to the species *Homo sapiens*; a "new species" would, by definition, be another, different species. This becomes even clearer when we consider that Victor says that this new species would "bless him as their creator and source." Part of the definition of a species is that its members can mate and produce young. Victor's created beings, on the other hand, would not be products of human mating but would come from a different source: Victor, operating on his own. But then when he says, "No father could claim the gratitude of his child so completely as I should deserve theirs" in the very next sentence, he seems to be back to considering that what he's creating would be human. He uses specifically human terms to describe the relationship he imagines between his creations and himself. Any male animal can father—as a verb—offspring, but the relationship words *father* and *child* are reserved for human beings.[4] At the very moment that Victor is planning his masterwork, the giving of life to a nonliving being, he seems both to want it to be human, a child, and to want it to be something else, a "new species." This reveals that while Victor claims to be making a human, the boundaries between human and nonhuman are blurred even before the Creature is born.[5]

The "so what?" is highlighted in blue. As you can see, **the "so what?"—the second half of the mini-claim—builds on all the exploratory work the student does, which is why it comes at the end of the module,** just as the essay's conclusion—the second half of the overall claim—comes at the end of the paper. If the student started the module by announcing the "so what?" the reader wouldn't have had any way to evaluate it. And if for some reason the reader was willing to go along with the claim, she'd have no real interest in seeing the evidence because she would have

---

[3] This is the **establishing claim.** Here the student is presenting his idea. Notice that this kind of claim about a phenomenon, just like an opening claim, requires more than simply pointing out that there is a contradiction. That would constitute an observation, not a claim. What makes this a claim is that it comes from a specific issue in the text and that the student has an idea about that issue that he wants to present, explore, and prove.

[4] All the work the student does from "According to *Merriam-Webster*" to "human beings" is his close reading and analysis of the specific language of his phenomenon.

[5] And this, at the end of the module, is the "so what?"—the explanation of why all of this matters.

already seen the "so what?" Good storytelling means that you don't tell the whole story at the beginning: If you did, why would your readers keep reading?

Using Mini-Claims to Get to Your Overall Claim

As we've said, one way to figure out your overall claim is to add up all of your mini-claims. So to get to your overall claim, you need to be able to see all of your mini-claims in one place. In a way, a list of mini-claims functions as another kind of outline: By eliminating the noise of the rest of the paper, it lets you see the key pieces of the story. When you can consolidate those pieces into a concise and coherent sentence or two and think through what they add up to, you'll have your overall claim.

So how do you do that? Start by listing your mini-claims, with both the establishing claim and the "so what." If you find it difficult to identify them in your draft, that's a sign that you're not ready to figure out your overall claim. In that case, go back to chapter eight and take another look at ways to get more analysis into your discovery draft.

It's also possible that you have everything you need but not in an order that tells your story as effectively as you want. If you find that this is keeping you from arriving at your overall claim, then try reordering the pieces of your essay. If you're not sure how to do that, you'll want to skip ahead to chapter ten.

To see how the process of using mini-claims to get to your overall claim works, let's look at the establishing claims and "so whats" for each module of the *Frankenstein* paper we saw earlier.

MODULE 1
ESTABLISHING CLAIM: Victor never knows what he's making.
"SO WHAT?": While Victor claims to be making a human, the boundaries between human and nonhuman are blurred even before the Creature is born.

MODULE TWO
ESTABLISHING CLAIM: Victor's human nature is degraded by his project.
"SO WHAT?": It's not just the project but also his loss of connection to others that makes him less human.

MODULE THREE
ESTABLISHING CLAIM: Once we understand what humanity is in the text, we can understand Victor's flight from the newborn Creature.
"SO WHAT?": Victor's flight is what makes the Creature nonhuman.

MODULE FOUR
ESTABLISHING CLAIM: But the Creature wants to be human.
"SO WHAT?": Unlike Victor, he figures out what it takes to be human—being in relationships with others.

MODULE FIVE
ESTABLISHING CLAIM: Knowing that the Creature understands human nature helps us understand why he doesn't just kill Victor.
"SO WHAT?": By keeping Victor alive, the Creature at least feels partially human because at least he's connected to someone.

Now that you've created this list, the next step is to see what all of these mini-claims add up to. There are a number of methods for doing this, but getting to your overall claim is almost always a process of trial and error: You're not likely to figure it out the first time around. Whichever method you choose, be prepared to take a number of runs at it.

Storytelling

If you're a person who thinks in stories, you might try connecting the mini-claims so that they look like a story. The key to this process is using connection words like *and*, *then*, and *thus*. **These words create causal relationships between ideas so you can better see where your ideas are leading.** And that, in turn, will help you figure out your overall claim. Here, for example, is the student's first attempt to tell the story of his *Frankenstein* essay.

> In *Frankenstein*, Victor Frankenstein claims to be making a man, **but in fact**, when you look closely at the text, you find problems with the definition of what a human is—**and even with** the question of Victor's own humanity. A close look at the story demonstrates that humanity in *Frankenstein* is dependent on meaningful connections with others—connections Victor has lost. **This causes** him to abandon his Creature, **which is what** turns the Creature into a monster. Ironically, the Creature, as shown by his search for connections, understands what being human is better than Victor does. **That's why** he keeps Victor alive, to keep himself even partially human, because even a terrible relationship is a relationship.

This first go at telling the story is thorough, but it has too much detail to be useful for establishing an overall claim. Rewriting it will help the student boil the story of his essay down to its most essential elements. Here's the student's rewrite.

> Victor's failure to understand if he's making a human or not, plus his own degraded humanity, lead him to abandon the Creature at birth, thus ensuring that the Creature will be isolated and nonhuman. Although the Creature tries to have relationships, he fails, and ultimately the only person he can relate to is Victor, which is why the book ends with the long chase between them—it's the Creature's way of having a relationship.

The act of retelling the story for himself lets the student see the key ideas. This, in turn, will help him figure out his overall claim.

The student's next step is to think about the key ideas in terms of his topic, humanity in *Frankenstein*. You'll see that he uses the words *human* and *humanity* below in several different ways. And you'll notice that his language is abstract: He's focused here on *ideas*, not *events*.

> While Victor Frankenstein claims to be making a human being, and of course thinks of himself as human, his experiment not only blurs distinctions between human and nonhuman, it reveals what humanity is actually based on, which is the ability to have relationships with others.

You'll note that the student isn't using exactly the same language as he did in the mini-claims. That's okay. This isn't a process of replication—it's a synthesis.

You might also find it useful to tell your story to someone else. By talking the story through to a listener who responds to what you're saying, you can often get to the "aha! moment" of figuring out your overall claim—that is, what your mini-claims add up to. When you get to the end, summarize what your story is about and why it matters, and then make sure that either you or your partner writes it down. Alternatively, try taping yourself and listening to the recording.

Flowcharting

Another way to figure out your overall claim is to engage in a more visual process of laying out the relationships between your ideas. You can do this in any way that makes sense to you, including using mathematical sentences ([mini-claim A] + [mini-claim B] + [mini-claim C] = D), but the simplest model is a flowchart. You may find it helpful to use a whiteboard or a chalkboard to do this.

Here the student begins by turning the list of establishing claims and "so what?" statements into a flowchart. By removing the labels and adding directional arrows between ideas, the student can see how these structural elements relate to each other as a story. He puts the topic at the top so that he can double-check that he's talking about the same thing all the way through.

Topic: Humanity in *Frankenstein*

Victor says he's making a human, BUT he never knows what he's making: human or not?

While Victor claims to be making a human, the boundaries between human and nonhuman are blurred even before the Creature is born.

Victor's human nature is degraded by his project.

He loses his connection to others.

It's not just the project but also his loss of connection to others that makes him less human.

Once we understand what humanity is in the text, we can understand Victor's flight from the newborn Creature: own humanity problematic.

Victor's flight is what makes the Creature inhuman.

But the Creature wants to be human.

Unlike Victor, he figures out what it takes to be human—being in a relationship with others.

Knowing that the Creature understands human nature helps us understand why he doesn't just kill Victor.

By keeping Victor alive, the Creature at least feels partially human because at least he's connected to someone.

If you find that you can't connect your ideas in this way or account for how you get from one place to the next, you'll need to go back to your draft and make decisions: Perhaps something doesn't belong, or perhaps you're missing an establishing claim or a "so what?" statement.

Next, the student makes a second flowchart that distills what he sees as the very basic throughline of his narrative and leaves out everything else. Once he's done that, he highlights all the ideas (as opposed to observations) in purple.

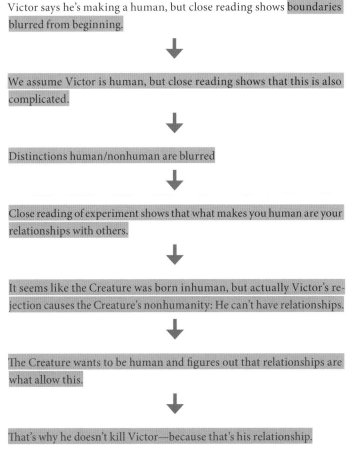

Victor says he's making a human, but close reading shows boundaries blurred from beginning.

↓

We assume Victor is human, but close reading shows that this is also complicated.

↓

Distinctions human/nonhuman are blurred

↓

Close reading of experiment shows that what makes you human are your relationships with others.

↓

It seems like the Creature was born inhuman, but actually Victor's rejection causes the Creature's nonhumanity: He can't have relationships.

↓

The Creature wants to be human and figures out that relationships are what allow this.

↓

That's why he doesn't kill Victor—because that's his relationship.

The student then creates a third flowchart. This one has only the ideas (the material in purple from the last flowchart).

The Creature's humanness is always blurred.

↓

Victor's humanness is complicated.

The distinctions human/nonhuman are blurred.

What makes you human are your relationships with others.

Victor's rejection causes the Creature's nonhumanity: he can't have relationships.

The Creature wants to be human and figures out that relationships are what allow this.

That's why he doesn't kill Victor—because that's his relationship.

This last flowchart allows the student to see the story he's telling, separate from the material he's observing and from the story the text itself is telling. To create his overall claim, he just needs to put this set of ideas in narrative form.

> While Victor Frankenstein claims to be making a human being, and of course thinks of himself as human, his experiment not only blurs distinctions between human and nonhuman, it reveals what humanity is actually based on, which is the ability to have relationships with others.

Checklist for Your Overall Claim

Any of these methods can produce a solid overall claim. If we look at our original list of what an effective overall claim does, you'll see that the student's claim now meets all the criteria.

- It makes the overall topic clear (humanity in *Frankenstein*).

- It shows what the student finds interesting or strange about this topic in the novel (Victor's experiment blurs distinctions between human and nonhuman).
- It declares the direction that the paper will pursue in exploring this topic (how does the experiment do this—and how does it affect both Victor and the Creature?).
- It shows why it matters (allows the reader to understand something about humanity: that it's based on relationships).

All of this offers the reader the chance to read the topic of humanity in *Frankenstein* in a new way, one that isn't obvious if you don't read the text with the student's argument in mind.

PRACTICING: GETTING TO AN OVERALL CLAIM

FINDING YOUR OVERALL CLAIM

- Print out your working draft.
- Highlight each of your establishing claims in one color.
- Highlight each "so what?" in another color.
- On another page, list your mini-claims module by module, including both the establishing claim and the "so what."
- Choose the method below that best fits your working style.
    - Connect the mini-claims so that they look like a story. The key to this is using connection words like *and*, *then*, and *thus*.

        OR

    - Use your list of mini-claims to tell the story of your essay to a friend or a classmate. When you get to the end, summarize what your story is about and why it matters. Write down that overall idea (or ask your partner to write it down).

        OR

    - Create a series of flowcharts that represents your narrative, recharting until you've isolated the idea chain and what it adds up to.

TESTING YOUR OVERALL CLAIM

Once you've figured out what your overall claim is, go back to the checklist above to test your claim.

- If any piece is missing, go back to your claim and revise.
- If you're having trouble putting all the pieces together using the system you started with, try again using a different method.

Overall Claims to Opening Claims

You now have an effective overall claim. But as we've said, you don't want to begin with an overall claim because then you're giving everything away up front. If the student writing the *Frankenstein* essay were to include the part of his overall claim about relationships in the first paragraph—that is, the exact information that his reading will reveal about humanity—he would spoil the story he's telling by revealing its ending. Instead he'll need to use his overall claim to derive an opening claim that doesn't spoil the ending.

To get to an opening claim, you'll need to look at your overall claim and do some division and refocusing. Here's the overall claim again.

> While Victor Frankenstein claims to be making a human being, and of course thinks of himself as human, his experiment not only blurs distinctions between human and nonhuman, it reveals what humanity is actually based on, which is the ability to have relationships with others.

The opening claim sets the terms for the whole paper: It defines the paper's topic and the strange or interesting thing about that topic in the text. But it doesn't set out to cover the entire paper. Instead **it takes you as far as the first major "so what?" of your paper, the first big thing you figured out as you moved through your analytical work**.

When we talk about the first big idea, we mean the first "so what?" that has repercussions outside the passage you're talking about. For example, the idea that Victor's humanity is compromised at the very beginning of his work, even before he abandons the Creature, affects how a reader would think about the rest of the book. That's why it qualifies as important enough to be the basis for your opening claim.

If you look back at the overall claim, you'll see that it, too, is based on this first big "so what." That's because when you're telling a story or building an argument, every idea rests on a prior idea and the work you did to support that prior idea. Nothing is assumed or taken for granted, and nothing is hanging in midair. Every module is built on the ideas in the prior module. So the opening claim sets up the whole story you're going to tell by setting up the first important piece of that story.

And that gives you the first piece of your opening claim: You've set up the topic and what's interesting about it. Now you need to tell the reader what's at stake here. You do this by looking at your overall claim once again and identifying the idea your reader will now be able to see—and that she couldn't see before. In our example, the student's overall claim says that the definition of humanity in the text is at stake and that humans are defined by the ability to have relationships with others. But the student doesn't want to put all of this in his opening claim because he doesn't want to give away his whole story. He needs to take what he's figured out and pull it back. You can think about this as a simple process of division: How can you divide the "so what?" in a way that lets you reveal some of the payoff of your ideas but not the whole story?

Here's an example of an opening claim for the *Frankenstein* essay. It's derived from the overall claim, but it doesn't follow it word for word because as we've said, the job of the opening claim is different from the job of the overall claim. Sometimes you can use more of the language of the overall claim, but you can't assume this will be the case. (To see an opening claim that looks more like the overall claim, go back to the beginning of this chapter and check out the two claims about the e.e. cummings poem.)

> In Mary Shelley's *Frankenstein*, it seems that the story is all about whether or not the Creature is a monster or a human. But if you look closely, you can see that the humanity that is in question is really Victor Frankenstein's.

This assertion fulfills the criteria for an opening claim.

- It makes the overall topic clear (humanity in *Frankenstein*).
- It shows what's interesting or strange about this topic in the text and points toward the problem that the paper will explore ("it seems that the story is all about whether or not the Creature is a monster or a human").
- It shows what is at stake ("But if you look closely, you can see that the humanity that is in question is really Victor Frankenstein's").

Let's take a moment to review the differences between the overall claim and the opening claim.

OVERALL CLAIM	OPENING CLAIM
tells the whole story	only tells part of the story
offers the topic in detail	offers a narrowed version of the topic problem or question you're working with

For example, in the opening claim in the *Frankenstein* essay, the topic has narrowed from "humanity in *Frankenstein*" to "the problematic nature of Victor's humanity in *Frankenstein*," leaving out the issues of the experiment and how Victor thinks of himself.

In this opening claim, the student has left out a big payoff: the idea that humanity is based on the ability to have relationships with others. That way the reader will encounter new ideas as she reads through the essay.

Here's another effective opening claim for the *Frankenstein* paper.

> Victor Frankenstein's experiment reveals that the definitions of human and monster are not natural but created.

In both examples, to show the direction he's taking, the student has made a move that's quite common in opening claims. This move can be boiled down to a *"seems/but actually" statement*: **In text X, it seems as though Y, but actually Z.** Here's how it works in each claim.

> There's a problem with humanity in this book. The problem SEEMS to be about the Creature, but it's ACTUALLY about Victor Frankenstein.

> OR

> The definitions of human and monster SEEM natural, but they are AC-TUALLY created.

In both, the writer has first stated the more obvious idea—the one that a casual reader could have—and then replaced it with a more interesting or unexpected idea. This immediately shows that the paper has something to say. Right away, it changes the reader's baseline assumption about the text. It also demonstrates what's at stake in this paper. If, for instance, your opening claim is that Princess Leia is actually the villain of the Star Wars movies, your reader can see what's at stake. The opening claim lets the reader know that this paper is about to upend the way she thinks about the films. Your claim may well not be that revolutionary, and that's fine. But it will set the stage for a change in the way your reader sees an important aspect of the text you're looking at.

The comparison can be either *implicit* or *explicit*. For example, let's look again at that first claim.

> In Mary Shelley's *Frankenstein*, it seems that the story is all about whether or not the Creature is a monster or a human. But if you look closely, you can see that the humanity that is in question is really Victor Frankenstein's.

If you wanted to be a bit subtler in your approach, you might say something like this.

> In Mary Shelley's *Frankenstein*, the question of what defines humanity is central, and the humanity that is in question is Victor Frankenstein's.

This claim does not explicitly say that the Creature's humanity is in question—which is what you would expect. That idea is only implied. The claim is streamlined, leaving more to be developed later in the paper, but the move is really the same.

PITFALLS AND PROBLEMS: OPENING CLAIMS

Opening claims can be tricky to pin down because it's hard to find the balance between being too indirect and saying too much. Here are some dangers to watch out for.

The Claim Is Too Obvious

> Victor Frankenstein's experiment has a negative impact not only on the Creature but on Victor himself.

Any reader of the book will see that things go badly for both Victor Frankenstein and his creation. While this claim may sound authoritative, it actually says nothing.

The Claim Is So General That It Asserts Nothing

> Virginia Woolf's "Professions for Women" is an essay that addresses the condition of women.

This claim is just a statement of a basic fact about Woolf's essay, and it's also too general to be meaningful.

The Claim Observes Something Without Asserting Why It's Significant

> In "next to of course god america i," patriotic sentiments are broken and unfinished.

This statement sounds as though it's taking up something important in the text, but really, it's just summarizing what the writer *sees* in the text: a series of broken-off quotes from patriotic songs. It doesn't tell the reader anything about what the writer thinks is going on with those statements.

The Claim Doesn't Take a Stand

> It's possible to see the Creature in *Frankenstein* as either a monster or as a victim.

This claim appears to look at an issue from both sides, but since it doesn't *choose* a side, it's not really claiming anything.

The Claim Pretends to Take a Stand but Actually Says Nothing

> Charles Darwin's *On the Origin of Species* is controversial in its claims about evolution, but it is an important landmark in the history of science.

While this claim seems to take up something important, it actually avoids the real issues it raises. No one is arguing that Darwin's text is unimportant.

The Claim Takes a One-Sided Stand

> In *Frankenstein,* Victor's problems come from his own ego.

This is a popular claim on "study aide" sites—but since the vast majority of readers would agree with this, there's really only one side to this argument.

The Claim Rewrites the Text

> In "next to of course god america i," cummings's narrator is a veteran of war.

This claim can never be convincing since you can't prove this through the text—it's not in there. The student has made it up.
This claim does something similar.

> If Frankenstein was a woman, relationships in the novel would have been very different.

It's hard to argue with this claim—but that's because it's both one-sided and based on a speculative rewriting of the text. You're obliged to honor what the text actually says and does.

The Claim Relies on the Reader to Know a Prior Idea That You Haven't Established Yet

> The fact that Victor Frankenstein's experiment is conceptually shaky from the beginning shines a light on the nature of Victor's relationship—or lack of one—to his creation.

This claim assumes that your reader already knows and agrees with an idea that you haven't demonstrated—that the experiment is "conceptually shaky," whatever that means—and goes on to a key idea based on that fact. Students often create claims like this when their ideas start to seem obvious to them because they've worked them out so thoroughly. But remember that your reader hasn't been with you throughout your process work, so you can't skip over the explanation. Nor can you just shoehorn it into the opening paragraph. That paragraph is the space for setting the overall terms of the essay, not for laying the specific groundwork for your ideas.

The Claim Includes Multiple Mini-Claims

> Although Victor seems human, the process of exploring death to figure out how to create life has dehumanized him, making him a lower species. And he never actually knows what he's going to create, plus in the process of creation he loses touch with every person he knows. So really, the Creature is more human than Victor because he knows that it's impossible to be human unless you have relationships with others.

This claim—we call this a "claim cluster"—is really a PowerPoint presentation of the entire paper. An opening paragraph like this ruins the story for the reader by telling him all of your big ideas at once. The first paragraph should introduce your ideas, not present them all as a compressed claim.

The Claim Gives Away Too Much of Your Story

> In *Frankenstein,* Victor Frankenstein famously sets out to build a human being. But the story of his creation of and relationship to his Creature really reveals the nature of monstrosity. More important, it reveals the nature of humanity itself: that it is based on relationships.

This claim is more like an overall claim than an opening claim: It reveals your whole story, which leaves the reader nothing to discover. A little mystery is a good thing.

CONCLUSIONS

Many students find conclusions to be the most intimidating part of the paper. This is one reason why they often leave out or impoverish their opening claims: They're afraid that if they say something important up front, they won't have anything left to say at the end. But the good news is that **once you've figured out your overall claim and your opening claim, you already have your conclusion.**

As we said before, the conclusion is the second half of your overall claim—the "so what," the payoff. It's the part that remains once you've taken out your opening claim. But even though you already know what you want to conclude, that doesn't mean you can just paste that phrase onto the end of your paper. You'll want to check to make sure that, now that you've reached the end of your claim draft, the conclusion follows from everything you've said. And you'll need to make sure it reads well, which may mean rewriting it a bit.

As an example, take a look at the overall claim, the opening claim, and the concluding paragraph of the *Frankenstein* essay we've been working with.

Overall Claim

While Victor Frankenstein claims to be making a human being, and of course thinks of himself as human, his experiment not only blurs distinctions between human and nonhuman, it reveals what humanity is actually based on, which is the ability to have relationships with others.

The highlighted portion of the overall claim is the payoff that will go in the conclusion—but not, as you can see below, in the opening claim.

Opening Claim

In Mary Shelley's *Frankenstein*, it seems that the story is all about whether or not the Creature is a monster or a human. But if you look closely, you can see that the humanity that is in question is really Victor Frankenstein's.

Here's the concluding paragraph, with the big payoff at the end.

By seeing how hard the Creature has tried to become human, the reader's idea of him changes: It becomes possible to understand not only that he wants to join humanity but also that he tries to do so by building relationships with others. This makes him, in fact, more human than Victor Frankenstein, who thinks he doesn't need relationships. The Creature's efforts to join the De Laceys and obtain a wife fail, but he has figured out something Victor once knew but keeps forgetting: that neither of them can be human without being in relationship with others.

This concluding idea:

- comes directly out of the overall claim.
- builds on ideas that the student has explored throughout the essay.
- demonstrates what those ideas add up to instead of restating them.
- emerges from the work the student has done in the paper (rather than coming out of nowhere).
- is still about the text itself, not the universe as a whole.

You'll note that while the student kept the idea from the overall claim, he changed the language so that he would have a sentence that made sense in the context of the rest of the paragraph.

Sometimes it's possible to move one step beyond your concluding idea once you've worked it out in the paper—that is, to build on your conclusion with a bonus move, as we mentioned in chapter four. This move allows you to show the reader how what you've figured out about your phenomena, in turn, allows you to understand the text as a whole differently. And if your assignment calls for it, you can use what you figure out in the bonus move to show how the text sheds light on the historical and cultural moment it emerges from. But you don't need to worry about this right now; we'll show you how to do it in chapter twelve. Your next move is to create a draft—with a claim and a conclusion—that tells the whole story of your essay.

CHAPTER TEN

ASSESSING AND WORKING WITH YOUR CLAIM DRAFT

In this chapter, we'll focus on a key element of essay writing: storytelling. As you'll remember from the "journey" metaphor in chapter four, an essay is really an act of storytelling: You convince your readers of something by taking them on a trip with you. In the last chapter, we talked about how to figure out your overall claim, your opening claim, and your mini-claims. In this chapter, we'll show you how to assess and work with your claim draft by figuring out the story you're telling.

STORYTELLING AT THE ESSAY LEVEL

Many students think that the best way to revise a draft at this stage is to work line by line, or at least paragraph by paragraph, editing language and tweaking ideas. But that kind of from-the-inside-out work is premature at this point because it won't help you figure out the throughlines of your narrative. If instead you spend some time figuring out where you're going and how the pieces fit together, each part of your paper will build on the previous part to tell your story.

Looking at storytelling first will save you time and work, too. After all, once you figure out the story you're telling, the order of ideas becomes clearer—you know where your paragraphs go and why. And it's much easier at that point to revise your individual paragraphs. We'll start by thinking about sequence.

Establishing the Sequence

It's a good idea to look first at the sequence of your story because once you know the story you're telling, it'll be easier to see if you need to reorganize paragraphs or modules. If that's the case, it's probably because the original sequence reflects the order in which you came up with your ideas and not a decision about the best possible order. It's just a relic of your original thinking process, and there's no reason to hold onto it.

You can see how this works in the *Frankenstein* essay. Initially the paper's first module was about how Victor's work was degrading his humanity, and the second was about what Victor thought he was making when he began the experiment. The two mini-claims looked like this.

> **Establishing Claim:** Victor's human nature is degraded by his project.
> **"So What?":** It's not just the project but also his loss of connection to others that makes him less human.

> **Establishing Claim:** Victor never knows what he's making.
> **"So What?":** While Victor claims to be making a human, the boundaries between human and nonhuman are blurred even before the Creature is born.

The problem with this original order is that the second mini-claim (Victor's understanding of the experiment) is an important building block for the first mini-claim (what the experiment does to him). This means that the current order needs to be switched. When you're looking at your claim draft to see if the order is working, ask yourself, *What do I need to say so that I can say this other thing?* Reversing the order so that Victor's compromised human status comes *after* the actual experiment allows the pieces of the paper to build on each other.

PRACTICING: SEQUENCING

- Print out your list of mini-claims.
- Cut the claims apart so that you can move them around.
- Look at your first mini-claim.
  - Is it truly laying the foundation for all the others?
  - Is there anything you say later that needs to come before it?
  - Test this by experimenting with the order; try out other claims before and after this first mini-claim.
- Once you've established what your first mini-claim is, test the order of the rest of your claims using this same method.
- If you realize that a piece of the sequence is missing, write through it.

Cutting Extraneous Material

Just as reorganizing the sequence makes the story clearer, cutting extraneous material makes the ideas in your essay stand out clearly. For example, here's what happens when the student writing the Woolf essay revises her first module.

She starts by reminding herself what her establishing claim and her "so what?" are. This is important because these will serve as her guides for what to cut and what to keep in this module. To avoid deleting material she may need later, she highlights anything she wants to cut in blue and anything she's not sure about in purple. (Everything else stays the way it was.)

Since she's interested in the big picture—the storytelling—she isn't looking at specific cuts in specific sentences. Her focus is on making her ideas as clear as possible. She makes notes to herself as she goes (in green). Here's what the module looks like when she's done.

> In Woolf's essay, the Angel in the House is a "phantom" that she has to "kill" in order to write what she wants to write with nobody getting in her way, including herself. Woolf takes the time to describe the Angel, since the "younger and happier" women in her audience in 1931 "may not have heard of her," because they're not Victorian women who grew up with these ideas. She writes,
>
> > She was intensely sympathetic. She was intensely charming. She was utterly unselfish. She excelled in the difficult arts of family life. She sacrificed herself daily. If there was chicken, she took the leg; if there was a draught she sat in it—in short she was so constituted that she never had a mind or a wish of her own, but preferred to sympathize always with the minds and wishes of others. Above all—I need not say it—she was pure. Her purity was her chief beauty—her blushes, her graces. In those days—the last of Queen Victoria—every house had its Angel. And when I came to write I encountered her with the very first words. The shadow of her wings fell on my page; I heard the rustling of skirts in the room.
>
> In this passage, Woolf seems to suggest that one of the things that makes her lose her patience when it comes to the Angel is that she "never had a mind or wish of her own," meaning she can't think for herself or have an idea of herself, or want anything for herself, or imagine what she might want, which is why she always puts other people first: She doesn't have

any sense of self—but when you look closely, that isn't exactly the case, and the distinction can change the way women think about themselves not only as writers but as women. [NOTE: ESTABLISHING CLAIM]

Woolf says that the Angel "was so constituted that she never had a mind or wish of her own, but preferred to sympathize always with the minds and wishes of others." *Constituted* means that this is the way she was made, which makes sense and fits with the Victorian idea that Woolf seems to be talking about of what a woman naturally was. It's interesting that she was "so constituted," not that she was "made by nature" or something like that because you don't know who or what made her. Also, according to the dictionary, *constituted* comes from *constitution*, which is about how your body works, like your digestive system—if you had a "strong constitution" it meant you were healthy, which is confusing since it doesn't seem to be about the way you act, which doesn't exactly go with the idea of whether or not you have a "mind" or "wish" of your own because that's about the brain. Maybe Woolf is saying that the brain and the body are the same thing, which is maybe what people believed back then, that your body and mind were exactly the same—not so different, now that you think about it, from the way we think about it now, where if you don't eat enough, for example, your blood sugar drops and then you can't think. Still it seems weird. But then the weirder thing is that there's something that seems like a big contradiction right in this sentence. Here it is: Woolf says that the Angel "preferred to sympathize always with the minds and wishes of others." But *prefer* means that you like something better, which means that you're making a choice about whether you like it or not—like if you prefer chocolate to vanilla or high boots to low boots. Maybe it's your taste, which is sort of inherent, but still you have to make a choice and decide. But this doesn't make sense if the Angel really "was so constituted that she never had a mind or a wish of her own." After all, how can you have a preference if you don't have a mind? And how can you like one thing over another if you never have a "wish," if you never want anything? So this is a place where if you look closely and really think about the language in relation to the content and what she's said before and after, Woolf is actually being critical of the Angel in a whole different way. While it seems like Woolf is saying that the Angel is a pain because of the way she's naturally self-sacrificing, what she's actually saying is much more serious: She's saying that while the Angel acts so much like she doesn't have a mind of her own or any wishes that people believe it, she actually does, and she's just making the choice to pretend and not use her mind. She "prefer[s]" to be brainless, probably as part of being self-sacrificing.

Then we get to "sympathize." According to *Merriam-Webster College Dictionary Online*, one definition of *sympathize* is "to be in keeping, accord, or harmony." So on the surface, it seems like Woolf is saying more of what she said before: the Angel always puts other people first, because that's how she's "constituted," meaning that's how she's made. "In short" makes it seem even more like it's just repeating what she said before because that phrase means summarizing briefly the thing that was said before. But *Merriam-Webster* says *prefer* is "to like better or best." If what she likes better or best is to "sympathize always with the minds and wishes of others," then it is not possible that she *also* "never had a mind or wish of her own." If she's deciding to sympathize, then she has to have a mind to do the deciding with. Just like animals don't decide, they only react (most animals); if she was naturally without a human brain, that would be the way she would act. She wouldn't be able to prefer to sympathize; she would just naturally do it. [NOTE: MAYBE I CAN KEEP SOME OF THIS AND MOVE IT UP.]

Then you can go back and read the beginning of the description of her again once you've figured out this idea, using it as a lens.

On first read, it seems like the description is pretty straightforward, but when you go back, you can see that it isn't—in fact it's weird. Woolf describes the Angel by saying she's "intensely sympathetic ... immensely charming ... utterly unselfish." These words seem very over the top when you first read them because of the way that they repeat themselves in three sentences that are almost exactly the same and because of the descriptive words that modify the characterizing words, which make the characterizing words themselves (*sympathetic, charming, unselfish*) even stronger. But when you think about them in connection with the idea that she actually has a mind of her own, but she's "preferring" not to use it, these sentences now seem suspicious, too, as though they're as fake as the idea that she does not have a mind. Now it doesn't seem over the top but very false, and the adjectives that describe the characteristics make them seem even more ridiculous and fake because they're so strong. When you look back, you think, *How could this possibly be real?* It's interesting also that "intensely sympathetic" is first used here and then later repeated in that she "preferred to sympathize always with the minds and wishes of others"—like in the first case it's a state of being, it's natural to who she is, but in the second case we've seen already that that's not true, it's a choice, and so the first case when you look back at it feels like she must be acting. [NOTE: MOVE THIS UP TO NEAR SYMPATHY STUFF EARLIER?] And when you keep reading, these sentences get less serious. "She sacrificed herself daily" sounds a lot less bad when you see that she's really talking about taking the least meaty cut of chicken or sitting in a draughty spot. It's kind of ridiculous—not like she's sacrificing herself by starving herself for somebody else or putting herself out in the cold to freeze to death so somebody else could be warm (even if that made any sense, as though giving up warmth could make somebody else warm). "Daily" sort of makes this clear, too, because if you really "sacrifice [your]self," you'd have to die, ultimately, or the equivalent because it's not making a sacrifice but sacrificing yourself, so it's like an Old Testament sacrifice, and that means you can't do it over and over. When you look at it like this, she's acting like a parody of a stereotypical Victorian good woman.

The idea that she's faking it becomes important when it comes to the idea that "purity" is "her chief beauty" because if everything else about the Angel is suspicious, then her purity must be, too. Woolf equates blushing to purity when she says "her blushes, her great grace" as parallel to "[h]er purity was her chief beauty," after the dash. Blushing is a physical reaction to anything that's shocking, so when the Angel blushes, that's supposed to show that she's innocent because she must be shocked by a lot of things. This is where that body-mind thing comes in again because her body reacts when she sees something that's shocking, and that's her "chief grace," so it's really about a characteristic of her character, so even if you buy that she has no mind of her own, there's still something that connects the body and the soul, so to speak. [NOTE: I THINK THIS MAKES THE ISSUE CONFUSING.] *Grace* means gracefulness like a dancer, but it also means a Christian idea of a kind of forgiveness or gift from God. So if "her blushes" are "her chief grace," then you can say that blushing is her main holiness. So her holiness is a physical reaction, which is different from the things she does earlier in the passage (sacrificing herself) and the things she is earlier in the passage (unselfish, etc.). So if purity is so important, and it's the same in the sentence as *blushes* because they're paralleled, then purity seems to mean this physical reaction, so even if the body and soul are connected, really what it's saying is that the body is the important part because it's what shows her purity, not what she says or what she does or her characteristics. This would make sense if she really was mindless because she would basically just be a body of natural reactions. But if that's what she "prefers" instead of how she's "constituted" ("made up or formed" according to *Merriam-Webster*), [NOTE: PROBABLY NEED THIS DEFINITION THE FIRST TIME I USE THE WORD.] then she's making her body more important than her mind on purpose. That seems like the opposite of being pure because the body is supposed to be less pure than the mind and it does what it wants and has to be controlled. The mind is the part that is supposed to be pure. And what happens if the purity that's "supposed to be her chief beauty" comes from all the things that Woolf has said before? That would mean her purity was even more fake because she's not really naturally mindless or self-sacrificing or without wishes—all of that is what she decides to be like. So that seems to say that blushes are just an external show of purity, on the skin, but they're not actually natural, or maybe that the Angel can manufacture them when she wants to—either way, she looks pure but it's just on the outside. So what Woolf is saying here is that the Angel's character isn't natural but fake and also that her purity is fake, too.

It's important that Woolf says, "In those days … every house had its Angel. And when I came to write I encountered her with the very first words." It seems like she's saying there's a different Angel in every house, so every woman has her own to deal with. This would mean that the Angel is personalized and that it was somehow part of what women are naturally, that all women had Angels to deal with that belonged to them. This would imply that women were naturally the things she first says the Angel is. But when Woolf says, "I encountered her," she changes that: Instead of saying, "I encountered mine," she says "her," which seems to say that there's only one Angel. So she's saying that women shouldn't feel like they're each responsible for their Angel because the Angel is actually one big thing that's the same for everybody, not your own part of yourself that you can't get away from because it's natural. So that means the Angel isn't something unique to every house, special to every woman, but the same thing. And that means she is sort of an idea of a woman being somehow beamed into every house. Woolf doesn't say where the idea of the Angel comes from, but we can assume if it isn't natural that it must be somehow made up, constructed, which means it's probably society that does it, which is where ideas of people's behavior come from if they aren't from nature. So Woolf is saying that women can't write because they are stopped by this idea created by society of what a woman is, that seems to be natural but that isn't really, which gets in their way. When she shows that the way the Angel isn't how women should be naturally but is a choice, and that the choice is socially constructed, she's saying, basically, that the Angel is a liar. And that means that women not only need to move this idea of women out of the way so that they can write—it also means that women need to see that the Angel isn't who they're naturally supposed to be, because it's a socially constructed lie that keeps them from speaking up. [NOTE: THIS IS THE "SO WHAT."]

Sometimes the material you cut doesn't seem very important, and it's easy to part with. But sometimes, you need to cut a really good idea that doesn't help you tell your story—that is, it doesn't help you prove your establishing claim or set up the "so what." Take the discussion of *constituted* in the Woolf essay. It's easy to see why the student cut the section where she compares the Angel to a drop in blood sugar. But the overall question of the relationship between the body and the mind is interesting—it would be possible to write a whole other essay on Woolf's speech with this as the focus. The ideas here are rich, and they're grounded in the text. But they don't really help the student tell the story she's trying to tell—and in fact, because they're smart ideas that are tangentially related to her story, they can potentially pull her and her reader off course.

Once the student has decided what to cut, she's ready to try out her new structure. To do so, she copies the whole essay into another file so that she can go back to the version she has now if she decides she wants to keep something she's cut.

The student begins the process of cutting things from her essay by getting rid of all the material she had originally highlighted in blue. Then she reviews the material she'd highlighted in purple to decide if she wants to keep it. Once she's cut out the material in blue, it becomes much easier to see whether or not the purple material does any work. In this case, even though she really likes some of these ideas, she decides that most of it can go. Her focus on the story she's telling lets her see that these pieces may be interesting but they're not useful. (Another way to do this: Print out the highlighted essay, cut out the parts that are marked as extraneous, and then put the remaining pieces together to see what you have.)

Deepening Your Story

Sometimes the process of figuring out the story you're telling helps you see sections in your narrative that need strengthening. For example, the student working on the cummings essay finds that one of her "so whats" is unconvincing. To arrive at a stronger "so what?" she needs to do some additional thinking about the ideas in the module.

Here's the student's first module with the establishing claim highlighted in green and the "so what?" in purple.

> In the very first line of e.e. cummings's poem "next to of course god america i," the speaker proclaims his love for America by saying "next to of course god america/i love you," which sounds like a very clear statement of patriotic pride and affection. But as he continues to speak, this patriotic pride gets less clear and definitive, and as the poem continues, it leads the reader to question what the narrator of the poem thinks patriotism is and whether he believes it's truly a way to show you love your country.
>
> After going through a number of quotations from patriotic American songs like "My Country Tis of Thee," the speaker says that "in every language even deafanddumb/thy sons acclaim thy glorious name." The *thy* refers to America, and at this point, he is one of those "sons," since all the songs he quotes praise her. Although he says that America's sons acclaim her "in every language," the one example he gives is *deafanddumb*, which is not actually a language. It's at this point that the mood begins to shift: Until now, the speaker didn't seem to feel any conflict about patriotism and love for country. Even the cut-off songs seemed like an effort to create the effect of a group of people, each singing one song or another. But if you acclaimed America or anything else in "deafanddumb," there would only be silence.
>
> What does it mean to praise a country in a way that can't be heard? And is unspoken, unheard praise really praise at all? The speaker started out sounding confident and excited about America, but now instead of a hubbub of people singing America's praises and acclaiming her "glorious name," there's silence. When the noise level goes down, so does the enthusiastic patriotism the poem started with. And by choosing *deafanddumb*, the speaker drains out all the sounds he created a minute ago, which indirectly raises the question of whether those snippets of

songs—which seemed positive before—are actually just noise. Now, not only does he seem less patriotic and excited about praising the country, but the reader is left wondering whether the speaker thinks patriotism might just be empty noise.

When the student looks at this module with a clearer sense of her overall claim—*by the end of the poem, the reader questions what the narrator of the poem thinks patriotism is and whether he believes it's truly a way to show you love your country*—she sees that the "so what?" is weak. It doesn't seem like enough of a payoff to say that "the reader is left wondering" whether patriotism is empty noise. So she goes back to her preliminary work and finds a freewrite that seems relevant.

Here's what she wrote in her freewrite.

> The chopped-up quotes—what's going on there? He puts enough that you can recognize it but doesn't finish any phrase. Does it matter that they are recognizable anyway? Does that say something about patriotism? What does cutting the phrases off do to their patriotism?

Looking back at this freewrite allows her to see the poem with fresh eyes and to generate new questions and ideas.

> So are the snippets patriotic? Hmm … yes, because they are so obviously from songs that praise America, including the official national anthem, and also because Americans reading the poem can recognize the phrases from just a tiny piece, which shows that they are part of American identity, and they are the songs that are sung when people are asserting their love for this country. BUT at the same time, by cutting them up in small pieces, the speaker takes away their sense and turns them into noise.

Then she goes back and adds this material to the second paragraph of the module to help make her case that the phrases are empty noise. As you'll see, some parts of her second freewrite don't need additional editing and others do.

> What does it mean to praise a country in a way that can't be heard? And is unspoken, unheard praise really praise at all? The speaker started out sounding confident and excited about America, but now instead of a hubbub of people singing America's praises and acclaiming her "glorious name" there's silence. When the noise level goes down, so does the enthusiastic patriotism the poem started with. By specifying *deafanddumb*,

a language that is neither spoken aloud nor heard, the speaker drains out all the sounds he created a minute ago, which indirectly raises the question of whether he thinks those snippets of songs—which seemed positive before—are actually just noise. And once that question comes up, the reader/listener can no longer avoid a question that's kind of built into the opening lines of the poem—what's the effect of taking these patriotic songs and breaking them into little snippets? They are absolutely patriotic—they are the songs Americans sing to praise our country and identify ourselves as belonging to it. But at the same time, by cutting them up in small pieces, the speaker takes away some of their sense and pushes them toward being a jumble of sounds, or noise. Seen in this light, the speaker not only seems less patriotic and excited about praising the country, but he also seems to be asking whether the familiar language of patriotism could be empty noise.

In her freewrite the student sees that two different things are going on at the same time: On the one hand, the song snippets are patriotic and instantly recognizable, but on the other hand, their sense is diminished. Sometimes when a student sees something that seems contradictory, she's tempted to leave out one part because it makes for a "cleaner" story. But as we've said before, a moment that seems to do two opposite things at once is often the most interesting—and most productive to look at. **If you simplify your story by taking out the oppositions, you'll diminish the depth and complexity of your story.**

STORYTELLING AT THE PARAGRAPH LEVEL

Once you've clarified the framework of the story you're telling, you can think about order *within* your paragraphs. This assessment process consists of the same moves that you made at the essay level: sequencing, cutting, and deepening. The idea here is to revise your work within each paragraph so that:

- the ideas are in the most logical order.
- each sentence builds on the one before it.
- there is no extraneous material.
- your storytelling is complete and convincing.

Establishing the Sequence at the Paragraph Level

Let's look, for example, at the cummings essay. The student prints out her first module and color-codes each first paragraph to see the ideas there. In the paragraph below, she highlights the discussion of heroism in blue, the discussion of "roaring slaughter" in yellow, and the discussion of war in purple. The establishing claim is in green. The first paragraph of her module now looks like this.

> Later on, the speaker asks, "What could be more beaut-/iful than those heroic happy dead/who rushed like lions to the roaring slaughter." At first he sounds like he's complimenting the dead men since he calls them "heroic" and "happy" and says they are like lions (lions are always portrayed as the brave kings of the jungle). But then comes an odd phrase, the "roaring slaughter." What should be roaring are the lions, but instead it's the slaughter itself. *Slaughter* means the killing of animals for food or the killing of a lot of people, like in a massacre. Although the speaker never mentions war, by creating the image of a massacre, he gives that idea. A "roaring" slaughter carries an idea of animals or people moaning and screaming and crying. Again the speaker is talking about sound, but now the noise isn't empty, it's terrifying. When he connects that sound to people he calls "the heroic happy dead," he indirectly brings up the subject of war. War is terrifying, but that part of it is often overlooked because of the way that war is seen as patriotic. There are two questions to ask here: Why would dead people be happy, and what made them heroes? The answers go together: They are heroes because they died for their country, and they are happy because they were heroic. When the speaker asks, "What could be more beaut-/iful than those heroic happy dead/who rushed like lions to the roaring slaughter," he is doing two important things: connecting patriotism to war and making his listeners think about what it means to die in a war, even a patriotic one.

Color-coding the paragraph lets her identify issues of sequence and places where she needs to do more work to make her narrative more convincing. Here's what she sees.

- She talks about the "heroic happy dead" twice. This repetition creates a sequencing problem: She needs to decide where that discussion is most useful.
- When she talks about "the heroic happy dead" in the beginning, she restates what the quote says but doesn't do much analytical work with it.

- She also talks about war in two different places. *This* sequencing problem is a result of a deeper issue in the paper: She hasn't yet figured out how to demonstrate her claim that the speaker is really talking about war. Because she doesn't know what she wants to say, she ends up circling around and repeating herself.
- She's not really addressing the issue of how patriotism connects to war. She needs to figure this out and get it on the page.

Here's the new paragraph, with the same color-coding (blue for the discussion of heroism, purple for the discussion of war, and green for the establishing claim).

> When the speaker asks, "what could be more beaut-/iful than those heroic happy dead/who rushed like lions to the roaring slaughter," war enters the picture. It does this because of the way he describes the dead. They aren't sad, they are "heroic happy dead." The obvious reason that someone who is dead could be both heroic and happy is that he died for a noble cause—for instance, in a war, fighting for his country. And what could show more patriotism, or love of country, than that? There's another connection, too, because the words "oh/say can you see by the dawn's early" are from the "Star Spangled Banner" which is about a war. Every time Americans sing that particular patriotic song, we connect ourselves to the idea of love of country and defending our country in war. By asking, "What could be more beaut-/iful than those heroic happy dead/who rushed like lions to the roaring slaughter," the speaker is doing two important things: connecting patriotism to war and making his listeners think about what it means to die in a war, even a patriotic one.

In her revision, the student does a number of things.

- She reorganizes the sequence so that the discussion of war is all in one place.
- She explains the connection between the "heroic happy dead" and war in much more detail and deepens that linkage by adding a new idea.
- She moves a lot of material out of the paragraph entirely. You'll note that she has moved the material that was highlighted in yellow out of the paragraph. That's because once the student did more work on clarifying the connection between the "happy heroic dead" and war, she could see that the discussion of "the roaring slaughter" didn't actually

belong in this paragraph at all. If your color-coding reveals that you have a lot of ideas in the same paragraph, you'll need to make some choices about what belongs in the paragraph and what could go elsewhere to avoid confusion.

As you can see, looking closely at sequence and connections at the paragraph level is just as important as looking at the big picture. When the student was only looking at how the paragraph fit into the overall structure of her essay, she thought it was fine because it moved the story forward. It was only when she looked closely at the paragraph that she saw the work it needed. It's crucial to make the internal story of each paragraph clear and coherent.

Cutting at the Paragraph Level

Cutting repetition and extraneous material at the paragraph level is also important: If you have a lot of unnecessary stuff in your paragraph, your reader may get bored or have trouble following the story. Often these unnecessary bits are relics of your thinking process that have survived from earlier drafts. Here are some examples from the Woolf essay. The cuts the student plans to make are highlighted in blue.

Repetition

> In this passage, Woolf seems to suggest that one of the things that makes her lose her patience when it comes to the Angel is that she "never had a mind or wish of her own," meaning she can't think for herself or have an idea of herself, or want anything for herself, or imagine what she might want, which is why she always puts other people first: she doesn't have any sense of self—but when you look closely, that isn't exactly the case, and what Woolf shows can change the way women think about themselves not only as writers but as women.

Here the student has repeated herself. She can easily see that she's using the same language over and over, and she knows she needs to cut something. But the decision about exactly *what* to cut is not straightforward: Each of the phrases she uses here has a slightly different meaning. *Thinking for yourself* isn't the same as *having an idea of yourself*, and *wanting something for yourself* isn't exactly the same as *imagining what you might want*. To decide what to cut, the student needs to pin down exactly what she thinks the text is saying rather than approximating it by creating multiple versions.

Don't automatically assume you have to cut whole phrases; you can always cut out the weak part of one phrase or idea and suture what remains to another strong piece.

Dialoguing with Yourself

> Woolf says that the Angel "preferred to sympathize always with the minds and wishes of others." But *prefer* means that you like something better, which means that you're making a choice about whether you like it or not—like if you prefer chocolate to vanilla or high boots to low boots. Maybe it's your taste, which is sort of inherent, but still you have to make a choice and decide. But this doesn't make sense if the Angel really "was so constituted that she never had a mind or a wish of her own."

Here the student has created an analogy that helps her understand what's going on in this moment in the text. That can be useful when she's still figuring out her ideas, but once she's moved to a draft that is trying to communicate a narrative, it just gets in the way and pulls the reader out of the story.

Narrating Your Process to Yourself

> But this doesn't make sense if the Angel really "was so constituted that she never had a mind or a wish of her own." After all, how can you have a preference if you don't have a mind? And how can you like one thing over another if you never have a "wish," if you never want anything? So this is a place where if you look closely and really think about the language in relation to the content and what she's said before and after, Woolf is actually being critical of the Angel in a whole different way.

Here the student is narrating her process as she goes: She's noting that she's looking closely, which is, of course, the definition of close reading. This sort of meta-narration takes the reader out of your story. While it can be useful to talk to yourself in this way when you're figuring things out, this conversation doesn't belong in later drafts. After all, the reader doesn't have to do all of this work—you've done it for her.

Summarizing Your Work

Woolf equates blushing to purity when she says, "Her blushes, her great grace" as parallel to "[h]er purity was her chief beauty," after the dashes. Blushing is a physical reaction to anything that's shocking, so when the Angel blushes, that's supposed to show that she's innocent. *Grace* means gracefulness like a dancer, but it also means a Christian idea of a kind of forgiveness or gift from God. So if "her blushes" are "her chief grace," then you can say that blushing is her main holiness. So her holiness is a physical reaction, which is different from the things she does earlier in the passage (sacrificing herself) and the things she is earlier in the passage (unselfish, etc.). So if purity is so important and it's the same in the sentence as *blushes*, because they're paralleled, then purity seems to mean this physical reaction, so really what it's saying is that the body is the important part because it's what shows her purity, not what she says or what she does or her characteristics.

Here the student sees that in the process of writing through her ideas about purity, she's included a summary of what she's figured out so far. This is actually quite useful in an earlier stage of writing: Restating what you've seen can help you build a platform on which to build the next idea. But there's no need to keep the summary as you move forward: Your reader can see your ideas because they're already on the page.

Oversummarizing the Text

Before looking at how Victor reacts to the Creature, it is useful to consider the way he describes the scene when the Creature is born. He calls the night gloomy, talks about how it was raining, how it was the middle of the night, and how his candle was almost burnt down to the end. Then he describes the moment the Creature comes to life. He spends a lot of time talking about how ugly the Creature is, especially his eyes, lips, and complexion. This makes it seem like the issue with the Creature's humanity is related to how he looks—but really, that's just an excuse that Victor is giving himself to justify fleeing.

In this example, the student has summarized the scene instead of focusing on the material that interests him. This overly detailed summary has no real connection to the point he's making. And since the summary begins the paragraph, it can mislead the reader into thinking that this is what the paragraph is really about.

BUILDING IDEA LINKS

After sequencing, cutting, and deepening at both the essay and paragraph levels, the next step is to assess the links *between* modules. These are often places where the story isn't sewn together as tightly as it needs to be. In other words, there is no clear analytical link between one module and the next, no reason why they are next to each other. It's not surprising that this happens: After all, your focus has been on developing your ideas in each module rather than on thinking through the exact connections between them. And if you've always written five-paragraph essays, you're probably not accustomed to focusing on these links because the five-paragraph essay doesn't require you to develop a connected narrative. But when you're writing analytically, you need to learn to spot weak links so that you can create strong connections, which we call *idea links*.

Spotting Weak Links

To make it easier to spot weak links, start by highlighting the first and last sentences of each module so you can see them in isolation. (You can also put each pair together on a separate page.) The following are some examples of common weak links.

Chronological Links

> **END OF MODULE 1:** *deafanddumb* changes the poem's mood: Before, you could almost hear a stadium full of people singing patriotic songs, and now, just nothing—silence.
>
> **BEGINNING OF MODULE 2:** Later on, the speaker asks, "What could be more beaut-/iful than those heroic happy dead/ who rushed like lions to the roaring slaughter."

Using phrases like *later on* (or *similarly, next,* or *also*) is a sign that the connection the student wants to set up isn't based on the story of his ideas but on the chronology of events in the text. Instead of showing how he moves from one idea to the next, the student is creating a false transition based on the fact that the second thing he's talking about comes later in the poem than the first.

No Transition

> **END OF MODULE 1:** It's Victor's flight from his creation, not the way the Creature was created, that makes the Creature nonhuman.
> **BEGINNING OF MODULE 2:** The Creature wants to be human.

Though there's clearly a relationship between these modules (both are talking about the Creature's humanity or lack of humanity), there's no actual transition. The student has moved directly from a discussion about what causes the Creature's lack of humanity to one about what the Creature wants, and he's left out a connection between these two ideas.

Repetition Instead of Transition

> **END OF MODULE 1:** In this way, Woolf shows that the Angel is lying.
> **BEGINNING OF MODULE 2:** Thus Woolf demonstrates that the Angel is untruthful. The Angel is lying about what she really is.

Here the student uses a word that seems to show that she's moving on—*thus*—but she's actually just repeating the last point she made in the previous paragraph.

Fake Transitions

> **END OF MODULE 1:** In this way, Woolf shows that the Angel is lying.
> **BEGINNING OF MODULE 2:** Similarly, Woolf makes it clear that her audience no longer has to deal with the Angel because history has moved on and women aren't controlled by the same social forces that were around in the Victorian era.

In this example, the student has used a word—*similarly*—that *seems* to link the two modules, but in fact, there's no real connection between the idea she finishes talking about in module 1 and the idea she starts talking about in module 2. (Other words that create fake transitions include *moreover, however,* and *in addition*.)

In order to address these kinds of problems, note the *idea* that you ended the first module with and the idea that you start the next module with. Now think about the relationship between these two ideas. If you find that no relationship exists, you'll need to make some decisions: Can you build a meaningful idea link between these two modules? Are you missing something in the middle that would help you connect your ideas more effectively? Do you need to move things around?

Thinking Through Relationships Between Modules

Sometimes a weak linkage between two modules exists because you haven't yet thought through how the idea in one module relates to the idea in the next. Here are some examples of how modules might relate.

Cause and Effect

END OF MODULE 1: In this way, Woolf shows that the Angel is lying, which discredits the idealized Angel.

BEGINNING OF MODULE 2: By demonstrating this, Woolf gives permission to her audience to leave the Angel behind. In fact, she implies that the new freedoms enjoyed by the young women writers in her audience are a result of this unmasking of the Angel.

Here the idea in the first module really is causing the thing you're talking about in the second module. The phrase "by demonstrating this" makes that relationship clear.

Commonality

END OF MODULE 1: *deafanddumb* changes the poem's mood: Before, you could almost hear a stadium full of people singing patriotic songs, and now, just nothing—silence.

BEGINNING OF MODULE 2: The issue of sound versus silence comes up again when the speaker mentions "those heroic happy dead/who rushed like lions to the roaring slaughter." The dead are silent, but there is also this "roaring" or noisy slaughter.

In this example, the two modules are connected because of something they have in common. (Earlier we pointed out that *similarly* is generally a fake link, but true similarity is a perfectly valid reason to put two modules next to each other.)

Opposition

END OF MODULE 1: Victor is convinced that it's the way the Creature was created that makes him nonhuman.

BEGINNING OF MODULE 2: But in fact, it's Victor's flight from his creation, not the way the Creature was created, that takes away the Creature's humanity.

In this example, the connection between the two modules is an opposition: The idea at the end of the first module sets up the unexpected new idea at the beginning of the next one. This is an effective way to build an argument, and, as you may have noticed, it's similar to the move we showed you for developing introductory claims.

PRACTICING: BUILDING IDEA LINKS

- Highlight the beginning and ending sentences of each module in your draft.
- Identify weak links.
- Determine whether there is a real connection between weakly linked modules.
- If there is no real connection, you need to decide: Do you build a new connection? Move things around?
- If there is an undeveloped connection, think through how these two ideas relate to each other. What exactly is their relationship?
- Rewrite the closing of the first module and/or the opening of the second module to reflect the relationship you see between the first idea and the following one.

Now that you've figured out the story of your paper and worked through your claims, you're close to a final draft. If, however, your paper involves research, you have one more major step before you've reached the end: You'll need to make decisions about what to research, find useful material, and incorporate it into your draft. We'll tackle this process in the next chapter. If your paper doesn't involve research, move right on to chapter twelve, where we'll talk about editing, polishing, and other things you'll need to do for your final draft.

CHAPTER ELEVEN

RESEARCH

So far in this book, we've focused on close reading and critical writing involving direct work on the text you're writing on. For many courses, this is all you'll need to do—but for some assignments you'll need to find and work with research. In this chapter, we'll show you how to choose research sources and how to incorporate research effectively into your essay.

WHAT IS RESEARCH FOR?

Many students begin every paper by going directly to the research step, regardless of the assignment. When you're doing research, you feel like you're getting something done—and you're amassing material, which is reassuring if you're worried you won't have enough to say on a given topic. But in almost all cases, research is not the source and sum total of the paper you'll be writing.

Instead research is useful for:

- taking up questions that can't be answered solely through your own analysis.
- finding information to help you analyze a text or phenomenon.
- finding tools or ideas to use as lenses to explore your text or phenomenon.
- in some cases, finding a text or phenomenon to look at.

Unless you're writing a *literature review* (a summary of what other people have to say on a given topic, such as a new medical innovation, for example, or a problem in political science), it's important to remember that **your paper is still primarily made up of your ideas,** even when you're using research.

In most cases, you'll be asked to use research:

- to inform your analysis using background information or factual material that can help you understand your phenomenon.
- to enter into a scholarly conversation on a given topic. (Academics spend much of their time in this sort of conversation. Scholar A says some-

thing about how trauma affects memory, Scholar B expands on this idea, Scholar C counters with her own idea, and so forth. This is an important way for scholarship to move forward.) When you write a research paper involving scholarly research and your own analysis, you, too, are entering into this conversation.

- to find an approach, a theory, or a methodology that helps you look at your phenomenon.
- to find material to explore, using what you've learned in your course. (For example, in a course on the history and theory of tourism in which you've been focusing on the nineteenth-century origins of American tourism, you might decide to focus on the development of Niagara Falls as a tourist destination.)

TYPES OF RESEARCH MATERIALS

There are many types of research materials you can use, depending on what you're trying to discover. These materials are categorized in a number of different ways.

Primary and Secondary Sources

One set of divisions that professors (and high school teachers) often use is *primary* vs. *secondary* sources. It's important to know what this distinction is and how it works—but once we've shown you this, we'll introduce you to another, more practical way of thinking about research materials.

The primary/secondary method of categorization draws a line between research sources that are **original** and research sources that **comment on the original**. For example, in a history course, you might see this breakdown.

> **PRIMARY:** the American Constitution
> **SECONDARY:** legal analysis of the Thirteenth Amendment
> a book on American politics in the 1780s

In a chemistry class, the primary/secondary source breakdown might look like this.

> **PRIMARY:** original published research

> **SECONDARY:** analysis of that original research by other chemists. (This is the case even if both are articles published in peer-reviewed scientific journals.)

In a literature class, the breakdown might work like this.

> **PRIMARY:** the novel *Moby-Dick*
> **SECONDARY:** a literary-critical article on masculinity in *Moby-Dick*
> a book on the history of whaling in New England
> a text on the psychology of obsession

This set of distinctions can be useful in determining what you're writing about—particularly if you need to do research to find the phenomenon that your paper will be about. It's important to know the difference between the *thing itself* and *responses* to that thing. But **the problem with defining sources as primary and secondary is that it doesn't necessarily help you figure out what to *do* with these sources.** For example, if you know that an interview with a musician is a primary source and a commentary on that interview is a secondary source, how does that help you put either of these documents to work in your essay? And the terms *primary* and *secondary* aren't absolute, either: Though commentary on the musician interview may be a secondary source in a paper on guitar players, it might be a primary source in an essay on music criticism. It all depends on what you're reading for.

So it's useful to understand what primary and secondary sources are (because you're likely to come across these terms in prompts)—but there is a much more productive way to figure out what kind of research materials you're looking for.

BEAM/BEAT

The method we like best is known by the acronym BEAM. It was developed by Professor Joseph Bizup.[1] BEAM stands for four kinds of sources.

> **B**ackground
> **E**xhibit
> **A**rgument
> **M**ethod

---

[1] If you'd like to read what he has to say about this method, see his article, "BEAM: A Rhetorical Vocabulary for Teaching Research-Based Writing" Review 27:1 (Oct 2007): 1–29.

Some instructors replace or supplement "Method" with "Theory," so you may hear the acronym referred to as BEAT or BEAT/BEAM.

The BEAT/BEAM method is based not on the issue of how original your sources are but rather on the question of what work each type of source can do for you. As the BEAT/BEAM methodology makes clear, your own analytical work is always at the center of the paper-writing process—even when you're using research. **The job of research is not to generate the paper: Instead it's to enrich, inform, or provide lenses for your work of analysis.** That means that your research questions emerge from your process of asking questions and analyzing your text.

As we've said, many students think that it's always a good idea to *start* the paper process with research. Sometimes that makes sense—for example, as you'll see below, if you need to find a subject to write about, you need to begin with research. But often, beginning with research is not a good way to go because, as we've shown throughout this book, it's not productive to begin the paper process knowing what you're going to say—you need to discover that as you go. And if you don't yet know what you're talking about, how can you figure out what research questions you need to ask? BEAT/BEAM is based on the idea that different types of research do different work—and that means that different types of research are useful at different stages in the writing process.

THE RESEARCH PROCESS

Here's a breakdown of how BEAT/BEAM works.

Background

Background refers to **information**: historical, scientific, biographical, musical, medical, or any other type of factual material. **If you reach a point where you**

can't proceed further in your analysis because you're missing information or you come across a reference in your passage that you don't understand, that's when you start looking for a background source. It's likely that you'll discover you need a background source early on in your process: You may get stopped in the dialogic journal process because you don't understand a term and need some background information. Or you may realize you need background information as you move deeper into your passage, perhaps even after you've finished a first draft. But don't leave it too long: It's important to have all the necessary information at hand so your analysis is as grounded and accurate as possible.

For example, if you're writing a paper about medicine in Bram Stoker's *Dracula*, you may find that you can't move forward with your analysis until you do some research on blood transfusions in the late nineteenth century—otherwise, you can't figure out whether Dr. Van Helsing is an innovative doctor or a dangerous quack when he transfuses untested blood into the vampire victim Lucy's veins.

Or if you're writing a paper on the rise of organic food in the Northeast and you're trying to figure out when people became willing to pay more money for organic produce, you might want to research the history of farmers' markets in northeastern cities.

Or if you're writing a paper on city planning responses to changing weather patterns in the Southwest, you might find it useful to do some background research on hurricane frequency and intensity in the area.

The information you discover by doing background research doesn't stand in for your analysis; it doesn't necessarily precede it. This information informs your analysis, giving you more information so that your analysis is more accurate and grounded. It's a basic step—much like looking words up in the dictionary—that gives you a greater understanding of your phenomenon.

Exhibit

Exhibit refers to **a phenomenon that you read closely and analyze: the primary subject of your paper. When you need something to write about, you need an exhibit.** If your assignment requires you to find an exhibit through research instead of using a class text, you'll need to do that early in the process—before you start drafting—because without an exhibit, to quote Gertrude Stein, "There's no there there." Until you have your exhibit, you have nothing to write about.

For example, if your assignment is to write an essay on a literary work in English from World War I, you might start by looking up lists of British World War I poets; then you'll need to look at some of their work so you can choose a poem to focus on.

Or if your assignment is to write an essay on a nineteenth-century Continental philosopher, you'll need to do some research on who those philosophers were and what they talked about in order to find a subject.

Or if your assignment is to write an essay on the introduction of the euro as a common currency in Europe, you could start by looking at opinion articles on the subject or at economists' writings on the euro or at political speeches or at historical analyses of the effects of the euro.

If you don't have an exhibit and you need one, you should do some preliminary work to help you figure out what you're focusing on. (If you don't need an exhibit for your assignment, skip to the Argument section.) The world of research materials is a very big place; the universe of online materials is vast, and academic libraries can be intimidating places. So here are some strategies to use before you go to the library.

Identify the Parameters of the Assignment

Sometimes your assignment will be very specific, so there won't be much for you to figure out. Take, for example, this prompt for the tourism class we mentioned earlier.

> In class this semester, we have discussed a number of theories and ideas about tourism and we've looked at a number of different types of tourist sites. In particular, we have looked closely at historical theme parks in America. Choose a currently operating historical theme park that we have *not* looked at in class as the focus of your essay, and use one of the methods we discussed in class to analyze this theme park in terms of its presentation of American history.

Your task here is to find an exhibit—but your job is limited by the parameters of the assignment. Your exhibit must be a historical theme park in America, and it can't be one you've talked about in class. So you might begin, for example, by researching lists of historical theme parks and then choosing a park that interests you, based on its region or its peculiarities or the historical period it focuses on.

In many cases, however, your assignment will be more open-ended. For example, a different assignment for the tourism class might read something like this.

> Based on our work in class, identify and analyze a tourist site that interests you.

In an assignment like this, you have lots of leeway (after all, the world is full of tourist sites). So how do you make decisions?

Faced with this kind of assignment, students often go to the library or online and begin looking around to find a starting point. That's an overwhelming and intimidating place to be. If you begin with techniques you already know and information and parameters from your class, you'll have an easier time of things.

Find a Topic

Start by finding a topic that interests you. The easiest way to do that is by looking back at your course materials.

- Review your syllabus, class notes, and reading notes to remind yourself of the key foci of the work you've done so far. In the case of our tourism course assignment, you might look for:
  - examples of tourist site analyses. (This will give you a method—an approach or set of questions you can usefully bring to the site you choose.)
  - key questions or issues the class has taken up. (This may give you a lens through which to choose or explore your site. If the class has focused on the environmental effects of tourism, for example, you may want to limit your research to sites sensitive to the environmental impact of tourism.)
  - mentions or brief discussions of sites that might interest you.
  - discussions of sites you found interesting that might provide you with a direction to find other sites of interest. (If, for example, you found the class discussion of Disneyland fascinating, you might want to think about finding another theme park to analyze.)

It's a good idea to make a list of criteria as you go: What ideas or sites or questions strike you as interesting? Listing them will help you pin down your interests. Don't edit your list as you go. Once you're done, winnow your list down to eliminate repetition and anything that isn't essential. Then reorder it, starting with the most important criteria.

For example, here's one student's list. The material in parentheses refers to material covered in class that the student found interesting.

- urban tourist sites in America (class discussion: Harlem bus tours)
- unenclosed sites (class discussion: Frank Lloyd Wright houses, Chicago)
- unintentional tourist sites → intentionally preserved (class discussion: downtown Charleston)
- tensions with community/poverty (reading: New York's Lower East Side)
- local history as part of site (reading: San Francisco's Chinatown)

The student sees from her list that she has some very specific interests. The class discussions on theme parks, resorts, and national parks didn't make her list; nor did rural vacationing or tourism abroad. Once she's made the list, she can see the commonalities among all of these different sites and get a handle on the categories that interest her the most. She realizes that she wants to look at an urban site that isn't specifically built and maintained only as a tourist destination, where the community has come into conflict with the developers and supporters of tourism—and perhaps with the tourists themselves. And she's interested not just in the contemporary state of this site but in its history.

The student might then make a list of all sites that fit these parameters—by brainstorming, by working from her notes and her textbook, or by doing some research on this subject. Eventually she decides that she's most interested in the redevelopment of Miami Beach as an active tourist destination, beginning in the 1980s—a site that fits all of her criteria.

If listing doesn't work for you, another approach is to ask yourself a series of questions about issues from the class discussion that interest you. For example, another student in the tourism class might write these questions.

- What's the difference between a community and a tourist destination?
- Is a remote tourist destination different from one that's easy to get to? In what ways?
- If a site does ecotourism, does it matter where the money goes? To individual entrepreneurs? The community? Outside developers?

- What's more important: money benefitting the community or ecological impacts that the community may not be so concerned about?
- What if the developer is using the term *ecotourism* to hide something detrimental to the long-term eco-health of the community?
- Does the tourist have a responsibility to the community?

This student is narrowing and focusing his interests by asking himself questions—not because he's setting out to answer them but because the questions show him what he doesn't know and wants to investigate. He sees that he's interested in environmentalism and its relationship to the local community and the economics of tourism, so he decides to focus on resorts that advertise their eco-friendliness as a selling point. He does some preliminary online research to find places that do this; then he uses the names and places he finds to do some online research on conflicts in these places. He eventually decides to write about an ecotourist resort in Costa Rica where water use is disputed.

If you feel like it's too soon to ask yourself questions, you might try just brainstorming or freewriting on anything from your class that grabbed you. Writing through this material will help you focus.

Use Your Topic to Find an Exhibit

Now that you've found a topic, you'll need to find an exhibit. This is a place where students often get confused: They think, *I've figured out what I'm talking about, so now I can just talk about it,* or, conversely, they decide to look at everything they can find on the topic. Neither of these approaches works very well. The first leaves you without a central text (an image, a recording, a book, an article …) to look at, which means that your paper is likely to be vague and general. The second, on the other hand, gives you *too* much to look at—which makes it difficult to explore any one thing in depth and may mean that your paper turns into a list or that you spend all of your time researching rather than writing.

For instance, the student who's decided to write on Miami Beach may think that she has an exhibit—but Miami Beach itself is just a broad topic. What exactly *about* Miami Beach interests her? What exact phenomenon is she looking at? If she tries to write about tourism in Miami Beach in general, she'll have so much information that she'll be overwhelmed. And if she tries to fit it all in her paper, she won't be able to actually say anything. She needs a specific phenomenon to analyze.

At this stage, you need to do some research to find a specific exhibit. What's available on your topic? (What happens, for instance, when you type "ecotourism in Costa Rica" into your library's search engine?) You also need to make some decisions—and this is where the primary-vs.-secondary-source distinction might be useful. It's almost always a good idea to start with a primary source because it gives you something to analyze. If you start with a secondary source, you're analyzing someone else's analysis. In the case of the tourism class, primary sources might include, for example:

- advertising for your chosen tourist site (brochures, print ads, websites ...)
- first-person travel narratives (diaries, books, Yelp reviews ...)
- films
- census data
- city-planning documents
- artworks
- documentary photographs
- family vacation photos
- personal histories
- interviews
- menus

How do you decide which exhibit to focus on? Students often find this difficult because they're looking for the perfect exhibit, the one that will completely encapsulate their interests and the class parameters. But just as there is no perfect moment in a text, there is no perfect exhibit—just the one you find most compelling. When deciding on your exhibit, consider the following.

- What's interesting to you? What catches your attention?
- What kind of exhibit are you comfortable looking at? (For example, a film student may be happy looking at a documentary film, while a sociology major may feel more confident looking at case studies.)
- Is your exhibit rich enough to sustain your analysis? Is there enough going on to give you lots of material for discussion?
- Does the exhibit raise questions for you? As with a passage in a text, is there something going on here that you don't understand? Is there something worth exploring?

You'll want to treat this exhibit the way you treat any other text: Look for phenomena that seem strange or interesting or contradictory. (Remember the train metaphor from chapter five: Look for the places where the main plot or message seems to be going in one direction while the specific language used to express that message seems to be going somewhere else. This works just as well for advertising, images, sound recordings, and other media as it does for printed words.) Use the methods we've shown you in previous chapters to look closely, ask questions, and analyze. Remember, except in very rare cases, a research paper is not just a report on what other people have said or a description of something that has happened. **It's still a work of analysis, and your questions and ideas are paramount!**

Argument

Argument refers to **critical analysis on the subject you're writing about.** (When we say "argument" here, what we're really talking about is "claim"—it's just that "BECM" doesn't have much of a ring to it.) **When you use an argument source, you're engaging with other voices in the field: You're looking at what scholars have claimed about your topic or text or phenomenon in order to test your own ideas**. Students sometimes think that the reason to use an argument source is to get a stamp of approval for their ideas, as if to say, *Look, this professor or scientist agrees with me, so my claim must be valid!* But you don't need this kind of validation: Your authority is based on your reading of the evidence in your text. Instead, argument sources are useful because you can engage with them in order to challenge your own ideas or move them forward. You might build on what another scholar has said. If, on the other hand, you disagree with a scholar's claim, you can use her argument as a "straw man"—that is, you can set it up in order to burn it down, to show why it's wrong and why your own claim is better.

In literature classes, you will often be asked to engage with literary criticism in your essays. In the sciences, you will often be asked to evaluate past research on a topic as part of your investigation. In the social sciences, you may be asked to enter into debates on a given topic or to engage with the work of historians about the implications of an event or phenomenon. In each of these cases, the key is to see how these sources can enrich or challenge your own work. Don't substitute someone else's argument for the work of developing your own.

nomenon you're looking at. Your choice will depend on your assignment and the aims of your project. And each choice will result in different types of analysis. It's a good idea to find a method early in your writing process—perhaps even before you write your first draft—since this provides the lens through which you'll be exploring your phenomenon.

For example, if you're writing a paper for an anthropology class on the experiences of single parents, you may want to use participant observation, a method in which you embed yourself within your subject culture, taking part in its daily life, or you might choose to interview subjects but maintain some distance from their daily lives. You might also use survey research or historical data.

In an economics class, you might choose to use case studies to explore a particular phenomenon among a particular population. You could create a field study, in which a theory is tested "in the field" with real-life participants, or you might use a meta-analysis, in which you look at the results of a number of studies in order to analyze and draw conclusions from them as a group.

Theory

Theory is similar to method in that it refers to a lens you're using to look at your idea. Where a method provides a way of working with the information or text you're looking at, a theory offers **a set of ideas you can use to help you unlock your phenomenon. A theory is not a set of facts but a way of thinking about something.** (Even scientific theories, which are adopted once they've been repeatedly tested, are called theories for a reason: They're not facts but collections of ideas, and they can be discarded if a better set of ideas comes along.)

Theories are used in all academic fields, from art to science to literature. Working with theories can be difficult because they are often very conceptual and they can be written in advanced disciplinary language. But they can be useful tools for unlocking the phenomenon you're looking at.

It's often a good idea to write through a first draft, and perhaps even a second draft, before bringing in a theory. That's because **you need to figure out exactly what questions you're unable to answer about your phenomenon through your own analysis before you turn to a theoretical lens.** Those questions, in turn, can help you figure out which theoretical lens makes the most sense to you. If you bring theory in too early, it's likely to overtake your own analysis.

For example, if you're working on a paper on the role of appetite in *Dracula* and you're trying to figure out why Lucy and Mina have such huge appetites for food, you might find it useful to read through the lens of the anthropologist Claude Levi-Strauss's *The Raw and the Cooked*, which offers a theory about how ways of eating correlate to social roles.

If, on the other hand, you're writing a paper about the effects of weight gain on American children between the ages of six and twelve and you're stuck on the question of why this population is gaining so much weight so quickly, you might want to explore glucostat and lypostat theories of appetite.

As you can see, BEAT/BEAM is a useful method for thinking about research sources because it's not based on absolutes: Instead it lets you focus on what you need the source to do for you. BEAT/BEAM offers a way to categorize sources so that you can get to something useful more quickly. And rather than allowing you to think of sources as generic items you're required to slot into your paper, BEAT/BEAM leads you to ask, "Why am I using a source here? What do I want to do with it?" That, in turn, makes your work stronger.

Peer-Reviewed Sources

Another way to categorize sources is by whether they are peer reviewed. Professors will often require students to use "peer-reviewed" research sources—especially in the case of argument sources but often in the case of background sources, too. (Your professor may also refer to "refereed" or "scholarly" sources. All of these mean the same thing.)

Peer review is the process by which articles and books by scholars are published. Let's say your professor submits his article "Hunting and Gathering: Food Resources, Killing, and Dystopian Humanism in *The Hunger Games*" to a journal called *Studies in YA Heroines*. The editor who first reads the article thinks it's a good fit for the journal, so she sends it out to readers for peer review. Peer-reviewed journals do not rely solely on the opinions of their editors: They depend, instead, on readers who work in the same field as the author and have expertise that relates specifically to what the article is about. They are "peers" of the author, hence the name. The readers evaluate the article on several fronts.

- Is it well-informed?

- Does it enter into current debates or discussions in the field? Where appropriate, does it cite the most relevant sources in the field?
- Does it say anything new, or does it only go over ground others have already covered?
- Does it use evidence effectively?
- Are there important sources or ideas the author has not yet taken into account?
- Are there objections to the author's claim or evidence that should be taken into account?
- Is it convincing?

If the readers have significant concerns on any of these fronts, they may recommend against publication or they may suggest publication only if the author makes specific revisions.

The final and most important question peer reviewers ask of a work is:

- Does it make a significant contribution to the field?

If they feel it does, they will recommend publication.

Your professor requires you to use peer-reviewed sources because, unlike newspapers, blogs, websites, and other sources that publish articles, peer-reviewed articles and books carry a stamp of approval from scholars in the field.

Identifying a Peer-Reviewed Source

Let's start by talking about sources that may be perfectly legitimate—but that are *not* peer reviewed. Primary sources fall into this category. If you think back to the primary-source-vs.-secondary-source division we talked about earlier, you'll remember that a primary source is the thing itself, not commentary on or discussion about that thing. Peer-reviewed sources, in contrast, are evidence-based sources that engage with debates in a given field and advance claims and ideas regarding these debates.

Newspaper, popular magazine, and blog articles are generally published quickly in response to the news cycle, so they can't go through a process of peer review; they are often not argument-driven, and they are assigned or bought by an editor (or self-published on a blog) rather than written by a scholar trying to advance the field. *Opinion pieces* are not evidence-based, so they can't be peer reviewed; neither can *autobiographies* or, usually, *biographies. Crowdsourced materials* like wikis are not peer reviewed because the contributors and reviewers aren't established as peers. *Encyclopedias and dictionaries* don't present arguments, so they don't count either.

Once you've eliminated all of these sources, you can look more closely at what remains. In terms of BEAT/BEAM, peer-reviewed sources may range across background, argument, methodology, and theory: If you're writing about *Dracula*, for example, you may use a peer-reviewed essay by a historian on gender roles in the nineteenth century as a background source, or you may use a philosopher's peer-reviewed book on time as a theory source. But it's most likely that your peer-reviewed sources will be argument sources.

All peer-reviewed sources have these basic markers.

- evidence, not just opinion
- claims, not just evidence
- citations or footnotes referring to other sources in the field
- a full, properly cited bibliography or works-cited page

In the sciences and social sciences, peer-reviewed articles also often have:

- an abstract at the beginning.
- a list of the author's credentials.
- subheadings.

But while these markers are signs that your source *might* be peer reviewed, they are not evidence that it *is* peer reviewed. And while it may seem like all claim-driven articles and books about your topic must be peer reviewed, that's not actually the case. For example, in the sciences, many journals will now publish scientists' work without requiring a peer review (and will charge the scientists for publication). There are also more "open-source" online journals, across many academic fields, which may or may not be peer reviewed. So how do you know?

The easiest way to check if a journal is peer reviewed is to use your library's online resources. Many university library search engine pages will have a box that allows you to limit your searches to "peer-reviewed" or "scholarly" sources. Once you check that box on your search screen, you can be secure in the knowledge that all the journal articles listed are peer reviewed. You can also limit your search in this way using many discipline-specific databases. Many journals also self-identify as "scholarly" or "peer reviewed" on their websites.

If your library search engine or database doesn't select for peer-reviewed material, take a look at the actual journal—either in print or on the Web. Is there a board that advises the journal? Are there multiple editors? Does the journal request that submitters send multiple copies of their essays? (This is a good sign that multiple people will be reviewing the work—which means the journal is probably peer reviewed.) All of this information is usually on the masthead page or somewhere linked to that page.

Books are also often peer reviewed. Your library's database may sort for peer-reviewed books; if that's not the case, you can generally find out by looking at the publishing information. **Critical, historical, and theoretical books published by academic presses** (University of California Press, Columbia University Press, Ohio University Press, and so on) **can be presumed to be peer reviewed**. Some of the big publishing houses (Routledge, for example) also have academic publishing arms. To see if books published by one of these presses are peer reviewed, it's best to look at the website.

A word of warning: Many students start their search process with a Google search because they're most comfortable with it. **But Google is not set up to find the best peer-reviewed research sources for you** (or really, the best research sources of any type), in part because it uses a search algorithm based not only on relevance but also on the number of views a page has had. When you're looking for research sources for an academic paper, the kinds of materials you need will almost never be the most popular or most searched for. And Google doesn't have any interest in whether you're looking for research-appropriate resources or not, and it can't sort for them. In fact, many peer-reviewed journals are behind pay walls and can't be accessed via Google (though they can be accessed for free via your college library).

Google Scholar, on the other hand, is a much better database if you're looking for peer-reviewed materials: It's set up to find sources useful for scholarly research. (Google Scholar is not the same as Google: It's a separate search engine, so you'll need to call it up specifically.) This does not mean, however, that you can access everything through the database—or that everything you'll find there is necessarily peer reviewed. (Conference proceedings, for example, are included in Google Scholar—but they're not peer reviewed since they're just the record of papers people give at a conference.)

The best way to use Google Scholar is to link it to your college library so that you can access full-text material you couldn't otherwise obtain. To do that, follow these steps.

1. Go to the Google Scholar home page.
2. Go to the "settings" icon at the top of the page on the right.
3. Go to the "library links" link on the left side of the page.
4. Enter your college's name to connect to your school library through Google Scholar.

You can then also use the filters on your library's search engines to determine if your sources are peer reviewed.

FIGURING OUT WHAT KIND OF SOURCE YOU NEED

Now that you're familiar with the ways sources can be broken down, you'll need to think about the kinds of questions you hope to address through your research. As we showed you earlier, different kinds of research resources are useful in taking up different kinds of questions in your analytical work. And as we've said, your choice of research resources is dependent on what you need to move your paper forward. For example, the student working on the Virginia Woolf essay may find that she doesn't really understand what it means for the Angel to be a false construction because she doesn't yet know enough about women and work at the end of the nineteenth century (the period Woolf is talking about in her essay). Without understanding what kind of jobs women were allowed to do and how women who worked were thought of, she isn't really confident that she knows enough about women's roles to write a thoughtful paper. Here are some questions she might have.

- Did many women have jobs?
- How were women with jobs perceived?
- Did women get to be writers? Was that socially acceptable?
- Did class matter when it came to work? (Were rich women allowed to work? Middle-class women?)
- Did it matter if you were married or unmarried? Were unmarried women allowed to work?

By exploring these questions, the student can get a better sense of what the Angel is all about, how powerful she is as a social force, and what the implications of seeing her as false and killing her off might be. **All of these questions require background sources**: They call for historical information that the student does not have.

A student in a sociology class, on the other hand, will need different kinds of sources. If he's writing about homelessness in his neighborhood, he might ask these questions.

- How many homeless people live in the neighborhood?
- Are they mostly men or mostly women?
- Is there a racial breakdown?
- Are they originally locals?
- Why are they homeless?
- Has anybody tried to house them?
- What are the challenges in housing homeless people?
- What effect do they have on the community?

Once he's created his list of questions, he realizes **he needs a method**—a means of looking at these questions. He asks himself, *How do I want to look at this? Should I …*

- do interviews with stakeholders (homeless people/workers for the homeless/city officials/community members)?
- research statistics on homelessness in this neighborhood over the last twenty years to see patterns and trends?
- research rental prices and the cost of living in the neighborhood over the last twenty years?
- look at studies on the causes of homelessness?
- look at theories on possible answers to homelessness?
- read case studies on what's been tried?
- look at the city government policy and the police policy on homelessness?

The student will need to choose an approach to his paper in order to move from his preliminary questions, observations, and analysis into a fuller exploration of his issue. He may find that he wants to use more than one method—perhaps, for example, he'll use interviews with homeless people and workers in conjunction with statistical analysis of trends in homelessness—but one method should be central. He'll need to decide which method is best suited to his questions—and he may need to rank his questions in terms of order of importance to help figure this out.

Sometimes an assignment will ask you to find several different types of sources. For example, look at this engineering assignment.

> Our task in this class is to design a green roof for a school building. We determined that we will focus on heat deflection and water circulation. Your task now is to research the best methods for heat deflection that can be applied to our particular building and made use of by our stakeholders and to find a means of explaining the philosophy of green roof building to skeptical stakeholders.

To fully address this prompt, a student will need to:

- use a background source to define heat deflection.
- find background sources on other work that's been done on this topic.
- use a methodology source to understand the premise of the green roof.
- use argument sources to help her explore the pros and cons of each method that's been employed.

All of this will help her tackle the analytical part of the assignment, in which she applies what she's learned to the building she's focusing on and the occupants of that building and decides which method is most effective.

THE RESEARCH PROCESS: A CASE STUDY

Finding research sources might seem straightforward, but the process of tracking down sources can be complicated, time-consuming, and frustrating. This case study will show you a research trajectory and some approaches that can make life easier for you.

Sometimes a professor will specify which types of resources you're required to use. For example, a literature professor in a course on *Dracula* may make the following requirements.

> In your research draft, please incorporate at least two peer-reviewed literary criticism sources, one background source, and one theoretical source.

In a case like this, your job is to find resources that fit the prompt's parameters. But many students assume that an assignment like this is just setting up a series of hoops to jump through, and they indiscriminately choose sources that basically fit the requirements without really considering whether the sources do any work for their essays. That's a mistake. Research requirements give you an opportunity to make your work stronger by incorporating other voices, ideas, and points of view. Don't waste that chance!

In the case of this *Dracula* prompt, a student could easily find two pieces of peer-reviewed literary criticism on the novel—after all, hundreds of books and thousands of articles have been written on Bram Stoker's work. But precisely for that reason, the student will want to choose carefully: Because there's so much material out there, it's doubtful that the first two articles he comes across will serve him well.

The process of research is generally not straightforward. It can require a multifaceted approach, and it will almost always require many steps and require you to work with different types of search engines, databases, or library resources.

Let's say the student starts out with an interest in communications technology in *Dracula,* particularly Jonathan and Mina's use of shorthand. He wants to look at this passage, written by Jonathan Harker in his journal while he's in Castle Dracula.

> Here I am, sitting at a little oak table where in old times possibly some fair lady sat to pen, with much thought and many blushes, her ill-spelt love-letter, and writing in my diary in shorthand all that has happened since I closed it last. It is nineteenth-century up-to-date with a vengeance. And yet, unless my senses deceive me, the old centuries had, and have, powers of their own which mere 'modernity' cannot kill. (40-1)

Gathering Basic Background Information

The student begins by doing some background research in order to figure out exactly what he's looking at. What is shorthand, anyway? **He starts, logically enough, with the dictionary.** This first move is necessary for the student: If he doesn't look up *shorthand*, his chosen passage won't make sense to him, so he needs some basic facts to be able to close-read effectively. To return to a metaphor we've used before, having this information lets him load his magnifying glass; when he looks back at the passage, he's more informed, so he can see more of what's going on. But this early information gathering is only for him: It doesn't belong in the final paper. (If he were defining something really strange that even his professor might not know, or if he were choosing an unusual definition of a word to use in his close reading, that would be another story—but this baseline information shouldn't be included. If he includes the definition in his essay, his professor will think he's trying to fill space.)

Merriam-Webster Online defines *shorthand* as a "[s]ystem for rapid writing that uses symbols or abbreviations for letters, words, or phrases." It also says that it's been around since Greek and Roman times, so the student is a bit confused: Why is it "nineteenth century up-to-date with a vengeance" if people have been using it for so long?

The dictionary definition lists two popular types of shorthand: Pitman and Gregg. So **the student types "Pitman shorthand" into Google** and finds a site called *Omniglot: The Online Encyclopedia of Writing Systems and Languages* (at www.omniglot.com/writing/shorthand.htm). The student copies the website onto a running list of sources he has created to make sure he keeps track of all his research materials. The site explains that Pitman shorthand was developed in 1837—and Gregg was first published in 1888, very much "nineteenth-century up-to-date."

But the site isn't peer reviewed: The "about" page on the website introduces the author and also makes clear that this page is open to submissions from the general public. Since he doesn't know what the vetting process is for the page, he can't use it as a background source: It may not be reliable.

Moving to Scholarly Background Research

Now that he knows some basic facts about shorthand, it's easier for the student to find scholarly work or reliable primary source material on the subject—that is, a background source he can actually use in his paper. That might be a primary source document, or it might be a scholarly book or article about his topic. Instead of deciding beforehand what kind of background source he needs, he casts a wide net: This allows him to really see what's out there. When **he types "Gregg shorthand history" into his library search engine**, for example, he finds a source by Dugald Mackillop called *Shorthand and Typewriting. Illustrated. Sketch of Shorthand History; Learning the Art; Suggestions to the Amanuensis; Description of the Various Kinds of Reporting; Typewriting in All Its Details, and Miscel-*

laneous Hints, published in London in 1891. This primary background source seems perfect. He downloads the citation information and heads off to find it in the library stacks. (It's possible that your college library will have scanned versions of historical texts like this to be viewed online, but in most cases, you'll need to find the physical book.)

If his college library hadn't offered anything useful, the student might have productively conducted the same search on *Google Books*. This resource, which collects books, sometimes makes full-source versions of historical texts available (for texts currently in print, you will almost always have to find the source elsewhere: Google Books will only give you a partial view). When you're looking for very old books that aren't scholarly works, Google Books is a better resource than Google Scholar.

Another way this student could find out about the history of shorthand is to look for a scholarly secondary text as a background source: For example, perhaps his college library search turns up a book titled *Revolution in Writing: Shorthand, Typewriting, and the Transformation of 19th Century Labor* by Arthur Robbins. The summary on the library search engine says that this text addresses the history of shorthand and discusses how it was used, by whom, and why it mattered in the late nineteenth century. It's different than a primary-source historical text because it explores and explains the phenomenon he's looking at from an academic point of view instead of presenting the phenomenon itself.

In either case, the student probably **won't want to read the entire book**— especially since he may end up using only two or three sentences on shorthand in his essay. Before he starts reading, he **makes a list of questions he wants answered.**

- What is Gregg shorthand?
- How does it work?
- Who used it and why?
- Why would Harker say it's "nineteenth-century up-to-date"?

He might also find a scholarly article on the subject titled "Clerking into Modernity: Shorthand in England in the 1890s" by Valerie Boggs. The student finds the article online through the library database. He scans it quickly, looking for subheadings or key words on his topic to see if it's useful to him. He can even do a search of key words if the site is set up for that. Searching *shorthand* might turn up too many results, but searching *Gregg, technology*, or even *modernity* might be helpful. If the article seems like a good fit, he'll need to print it out. It's tempting to just download the link, read the article online, and make some basic notes—but, as is the case with a text you're reading for class, that's not the best way to go. When you read an article onscreen, you tend to read more quickly and to acquire only a surface understanding of the material. By printing it out, physically marking it up, and employing the close-reading techniques we've shown you in earlier chapters, you'll gain a much more thorough and nuanced understanding of your source. This will allow you to do much better work with the material in your paper.

Finding a Theory Source

Once the student has researched the background material he needs in order to work with his passage, he's ready to find a theory source. He doesn't want to wait until he has a claim to do this because he needs to use his theory source as a focusing lens through which he can read his passage. The theory source *informs* your claim; it's not the source of the claim but instead helps to focus your thinking about your passage so you can get to your claim. If you're asked to find a theory source, it's a good idea to do so after your discovery draft.

As you'll remember, when you're looking for a theory source, you're looking for something *conceptual*: a piece of writing that offers a concept or a way of seeing rather than a discussion of an event or moment in the text. To figure out what kind of theory source would be useful, it's a good idea to focus on the conceptual questions that might be hiding out in your discovery draft.

In this case, the student knows that he's interested in shorthand in *Dracula*—but that topic isn't yet a *concept* because it's about a set of *things*. He returns to his discovery draft and reads through it, highlighting different types of material in different colors. He marks his writing about concrete things—physical objects, events in the text, and so forth—in red. He marks passages that contain concepts and ideas in blue. Anything transitional—showing a move from the physical to the conceptual—is marked in yellow. Here's what one section in his discovery draft looks like.

> I'm interested in what "it" refers to in the second sentence. Is it shorthand that's up to date, or is it using shorthand at the table where the fair lady might have written her love letters? If it's the first, then it's the technology that's up to date, but if it's the second, that's interesting because it says the technology is only up to date because of the way it's compared to the old stuff. And "with a vengeance" is interesting because that means the

technology of shorthand in either case is committing vengeance—getting back at someone, revenge—on the old stuff. So the old stuff, associated with Dracula, is dangerous, even when it's a lady writing love letters, and needs to be revenged by technology: Here Jonathan seems to be saying technology will save him. But then in the last sentence there's that "and yet," which seems to say that the new technology can't really bring revenge, because of the power of the past—which still exists in the present. And he puts "modernity" in quotation marks, as though it's not real. So maybe he doesn't really believe in technology after all?

When he looks at his markings, he realizes that the conceptual work he's done so far focuses on the relationship between technology and time in his passage—and, in particular, on the idea that the past somehow still exists in the present.

Using his highlighting as a guide, he makes a new list of questions.

- What does it mean for the power of the past to still exist in the present?
- What's the relationship between technology and the past?
- What's the relationship between technology and the present?
- What does modernity mean in relation to time?
- What exactly is "the past," anyway?

Based on these questions, the student makes a list of terms that are about abstract ideas, not about things. His list includes:

- how time works
- modernity
- relationship between past and present
- boundaries of time

Note that he doesn't include anything concrete (*technology, shorthand, desk*). Looking back at his list, he sees that all of these ideas are really about time, so he chooses that as his key word and pairs it with *theory*.

Once the student has chosen his focus, **he searches for "time theory" on the library website.** (When you're looking for a broad topic like this, it's more useful to start with the library website than with Google Scholar because Google Scholar will probably turn up far more material than you can process and the useful material may get buried.) But even the search on the library website results in thousands of books and articles. The student scans down the list to find a book that seems related to what he's working on. To do this, he focuses on titles that seem to address the concept he's chosen most directly. To figure out whether or not a book will *actually* be useful, the student needs to click through and look at a description of the text and perhaps a preview of the table of contents or the first few pages. (If your library doesn't offer these resources, this is a good time to use Google Scholar.) This takes some time and leads to some dead ends: He clicks on six or seven sources that actually have nothing to do with what he's interested in before he finds a book that's useful. This is typical of this stage of research. Be patient—eventually you'll find something that works.

The student finds a book that seems related to his interests, and he clicks on the **"more info" tab** and looks for **Library of Congress subject headings** (the delineations that show you how a book is classified in all American libraries). All books have Library of Congress subject headings; some have many because they take up a range of topics. He sees "time perception" and clicks on that because it's the most closely related to what he's interested in. This time, only twenty-two sources come up. This is much more manageable and more likely to be relevant than the big list.

He scrolls through the list, looking at titles and short descriptions until he comes across a book called *Real Time* by D.H. Mellor. The description notes that "the author argues that although time itself is real, tense is not." The student isn't sure of what that means, but it seems like it might be useful for him, so he scrolls down to the preview. The first sentence of the introduction reads, "This book is about such of the metaphysics of time as follows from settling the significance of text, i.e., of the distinctions we draw between past, present and future." Though he's not sure what "the metaphysics of time" is all about, the stuff after "i.e." seems like it takes up exactly the questions that the student is thinking about in his passage. (The student is doing something really important here, especially in the case of a theory source: He just keeps reading past the things he doesn't understand. If you don't understand the first few words in a source, don't panic. Keep reading; often you'll get to something that makes sense.)

In basic terms, Mellor's theory is that present time is no more real than future time (because future time already exists) or past time (because past time never goes away and hence isn't really past). This theory offers the student a new way to think about time in his passage. Now he can consider the idea that the past continues to exist, which means that "modernity" doesn't leave the past behind. That helps him read what Jonathan is saying in the moment from

Dracula and think about what it would mean for a rational London lawyer to say what he does. In other words, this theory acts as a lens to help the student look again at the passage.

Finding an Argument Source

The student moves on to write a claim draft in which he argues that the real horror of the novel is that the past keeps threatening to move into the modern world of London. Now that he has a claim, he's ready to find his two argument sources. Before he starts this stage of his research, he makes a list of questions he thinks argument sources can help him with.

- What's the significance of the failure of all the modern technology in the novel?
- What's going on with the idea that Transylvania seems to be stuck in the past, even though Jonathan suggests it isn't?
- Is the England in the novel in the present or in the future? Can it also be in the past?
- Does it matter that the telegram from Van Helsing to Dr. Seward arrives late?
- If technology is modern and the vampire is old, how exactly does the failure of technology relate to what's going on with time in the novel?

These questions are different than the kinds of questions he had back when he was doing research about shorthand. Those earlier questions were factual; here, his questions are analytical. He's testing his idea and trying to figure out the implications of what he's seeing.

So how can he narrow his search so that it only brings up literary criticism? If he just types "time in *Dracula*" into his school library's search engine, he'll find some books but his results will be limited. Instead he goes to the list of databases on his library website, limits the category to "humanities" databases and then to "English language and literature" databases, and scans the list. Based on the description, he chooses the "MLA International Bibliography," a database that compiles articles, books, and dissertations on literature in English and other modern languages. Since the database compiles material *about* literature, it won't turn up very much primary source material.

Similar databases exist in all academic fields. These databases are different than online collections of articles and books. A database is a searchable list of resources rather than a collection of the resources themselves (though databases often link to such collections). It's possible to do limited searches on online collections of scholarly material, but you won't find very much because these collections aren't designed for searching. For example, if the student searches JStor, an online repository of peer-reviewed articles on a wide range of academic subjects, he'll have a challenging time finding articles on "time in *Dracula*." JStor might have a number of articles on the subject, but since it isn't a database, it isn't particularly good at pulling up comprehensive lists of material that are relevant to your search.

When the student tries the same search on the MLA database, on the other hand, he finds pages of potentially relevant material. Since the student has accessed the database through his library site, he might very well be able to link directly to articles he's interested in, depending on whether his library has digital access to the journal in which the articles are published. But the database itself does not contain articles: It's only a list.

Using the MLA database, the student finds a chapter in a book and an article that seem like useful sources for him. He copies each full citation into his running list of sources.

> Barrows, Adam. *The Cosmic Time of Empire: Modern Britain and World Literature*. Berkeley: U of California P, 2011. "At the Limits of Imperial Time; or, Dracula Must Die!" 75-99

The student won't need to cite the specific chapter in the works-cited list in his paper—just the book itself—because the work is written by only one author, but he wants to make sure he remembers what the relevant section is and where he can find it.

> Richards, Leah. "Mass Production and the Spread of Information in *Dracula*: 'Proofs of so wild a story.'" *English Literature in Transition, 1880-1920* 52:4 (2009): 440-57.

Each of these sources is useful to the student: One is concerned with time, the other with information technology. The student's task here is to read each article carefully. He must note the moves each author makes to substantiate his or her claim to see what he thinks about each author's claim, evidence, and conclusion and, using his list of questions, think carefully about how each author's ideas might be useful to him.

The most important thing for the student to remember as he works his way through each article is that **he isn't obliged to buy what the author says.** Remember that argument sources take part in a conversation—an ongoing argument—among critics about a given text, question, or issue. Every critic builds on the work other critics have done; every critic sets out to prove that she's right and others are wrong, if not wholly, then in part. Your task is to test your claim to see how it stands up to what other writers have to say—not to bow to their expertise and replace your hard thinking with theirs. And it may well be that what the critics have to say is not as compelling as what you have to say: Just because work is published doesn't mean it's good. In your paper, you're free to criticize or question your argument sources as long as you do it through convincing analysis.

If, on the other hand, the student finds that an argument source is right on point, he can also make use of that material—not to replace his own ideas but to work through them further. How does the idea the source puts forward help him find the nuances in his reading? How is his analysis made better by what the critic has to say?

For example, the student thinks Barrows's idea that Dracula is defeated by the protagonists because they can use modern time (timetables, scheduling) in a way that Dracula can't is really interesting. The student cites that idea and then goes on to say that while Dracula, a force of the dangerous past that threatens England, is beaten back, that destruction is incomplete. This is because, he says, if the past is never completely cut off from the present, "modernity" can never be enough to save the protagonists.

HOW TO WORK WITH RESEARCH MATERIAL

Once you've figured out the basics of what you need in terms of research, you might think you're finished. But homing in on a source, reading it efficiently, and culling useful material from it can be difficult if you dive in without a plan. Here are some approaches that can help you out.

- Before you start reading, **make a list of questions you want answered.** It's a good idea to reread your draft, noting questions and unresolved issues as you go. Keep in mind where you are in the drafting process and which kind of source you're looking for: If your assignment is to find a background source, don't waste your time trying to pin down questions that will help you find an argument source. Then read over your notes and create a list of questions you think could be best answered not by further close reading but by research. If you need to return to the research process more than once—to find a background source and then an argument source, for example—repeat this rereading and listing process each time.
- **Find more sources than you think you need.** If you're required to include two sources in your paper, you may need to read six sources to find the material that's best for you. Never stop at one source—you'll just need to go back and find more material later.
- **Print out the material, or find a hard copy in the library stacks.** As we've said before, you read differently onscreen than you do on the page. Give yourself the advantage of a mode of reading that allows you to slow down, concentrate, and annotate effectively. (If you're working with a library hard copy, of course, you'll need to make all of your notes on a separate sheet of paper or photocopy the pages you're working with. Don't be the troll who marks up the library book … .)
- **Print out your list of research questions, and keep them close at hand.** Pick a highlighter color for each research question. Mark each question in its color. (Alternately, give each question a letter code.) This will make it easier for you to mark up your research text as you move through it.
- Read through your research text more carefully. As you go, **note the main point of each paragraph in the margin** (or on a separate page if you're using a library copy). If you're working with an argument source, trace the development of the author's claim through the paper as you go. **When you come across material that seems particularly relevant to one of your color-coded questions, color-code that material.** If you have questions, comments, or words to look up, note all of that briefly in the margin as well, just as you would with a class text. You have to go through this process to see if a source will be useful to you. If it's not, stop here and find another source—but still be sure to check the source's works-cited page

or bibliography for other potentially useful sources. Don't be afraid to drop a source if you don't think it's interesting or useful: Even research material written by important scholars and published in scholarly journals can be bad. Trust your instincts! If the source is useful, continue on with the steps below.

- If you're working with a scholarly source, **mark any sources your source refers to that seem like they might be useful to you.** Since scholars cite one another as they build their arguments, using your source's bibliographic sources can save you a lot of time—and often this technique leads you to the key work on a given subject. Color-code these sources to correspond with your questions as well—and be sure to color-code their bibliographical information so you can find them easily.

- Take a moment to **do a brief wrap-up of what you've read** (see chapter one). Mark down what the source is saying and how you think it could be helpful to you, as well as any initial questions the material raises for you. If you're working with an argument source, be sure to also write a brief synopsis of the author's claim and what you think of it.

- **Slowly and carefully reread the material you've color-coded as useful.** Look up words that are unfamiliar or used in unfamiliar ways, highlight anything that seems important or strange or interesting to you, and make brief notes in the margins or on a separate page. (If you're working on a separate page, make sure you indicate exactly what these notes refer to.)

- Focusing on only the material that you've color-coded as useful, **create a brief dialogic journal**. This is a slightly different dialogic journal than the one you create for a text you're analyzing. Here's how it works.

  - On the left half, in addition to quotes or paraphrases, note the exact source of this material, including the page number or URL. Nothing is worse than incorporating the perfect research quote into your paper and then realizing you have no idea where it came from.

  - On the right half of the journal, talk to yourself about how you'll use this material. Does it raise new questions for you about your moment or about your claim? If it provides background information, how might it be useful? If you're reading an argument source, what do you think about the argument at each relevant point and why? How might this source be helpful to your own reading? If you're reading a theorist, what questions or ideas does the theory raise for you? If you have an idea of where it should go in your paper, note that, too.

- This is also a useful place to note things you don't understand or need to think more about for the source you're reading.

This process may seem tedious—but it will help you figure out how to use this material in your paper, which will save you time later. And—another big timesaver—it will help you find this material quickly when you're ready to incorporate it into your draft.

- If your work leads you to an idea that you need to work through, use the tools we've shown you for figuring things out in your moment: Do a quick freewrite, a mind map, or some brainstorming.

- If you need to find more material, or if you want to deepen your understanding of a concept or an event or an argument, make a list of the sources you marked in your source's bibliography and track them down through your college library. Sometimes it can be useful to read several sources on the same set of issues to find the material you want; sometimes different writers have different ideas about the same thing, and it can be useful to put them into dialogue with one another. And sometimes a source you're reading will make a reference to a primary source document that clearly belongs in your essay. Follow the procedures above with any new material you find.

Working with Books as Research Sources

While you'll need to read articles you plan to work with in their entirety, this is not the case with books. As we said earlier, **very few situations come up in which a student needs to read an entire book as a research source.** (Exceptions include exhibits—which must always be read in full unless your professor tells you otherwise—and specific assignments from professors.) If you feel unsure about this, it's worth remembering that you probably won't use more than a paragraph or two of any one research source in your essay, so reading a whole book can really be overkill. (Of course, if you're interested, by all means go ahead!) Here are some steps for narrowing down the material in books you're using as research sources.

- Scan the **table of contents**, looking for **chapter headings** that correspond to your questions.
- Scan the **introduction** for information about the book's contents and where it can be found. Many scholarly books include introductions that begin by posing the basic question or argument of the text and conclude by giving an idea of what each chapter discusses. These can be helpful in figuring out which areas of the book might be useful for you.
- At the top of each chapter, look for an **abstract** or **list of topics covered** to pinpoint your search more specifically. (These aren't included in all texts, but it's always worth checking.)
- If there's an **index**—an alphabetical list of topics mentioned in the text, with corresponding pages—at the back of the book, use that to find relevant pages. (For example, an index entry for "shorthand, Gregg—history" lists these pages: 23, 67, **84-87**, 92. The page range in bold indicates that this is a major topic, and the fact that there's a three-page range reinforces this, so the student will start looking on page 84.) One important hint: **If you can't find the topic you're looking for in the index, ask yourself whether it could be indexed under something else.** For example, if you look up *Dracula* in an index and can't find it, be sure to look up *Stoker, Bram*.
- Go directly to the material that seems relevant to your questions. If you're working from the index, you may need to back up and read a little bit earlier in the text to gain some context, but otherwise, it's perfectly okay to stay narrowly focused. Once you've found something useful, use all of the reading and note-taking techniques we've discussed in this section.

Working with Theory Sources

Theory sources can often be tough for the layperson to understand. Theory is written in dense language generally used only by people in the field. Often it doesn't tell a straightforward story. Because theory texts deal with complicated ideas, they are often written in complicated language. And sometimes they're translated from another language entirely, which can add to the confusion. But if you have to use a theory text, don't freak out. Just because a theoretical text is difficult, that doesn't mean you can't read it. Here are some approaches to help you get through it.

- Make a list of questions before you start. As is the case with other kinds of sources, if you know what you're trying to figure out through a theory source, it will be much easier to find relevant material—and you're less likely to find yourself drowning in incomprehensibility.
- Before you dive in, use information that the text comes with—the online description, the description on the back of the book, the preface if there is one, biographical information, abstracts, the table of contents—to compile as much information as possible on what the text is saying. This material will give you a head start on figuring out what the theorist is talking about. You may also want to look up some basic information on your source online—but don't over-rely on what you find. Remember that you'll still need to read the source itself.
- **Make sure you're reading a hard copy.** All of the issues we've talked about regarding reading onscreen are multiplied when you're working with a difficult text.
- If you're working with a whole book, use the table of contents and index to find useful material.
- Read the introduction. Often that's where the theorist explains her theory most clearly.
- Scan each page you're reading for words that relate to your topic or questions, and then slow down and read that section carefully.
- If your eye is skipping around on the page, or if you're reading without actually taking anything in, slow down by using a piece of paper to block the lines below the one you're reading. Move the paper down as you go. This simple technique can help you focus and absorb what you're reading.
- **Keep reading until you get to the example.** Theorists often present a big idea first and then, sometime later, give you an example of what they're saying—which makes everything much clearer. Once you understand the example, make some notes about what's going on, and then go back and reread the chunk of theory that preceded it. Chances are it will make much more sense.
- **Don't look up every word.** Even if you're feeling really lost, read in big chunks, marking anything that seems important as you go. Don't stop in the middle to look things up: You're likely to lose the thread of the discussion, and it may turn out that what you're looking up is explained by

context or that it isn't important after all. You don't need to understand every word in order to understand the basics of the theory. But once you find a passage that's useful to you, you'll have to slow down and look up all the words you're not sure about, just as you would with a moment you're working with in your exhibit.

- Each time you stop reading, be sure to create a wrap-up of what you've read. Jot down a very brief summary of what you've just read, plus any questions or comments you have on it. This will save you the trouble of continually rereading because you can't remember what you just read— a real issue with complex texts.

Working with Argument Sources

Argument sources are usually a bit more straightforward than theory sources: After all, they're about something specific (a text, an idea) and they're advancing a claim about that thing, so their framework is clear. But argument sources can still be filled with jargon, and they can be confusing precisely because, as we've said, each source is part of a bigger conversation among scholars. That can mean that reading an argument source can feel like walking into the middle of a conversation without knowing what's going on, who's been talking, or even what they're talking about. To make things easier, use these tips.

- **TRACK THE ARGUMENT.** It's a good idea to keep a running outline of the argument on a separate piece of paper as you read. Note each point the author makes, the evidence she offers to substantiate it, and the conclusions she comes to about it. You can also note questions or issues that come up for you as you trace the argument. This will help you clarify what the source is saying, what you think about it, and how it can be useful to you.
- **READ CLOSELY.** Put your close-reading skills to work: All of the techniques you use to read your central text will be useful here in helping you evaluate the source's claim, look for inconsistencies and weaknesses, and find something to say about it.
- **KEEP READING PAST THE JARGON.** Like theory sources, argument sources often provide specific examples, and since these examples are on your topic, they'll be easier to understand. You'll probably be able to figure out

what the jargon means from the context, and in many cases, you may find the exact meaning of the word doesn't matter.

- **IF YOU DO HAVE TO LOOK UP JARGON, BE SURE TO CONSIDER IT AS IT IS USED IN ITS FIELD.** A word that means one thing in general usage can mean something quite different in specialized usage. Let's say a critic uses the term *abject* to describe a character in a text. *Merriam-Webster* defines this word as "extremely bad or severe; very humble : feeling or showing shame; very weak : lacking courage or strength." But when you search for a definition of *abject* with the added terms *theory* or *literary criticism*, you'll find a number of sites that define the term as the theorist Julia Kristeva does but in simpler language. For example, Purdue University's English department site defines it as "our reaction ... to a threatened breakdown in meaning caused by the loss of the distinction between subject and object or between self and other."[2]

  Sometimes the definition you find can be fairly intimidating or obscure (like this one). If that's the case and you really need to understand the term, take a few minutes to do some background research. Who is this Kristeva, and what is she talking about? Google is your friend here: Commonly used theoretical terms are often defined and explained on professors' pages, for example.

- **IF THE PAPER SEEMS TO START IN THE MIDDLE OF A DISCUSSION, JUST KEEP GOING.** You know the basic topic from the title of the article; don't let references to other work you haven't read or ideas that haven't been explained to you scare you. If you feel overwhelmed, go back to your list of argument questions and focus on finding material that specifically takes up those questions.

INCORPORATING SOURCES

Once you've found and read all of this material, how do you work it into your paper? The method we'll show you here will help you keep track of everything while keeping your own analytical work front and center. Remember that you never want your analysis to be overwhelmed by your research work!

---

[2] www.cla.purdue.edu/english/theory/psychoanalysis/definitions/abject.html

- Reread your draft.
- Return to the research dialogic journal that you made (and any other material you've generated). Highlight material you want to use.
- Print out a draft of your paper, and, working with your dialogic journal and your draft, use color-coding, numbers, or letters to mark the places you'll incorporate quotes or paraphrases from your research. This is another place you might want to cut up your draft: When you know you want to incorporate research material, leave space and then write (or cut and paste) the material from the source that will go in that spot, along with an introduction to the material and a brief summary of what the source is saying. Then write (or cut and paste) what you have to say about this source. What work is it doing for you? What question does it take up? And how does that advance your discussion?

Like research itself, the process of incorporating research often needs to be done in stages: You can usually incorporate a background source fairly early in the process, for example, but an argument source will likely come later in your drafting process. Once you've found and incorporated all of your research and you've drafted and redrafted to make your narrative as clear and compelling as possible, you're ready to move on—finally!—to the final draft. In the next chapter, we'll take you there.

CHAPTER TWELVE

FINAL DRAFTS

At this point in your writing process, you've done all the truly hard work of creating an essay, from reading actively through asking questions and analyzing to figuring out what you're actually talking about and making some claims about that issue. In other words, you've come up with an argument about the phenomenon or text that you're looking at, and you've figured out how to convince others of your argument by crafting a narrative that communicates your ideas. Now that you've done all of this, you're ready to smooth out your essay and make it a strong product. That's what this chapter is all about.

Students often imagine this stage as a single operation, so they try to do everything at once. That creates problems: A student may look so closely at individual word choice that she misses some big connection issues, for example, or she may skip over sentence structure issues because she's only evaluating the big moves her essay makes. That's why we prefer a systematic three-step approach. In this chapter, we'll show you how to look at your paper on three levels.

1. macro or whole-essay level
2. medium or paragraph level
3. micro or sentence level

This process requires you to reread your essay at least three times. That may seem like overkill, but trust us—it's worth it. By the end, you'll have a handle on what you've said and how you've said it, and you'll have produced a final product that is as clear, well structured, precise, and convincing as possible.

1. EDITING AT THE MACRO (WHOLE-ESSAY) LEVEL

Start by doing one last inventory and reverse outline of your paper to check on the big moves your paper is making. You'll want to make sure that things are where you expect them to be and that you haven't left anything out (or put it in twice!). Here's how to do that.

- Print out your whole paper.
- Mark the beginning and end of each module.
- Highlight the establishing claim and the "so what?" for each module.
- Write a brief (two- to four-word) summary of the main idea of each paragraph in the margin; in other words, make an inventory of each paragraph.
- Note any places where you have more than one idea in a paragraph or where one idea carries over into more than one paragraph without changing or progressing.
- Copy your establishing claim and "so what?" for each module onto another page.
- Copy each sentence or phrase from your inventory onto this page, placing it below its corresponding establishing claim. Each piece of the inventory should follow the one that preceded it.
- Add arrows to make this a reverse outline. If you can't add arrows, you need to go back and make some decisions: What's not following logically here? Are you missing connections?

The key here is to make sure that you now have a single, coherent narrative that moves effectively from one idea to the next. Look out for places where:

- you're missing an establishing claim or a "so what."
- your establishing claim or your "so what?" seems unconvincing or incomplete.
- you can't connect one idea to the next.
- you repeat your ideas.
- you realize that you're telling a different story that splits off from the main story.

If you find these issues in your draft, you'll need to make some changes.

- If you're missing material, you'll need to write that material.
- If you're repeating yourself or going off on tangents, you'll need to decide what to cut and what to keep.
- If one of your mini-claims or "so whats" isn't working, take the time to add up the work you're doing in the module and summarize it to yourself

in order to re-create a mini-claim. Then break out the establishing claim and the "so what."

If your establishing claims or "so whats" aren't working, it may mean that what you're saying in a given module has changed over the course of the drafting process. No need to panic. Take stock of what you have, and rewrite the mini-claim for the changed module. **Remember that the ideas you figure out are the source for the mini-claim—not the other way around—so you don't want to change your ideas to fit an outdated mini-claim.**

THE AUDIENCE FOR YOUR PAPER

Even though your professor is likely the primary reader of your paper, you'll need to write in a way that's comprehensible to any casual reader who knows basic information about the text or subject you're writing about. Your professor undoubtedly knows a lot about your text, so if you keep her in mind as the reader, you may skip over important context or explanatory material, rationalizing this by thinking, *Well, the professor knows this already, so I don't need to explain it.* Sometimes students assume ideas are transparent to the professor when they're actually not. But the professor needs to follow your thinking from beginning to end to evaluate your work. That's why it's important to get your whole story onto the page—even if you think the professor already knows part of it.

Incorporating Research Materials

If you're working with research materials in your paper, you've already incorporated these materials into your draft (see chapter eleven). In your final draft, make sure that your research materials are in the right place and doing work for you. Follow these steps.

- As you create your inventory, pay particular attention to your research materials. Each time a research source comes up, note in the margin what the source is saying and what it does for you in this particular spot.
- In your reverse outline, make sure your secondary sources are doing work for you. What do they let you explain, question, expand on, or develop?
- In your reverse outline, make sure that you can link to and from each research source with arrows.

- If your source material doesn't do enough work in its present position, use your reverse outline as a guide to figure out where it could usefully go—or if it needs to be cut.
- If you're moving material around, smooth out the links between ideas when you've taken a piece out and incorporate the material effectively into its new home.

Once you've made sure you have all the pieces of your discussion in the right order and you've checked that your research is doing effective work, take another look at the connections between modules. This is often a difficult transition because you're making your biggest moves between ideas. It can be tempting to make these moves very bare bones, jumping from one module to another simply by saying, "In my next passage" or "On page 43." But these weak links take your reader out of your story and undercut the process of building an argument. Pay particular attention to the links in these places—and make sure that the "so what?" of your last module and the establishing claim of your first module are joined clearly and effectively by your link. If you're having trouble with this, take another look at our discussion of this topic in chapter ten.

Fine-Tuning Your Introductory Paragraph

You're now ready to rewrite your introductory paragraph. You'll remember that when you first focused on this paragraph in the claim draft, your task was to figure out how to make your opening claim clear without revealing your entire overall claim. Now that you understand how the paper moves and the story you're telling, you can think more fully about the work an introductory paragraph does.

- **IT SHOULD ORIENT YOUR READER.** What's the subject, broadly speaking, of your paper? If you're writing about Woolf's essay "Professions for Women" and you leave out the writer's name or the title of the essay in the first paragraph, it's difficult for your reader to get a grasp on what you're talking about. It's also a good idea to provide a genre or field (Woolf's work is an essay, not a novel) and, perhaps, a year of publication (it might matter that Woolf is writing in 1931, not back in the Victorian period she's talking about). To return to the "journey" metaphor we talked about in chapter four, this is the place you tell your reader where you're going.

- **IT SHOULD MAKE THE TOPIC OF YOUR ESSAY CLEAR.** Woolf's essay may be about how women writers find the courage to work, but that isn't necessarily the topic of *your* essay. If you're writing about "honesty in Woolf's 'Professions for Women,'" that essay will be different than an essay on "family in Woolf's 'Professions for Women.'" You'll want to make your topic clear to your readers so that they know what kind of journey this will be and what kind of things you'll be paying attention to on the road.
- **IT SHOULD PRESENT THE OVERALL PHENOMENON THAT YOU'RE TALKING ABOUT IN YOUR PAPER.** To do this, you may need to offer **a very brief summary**—just enough to make basic sense of the phenomenon you're exploring in the paper. A student writing about honesty in the Woolf essay might write, "The speaker seems to be saying that the Angel is a powerful social force that keeps women writers down—but she also says that the Angel is a liar." **Don't give too much summary—either of the text you're writing about or of your paper.** The opening paragraph is not the place to give your reader all the background information or to summarize your essay; it's an *introduction* to what you're talking about and what you're saying about it.
- **IT SHOULD OFFER YOUR OPENING CLAIM**—the section of your overall claim that introduces your argument and points in a direction.

Here's an example of an effective opening paragraph from the student essay on *Frankenstein*. We've marked the pieces of the introduction with different colors: the subject that orients the reader in blue, the topic in green, the summary leading to the phenomenon in yellow, the phenomenon in purple, and the opening claim in red.

> Mary Shelley's 1818 horror novel *Frankenstein* explores the issue of what it means to be human. The novel's protagonist, Victor Frankenstein, is a science student who sets himself the project of creating a living being. He describes the difficulties and excitement of this process in great detail. But when his creation comes to life, Victor finds himself upset and horrified—apparently because the Creature is unexpectedly ugly. Instead of celebrating his success, Victor abandons his creation just as that creation is trying to make contact with him. In this way, Victor Frankenstein creates not one but two creatures: first a living being formed out of human parts, and second, a monster. This double creation process lets us understand what, in *Frankenstein*, makes a person truly human.

It's a good idea to use this highlighting technique once you've rewritten your opening paragraph: That way, you can ensure that you haven't left anything out (or added anything extra).

It's also useful to use this technique for each module's opening paragraph. While the first paragraph of the module doesn't have to carry as much weight as the opening paragraph of the essay, it still does a lot of the same work. The first paragraph of the module should:

- orient the reader to the moment (or idea) you're talking about—where we are in the text.
- provide a brief summary of this moment.
- present your phenomenon.
- offer your establishing claim.

You'll note that we've left the word *topic* off this list. That's because the topic of your essay shouldn't change: It should be consistent across the essay. If you begin by talking about gender in *Frankenstein* but your first module is about science, you've lost that single coherent story. To use our "journey" metaphor, you're talking about France and Italy at once. They may have some things in common, but they're not the same place.

Fine-Tuning Transitions Between Paragraphs

In chapter ten, we talked about creating meaningful transitions between modules, and you checked to see that your ideas build on one another when you created your final reverse outline. But it's important at this point to take one more look and make sure that all of your transitions are effective. Watch out especially for links that read smoothly but don't actually do the work of moving your reader from paragraph to paragraph.

To do this, it's a good idea to return to the technique we showed you in chapter ten. Pull out the first and last lines of each paragraph, and check that the last line of a given paragraph leads smoothly into the first line of the next one.

For example, the student working on the *Frankenstein* essay considers the link between his third paragraph, which talks about how Victor's process of building the Creature seems to diminish his own humanity, and his fourth paragraph, which discusses the moment of the Creature's birth and Victor's reaction to it.

> **END OF PARAGRAPH 3:** In this way, Victor loses touch with his own humanity as he builds the Creature.
>
> **BEGINNING OF PARAGRAPH 4:** One night, Victor finally plugs in the electricity and animates his creation.

This reads very smoothly and makes sense: We're moving from the idea that Victor is less human as a result of his experiments to the idea that he refuses to see humanity in the Creature. But since the chronology of the text has taken the place of an actual idea link, the reader doesn't know why you're talking about a specific night at the beginning paragraph 4. You've lost the story of your essay and are instead telling the story of the novel.

Another common transition issue in final drafts is the single word that stands in for a more complicated relationship. Take this link, for instance.

> **END OF PARAGRAPH 3:** In this way, Victor loses touch with his own humanity as he builds the Creature.
>
> **BEGINNING OF PARAGRAPH 4:** Similarly, when Victor's Creature awakes, Victor can't see him as human.

This link may seem to be effective because *humanity* is in the last sentence of paragraph 3 and *human* is in the first sentence of paragraph 4. These words *are* similar, so *similarly* seems to do the job. But the idea that Victor loses touch with his own humanity isn't the same as the idea that Victor can't see the Creature as human, though it may be related. As we said in chapter ten, *similarly* is one of those words that students are taught to use to link ideas in a five-paragraph essay; if you don't have a real connection, these words can end up making the ideas harder to follow, not easier. In this case, *similarly* is simply the wrong word: the link is cause and effect, not similarity.

Another common mistake students make in linking paragraphs is repeating the end of the last paragraph in the beginning of the next one.

> **END OF PARAGRAPH 3:** In this way, Victor loses touch with his own humanity as he builds the Creature.
>
> **BEGINNING OF PARAGRAPH 4:** So Victor loses touch with his own humanity as he builds the Creature, and that means that he has trouble seeing the Creature's own humanity when he awakens.

Although this link is effective in one way—it does clearly show the relationship between the two ideas—the repetition slows the reader down. Students often build links like this because they don't entirely trust their own narratives. At this stage, you need to trust that you can move from one idea to the next without leaving your reader behind.

The student writing the *Frankenstein* essay tries out a number of links between these paragraphs. He finally settles on this link.

> **END OF PARAGRAPH 3:** In this way, Victor loses touch with his own humanity as he builds the Creature.
>
> **BEGINNING OF PARAGRAPH 4:** It should not be surprising, then, that Victor also has trouble seeing any humanity in the Creature himself.

This link is effective for several reasons.

- It moves the story forward and shows the move from the first idea to a second, related idea that builds on the first.
- It sets up the student's discussion of Victor's perception of the Creature's humanity so the topic of the new paragraph is immediately clear.
- It doesn't repeat what the student has already said.
- It doesn't rely entirely on a "transition" word instead of demonstrating an actual connection.

As you're reading through your links, pay attention to **repetition of linking terms**. Links hold meaning, so you can't rely on one term to do different work. If you find yourself using the same words or phrases over and over (*thus*, for example), it's a sign that you need to think through the connections between your paragraphs and edit accordingly.

PRACTICING: SMOOTHING OUT YOUR TRANSITIONS

- Copy each transition from your draft into a new document. Set up your transitions in pairs so you can see the move from one paragraph to the next.
- Next to each transition, note the point you're making in the relevant paragraph. (This will help you keep the point of each idea link in mind.)
- Evaluate each of your transitions. Read the transition sentences out loud so you can slow down and step back a bit from the work you've done.

- Is the connection between paragraphs (and between ideas) clear?
- Does the link set up the new idea while showing how it builds on the previous one?
- Does the link help the reader move forward?

- If your link isn't working, rewrite it. You'll probably need to do this several times before you get to a link that you're happy with.
- Rewrite all of your links in sequence. Make sure that you can follow the story you're telling by reading through your links.

The Payoff: Building on Your Conclusion

Once you've reread your paper and thought about connections and storytelling, you can re-address your conclusion. You'll remember from chapter nine that the conclusion is where the second half of your overall claim is made—that is, the "so what?" for the essay, the payoff for the story you've told. In your conclusion, you show your reader why it's useful to think about the text in the way you're thinking about it. You're demonstrating to your reader how he might understand the text or subject you're discussing differently, now that he's learned everything you've taught him.

Your conclusion should, as we've said, go beyond the opening claim. If you just demonstrate the opening claim, you've left out the payoff. In the *Frankenstein* essay, as you'll recall, the overall claim reads like this.

> Victor Frankenstein creates not one but two creatures: first a living being formed out of human parts, and second, a monster. This double creation process lets us understand what, in *Frankenstein*, makes a person truly human.

In this paragraph, the student arrives at the place that his opening claim pointed toward.

> If relationships constitute what makes someone human in *Frankenstein*, it makes sense that Victor flees when the Creature awakes and looks at him. Seeing and being seen is a relationship; if Victor stays and looks at and is seen by the Creature, he would be opening the door to a connection to another being, and Victor is no longer capable of that. So he *has* made a "being like [him]self" (81) in two ways. The Creature is "like" Vic-

tor because he's made of human parts. But, more important, Victor also makes the Creature "like" himself by depriving him of the possibility of a meaningful relationship. As a result, the Creature, like Victor, becomes a being that is less than human, an uncertain, indefinable species—in other words, a monster.

This paragraph works through the opening claim: The writer has made his case, explained his meaning, and shown how his opening claim is correct. But he hasn't yet moved *beyond* that opening claim to an overall "so what?" that provides the payoff for the work he's done in the essay. He does this in his conclusion.

The Creature, over the course of the novel, becomes aware of the nature of his lack of humanity—he comes to understand, through his attempts to find friends, that his monstrosity grows out of his lack of connection with others. This is what makes him insist that Victor create a companion for him. When Victor destroys the companion, the Creature embraces his monstrousness and sets out to confirm Victor's, too, by killing everyone that matters to him. But a strange thing happens near the end of the text. As they go on the long chase that ends in both their deaths, the Creature leaves food for his pursuer. Why? It's possible to argue that he does this to extend Victor's punishment—to keep him alive and suffering. But another, more compelling reason he does this is because they are two of a kind. All they have is each other—no one else would believe or understand their histories, and without the other one, there's no point in continuing to live. So whether Victor likes it or not, he and his Creature have a relationship with one another. In other words, paradoxically, Victor and his Creature, both alienated from humanity by their lack of connection, finally make one another human. This is why we see the Creature weeping over his dead creator: In this moment, the Creature becomes fully human as, at last, another human, Walton, connects to him with sympathy.

The student has gone a step beyond his opening claim by making use of the second half of his overall claim. Over the course of his paper, the student has shown that the Creature possesses the double identity he references in his opening paragraph (he is physically human and is monstrous because he is abandoned); he has demonstrated how the lack of connection causes the lack of humanity, and in the process he has shown that Victor, too, is inhuman in this way. In his conclusion, the student gives us the payoff: In the end, the Creature and his creator are re-deemed by their relationship with one another.

And then the student goes one step further because now that he's written through his conclusion, he's able to see the "so what?" of *that* idea.

> And this in turn explains the frame story involving Walton: It is Walton who turns back from his Arctic adventure, saving his men from almost certain death and his sister from grief, instead of pursuing his ambition at the cost of human relationships. So in the end, the novel reaffirms the possibility of choosing human relationships over ambition.

Here the student realizes that the idea he's explored about how relationships make people human actually helps him make sense of the novel's frame narra-tive, in which the adventurer Walton ultimately chooses human relationships over ambition. This bonus step isn't always available, but when it is, it can really help you show your reader how your reading changes the way you understand the text as a whole. Once you've written your conclusion, ask yourself, *Is there another "so what"*? It's a good idea to ask that question in a freewrite, brainstorm, or mind map. These generative techniques can help you see how your reading lets you—and your reader—understand the text or phenomenon you're looking at in a different way.

This may very well be the end of the essay. If the student's assignment is to explicate the text, he's probably finished. But sometimes the assignment asks the student to go a step further and think about how his claims and explorations show him something about the world that has produced the text. How does the text shed light on the historical and cultural moment it emerges from?

In this case, the student knows a little bit about the historical moment in which Shelley is writing: His class has discussed the Industrial Revolution. (In the context of a different assignment, he could have found out this information in the course of doing research, in which case he would need to cite his sources.) Here's what he writes.

> In this way, Shelley's text offers a particular view of early nineteenth-century Europe. The novel's focus on the importance of human connec-tion and the failure of that focus in the context of science and industry suggests that there is a problem with the Industrial Revolution that is going on at that time. Ambition can make work more important than

relationships and can change people from workers to cogs in factory machines. The text seems to suggest that humanness is about relationships and that an increasingly industrial Europe needs to get back to these authentic connections—or else dangerous things will happen.

Here the student has linked the text closely to what he has learned about the period in which it was written. It's important to note that, instead of applying the history to the text and coming up with a circular reading (i.e., *industrialism leads to isolation and dehumanization; therefore the novel is about isolation and dehumanization; therefore the novel is about industrialism*), **the student has worked from the inside out**, starting with his close reading and, through his analytical work, building an argument that ultimately lets him look at history. This allows him to craft an argument that has depth and complexity—something he couldn't do if he simply "applied" history to the text.

2. EDITING AT THE MEDIUM (PARAGRAPH) LEVEL

Now that you understand how your narrative moves, where it begins, and where it gets to, you're ready to look more closely. Since you've now cut out or moved paragraphs that weren't doing any work, you won't waste time repairing material that might not make it into the final draft.

One Idea Per Paragraph

It's useful at this stage to think about what a paragraph *does*. A paragraph is a unit of thought: It explores or plays out one idea or concept. That means that every paragraph should have no more than one idea. You can use the inventory you did at the essay level to check this; if you suspect that you might have glossed over this issue in your inventory, however, do another inventory focusing on this.

If you find more than one idea in a paragraph, you might be able to break the paragraph at the place where the second idea starts, thereby creating a new paragraph and keeping your ideas clear. Here's how this might work in the Woolf essay.

> The Angel here shows that she's not genuine: she's faking the way she seems to be. Instead of using *is* words, like the ones Woolf used in her description of her in the first passage ("She *was* immensely sympathetic"),

she tells Woolf what to do using *be* words. By saying "you should be this way," the Angel tells Woolf, and by extension women, how to behave. This shows that there is nothing about women that is inborn and always "sympathetic" or "tender"—they have to be instructed to be this way. The Angel also announces that it's the woman writer's job to "deceive," telling her to "use all the arts and wiles of our sex." In other words, the Angel is demanding that the woman writer lie—and suggesting that this is what all women are supposed to do. At the end of this list that begins with nice words and ends with lies and trickery, she says, "Above all, be pure." When she says this, she transforms purity into something that comes from your mind instead of your body. And since the Angel has already shown that her mind is full of lies and is attempting to fill the woman writer's mind with lies, she makes purity into a lie, too. In response to this, Woolf sets out to kill the Angel. Interestingly, she uses the word *credit* twice to talk about what she does to stop the Angel. One definition for *credit* is "recognition, acknowledgement" (*Merriam-Webster*), and that makes sense for how it's used here. But most of the definitions for this word are about money: "the balance in a person's favor in an account" or "an amount or sum placed at a person's disposal by a bank and so forth." Woolf does talk about money here: She says that the reason she's able to kill the Angel is that she has money. She says that because she has some money, "it was not necessary for me to depend solely on charm for my living." That's why she can kill the Angel.

The student has followed her own train of thought and has ended up putting two ideas together in the same paragraph: the false nature of the Angel and the role of money in killing the Angel. Since each of these ideas is explored fully and distinctly, she can easily fix this problem by cutting the paragraph in two.

It's possible, however, that your ideas are intertwined in your paragraph, in which case you may need to cut out some pieces. Those pieces might go elsewhere, perhaps in their own paragraph, or they may be extraneous. Decide what work they're doing. Take this paragraph, for example.

The Angel here shows that she's faking it, or at least being the way she is on purpose. Instead of using *is* words, like the ones Woolf used in her description of her in the first passage ("She *was* immensely sympathetic"), she tells Woolf what to do using *be* words. By saying "you should be this way," the Angel tells Woolf, and by extension women, how to behave. This is connected to the idea of *credit*, which she then talks about, and how money plays a role in relationships between men and women. When the Angel tells women how to behave, this shows that there is nothing about women that is inborn and always "sympathetic" or "tender" since they have to be told to be this way. The Angel also announces, without apology, that it's the woman writer's job to "deceive," telling her to "use all the arts and wiles of our sex." In other words, the Angel is demanding that the woman writer lie—and suggesting that this is what all women are supposed to do. This is again connected to the idea of credit and money, which is what the woman writer should be trying to achieve, but also what lets the speaker kill the Angel. At the end of this list that begins with nice words and ends with lies and trickery, the Angel says, "Above all, be pure." When she says this, she transforms purity into something that comes from your mind instead of your body. But what seems strange to me is the way Woolf uses the word *credit* to talk about what she does to stop the Angel.

As you can see, the student needs to untangle the idea of credit and money from the notion of the Angel as deceitful: Because these two ideas are intertwined, neither one plays out clearly. In fact, the discussion of credit and money is confusing because the student has integrated this idea before she's actually explained what the phenomenon is or why it's interesting. To explain her ideas clearly, she'll need to separate the discussion of deceit from the discussion of credit.

You may also find that once you divide or cut out your second idea, you don't have enough material left in your paragraph. If this is the case, you'll need to explain your first idea more fully.

Cutting Extraneous Material

Another way to streamline your paragraphs is by cutting repetition and filler. Now that you're clear on the point you're making in a given paragraph, is there material that doesn't move that point forward?

After Victor Frankenstein is picked up by the explorer Walton in the middle of the ocean, he tells Walton how he came to have the power to generate life and how he went about the project that led to the birth of the Creature. Walton has been traveling in the ocean on a quest to find a passage across the North Pole. In this important moment, set in the wild and picturesque environment of the isolated ship on the ocean, Victor explains to Walton that, though at first he considered animating not a human but a being "of simpler organization," in the end he began the "creation of a human being." He claims that he started by working on something very simple, perhaps an animal or an insect, but finally decided that he wanted to build a human, even though it would be more complex. But what's interesting is that a few lines later, he says that what allowed him to keep working, even when the project was difficult, was the idea that "[a] new species would bless me as its creator and source; many happy and excellent natures would owe their being to me. No father could claim the gratitude of his child so completely as I should deserve theirs." But the idea that what he is making is a "new species" raises the question of what Victor actually thinks his experiment will produce.

Here the student has padded his paragraph with a number of extraneous pieces: unrelated story narrative (marked in yellow), unnecessary flowery description (marked in green), and repetition (marked in red). All of these pieces share a common problem: While they may be interesting or evocative, they don't do any work for the student because they aren't advancing his ideas. And if they don't do any work in the paragraph, then they should be cut. In your final draft, every sentence in every paragraph of your essay must be there for a reason.

Paragraph Length

It's also useful to look at the length of your paragraphs. A good rule of thumb is that a paragraph shouldn't take up much more than half a page but should be at least three sentences long. Your paragraph might have a single idea, but it can still be too short or too long.

A very short paragraph is probably a sign that you haven't explained your idea fully.

cummings's poem ends with silence after the speaker speaks and then "drank rapidly a glass of water." Since you cannot speak while you drink water, the speaker's voice disappears, which undercuts the whole idea of speech and noise in the poem.

In this paragraph, the idea about the speaker's relationship to sound is present, but it's so rushed that it's hard to figure out what exactly that idea is or what its implications are. The student will need to expand on her ideas here.

On the other hand, a very long paragraph can be problematic not because it implies a thinking problem but simply because it is too long for the reader to follow. If all of your sentences and ideas belong in the paragraph but the paragraph is still very long, you need to find a place to break the paragraph. Since a paragraph is a unit of thought, a reader approaches it by assuming she can swallow it in one bite. She expects to understand one reasonably compact idea in the space of a paragraph. When she gets to the end of a paragraph, she can take a moment to digest before moving on to the next bite. When your paragraphs are very long, the reader becomes mentally overloaded and she may have a hard time following your ideas all the way to the end.

Take, for example, this long paragraph.

> Victor claims that he's producing a human being, but his own language seems to make that idea less clear. He refers, for example, to "a new species" when he talks about what he hopes to create. According to *Merriam-Webster*, "a species is a group of animals or plants that are similar and can produce young animals or plants." Scientifically speaking, humans belong to the species *Homo sapiens*; a "new species" would, by definition, be something different from *Homo sapiens*, another type of being. This becomes even clearer when we consider that Victor says that this new species would "bless him as their creator and source." Part of the definition of a species is that its members can mate and produce young. Victor's created beings, on the other hand, would not be products of human mating but would come from a different "source": Victor, operating on his own. But then, when he says, "No father could claim the gratitude of his child so completely as I should deserve theirs" in the very next sentence, he seems to come back to the idea that what he's creating will be human. He uses specifically human terms to describe the relationship he imagines between his creations and himself. Any male animal can father—as a verb—offspring, but the relationship words *father* and *child* are reserved for human beings. So Victor seems to want things both ways: Even at the very moment that he is planning his masterwork, the giving of life to a fabricated creature made of dead parts, he seems both to want it to be human, a child, and to want it to be something else, a "new species." He

seems untroubled by this contradiction: There is no evidence from his own speech that he's aware of it. This reveals that while Victor claims to be making a human, the boundaries between human and nonhuman are blurred even before the Creature is born.

This paragraph explores one idea; it doesn't move beyond the notion of category confusion regarding humans and nonhumans in the text. But it's too long for the reader to absorb in one go. The highlighting shows where we've decided to break the paragraph. "Time" words and phrases and those that show a change in direction (*but*, *however*, *in this way*, *for this reason*, *so*) often signal logical places to break your paragraph. These are good spots for your reader to catch her breath.

Moving from Sentence to Sentence

Keep the logical progression of your ideas in mind as you move from sentence to sentence within each paragraph. Take a look at this section of a paragraph, for example.

cummings's poem raises interesting questions about war through its use of sentence fragments and silence. At the end, the speaker stops speaking and drinks a glass of water. The contrast between one and the other is what makes the poem's point.

Here the sentences don't follow logically. The student has lost the thread of her storytelling: The middle sentence is a *non sequitur* (it doesn't follow from the one before it and doesn't take you to the next one). That makes it hard for her reader to follow her ideas.

To make sure your paragraph comprises sentences that follow one another in the most logical progression possible, do the following.

- Print out your paragraph, and cut out each sentence.
- Spread the sentences out on a big piece of paper in no particular order.
- Without looking back at your draft, assemble your sentences in the order that makes the most logical sense.
- Once you've made decisions, tape the sentences down on the page.
- If there are gaps between sentences, leave spaces.
- If there are missing connections within or between sentences, leave space or write them in.
- Compare the reassembled paragraph to your original paragraph. If they aren't exactly the same, rewrite the paragraph to fit your new structure.

A common problem that students encounter in final drafts is a lack of connection between pronouns and the nouns they refer to. For example, a student might write, "This is the most important thing she does," but it's not entirely clear what *this* refers to or who *she* is because the nouns that go with these pronouns are too far away. A good rule of thumb: If you are referring to a noun that is two or more sentences away from the current sentence, or if there are multiple possible nouns, use the proper word or name for the person, place, thing, or idea you're referring to.

To spot floating pronouns, try this.

- Triple-space and print out your paragraph so you can see it clearly.
- Highlight all pronouns: *this, it, they, he, she, we, his, her, their, our, these, that, those*
- Use another color to draw a line connecting each pronoun to its noun (the person, place, thing, or idea to which it refers).
- Check for distance and clarity. Is the pronoun too far away from its noun to be clear? Pay special attention to situations where you mention multiple people (for instance, characters or research sources) of the same gender. You might need to repeat the nouns you're referring to (names, job titles) more often.
- Replace pronouns with nouns anywhere confusion occurs.

Integrating Research at the Paragraph Level

If your paper involves research, make sure that you've integrated it effectively. In each instance where you've included research, check that you've introduced your source in a way that integrates your source work into the text of your essay. For example, here's an effective way of integrating a source into your paragraph.

> While it is possible to see "next to of course god america i" as an antiwar poem, Russell Smith argues that cummings's poem "talks around the idea of war without ever getting there" (43).

Here the student smoothly introduces the source material by making it a part of her discussion. She provides the source's name, a direct quote, and the page number—all in a sentence that allows the narrative to progress. This is effective because it makes her story more important than Smith's work. As we said in chapter eleven, your ideas are always the primary story in your essay: Your research is there to enrich *your* ideas.

In this next example, the student uses the end of her paragraph to introduce a block quote. (Any quote that takes up more than five lines of text in your essay should be turned into an indented block quote that stands alone.)

> Woolf's speech on the Angel is really about the idea of the woman as artist in a society that doesn't know what to do with woman artists—but she is definitely talking to upper-class and upper-middle-class women. In her book, *Thinking About Art in Virginia Woolf,* Rosamund De Grazia writes,
>
>> Women artists of all types are highly visible in Woolf's fiction as well as in her essays. She is perpetually interested in the problem of how women can find space to make art of all types when they're supposed to be busy doing other things: raising children, running households, taking care of the men in their lives. She is very clear about the connections between privilege and art-making, arguing over and over again that having access to money, leisure and privacy is the key for women artists (the most famous example of this in Woolf's writing is, of course, *A Room of One's Own*). But while her argument for female economic emancipation in regards to art production is important, it also reveals Woolf's class biases. (125)
>
> De Grazia points out that while Woolf seems to be talking about all women in her work on women as artists and writers, she's really focusing on women with financial security. And since her audience for the speech is made up of female college students, it's possible to assume that she's also speaking to women with some financial privilege. So Woolf seems to be claiming that women need to seize the right to be artists—but as De Grazia suggests, only some women get to do that.

Once again, the quote is properly set up: The student provides the citation information for the source and connects it to the idea she's interested in. Then she briefly explains it and puts it to work in her essay.

In contrast, look at this example.

> Victor's anger at the Creature seems unfair since he is the one who abandoned the Creature in the first place. "Victor Frankenstein is prideful, and in Shelley's work, pride is the deadliest sin" (Stevens 42). It is not

> surprising that the Creature becomes a monster since he raised himself without a parent and without human love.

Instead of integrating the source material into the paragraph, the student has just dropped it in without explaining how it relates to his ideas or explicating the source in any way. This use of source material may fulfill the requirement of including a source, but it doesn't actually do any work for the essay: Nothing is explored or clarified through this use of source material. In fact, the quote simply interrupts the essay.

As you can see, once you've introduced your source, quoted or paraphrased, and cited appropriately, you'll need to make sure that you:

- briefly summarize what the source is saying. (Don't rely on the source to do the work for you.)
- put the source to work. Why are you citing this source? Do you agree with it? Disagree? In part or in whole? What does the source help you illuminate, explicate, explore, or argue?
- cite your source properly with in-text citation. If you're using MLA format (common in many English and humanities classes), cite as the students do in our examples above: Put the page number in parentheses at the end of your quote or paraphrase. If the author's last name has not been recently and clearly mentioned in relation to the referenced material, it goes in the parentheses, too. If your quote is in the body of your paragraph, the parentheses go inside the sentence's punctuation; if you're using a block quote, the parentheses follow the punctuation at the end of the referenced material. In all cases, the full citation information goes in a works-cited page organized alphabetically by author name at the end of your paper.

In the *Frankenstein* essay example, though the source is not used well, the student does cite correctly. When you don't mention the author's name in your setup, you need to include it in the parenthetical citation, as he does here: "(Stevens 42)." Note that there is no comma between the author's name and the page number and that the punctuation that follows the citation (whether it's a period, a semicolon, a comma, or any other form) comes *after* the parentheses.

In the Woolf essay example, by contrast, the student provides her source's name, Rosamund De Grazia, in the sentence introducing her material. Because we already know the critic she's talking about, the student doesn't need to include the critic's name in the parenthetical citation.

MLA is only one form of citation: Every field has its own preferred form (or forms), and some professors have a form they like students to use even if it isn't the usual form for their discipline. Check on what's expected for each course. Resources for formatting and citing properly in each form are widely available online and in print; a good source is the Purdue Online Writing Lab (https://owl. english.purdue.edu/owl).

3. EDITING AT THE MICRO (SENTENCE) LEVEL

Once you've worked through the big issues in your final draft, you're ready to work at the sentence level. That means making sure that your sentences say precisely what you want them to say and that they don't contain any grammatical or punctuation problems that will confuse your reader.

You've probably noticed that we haven't talked much about grammar or punctuation so far. It's not that we don't think grammar and mechanics are important; we just don't want you to waste time worrying about them when you're working on process rather than product. If writing is thinking (and it is), you can't think freely if you're also worrying about your mechanics. And as we've said before, if you think of your essay as a product too early in the game, you may write a paper that—although grammatically perfect—is idea starved. But grammar and punctuation and other issues of mechanics are important, and once you're ready to think of your essay as product, it's time to think about them.

Grammar and Punctuation

Lots of people think they don't like grammar. That's either because they were badly taught, so that grammar seemed dull and rote, or because they weren't taught it at all. And because people feel uncertain about grammar, they avoid focusing on it. But actually, **grammar is power.** We mean that in two ways: First, when you know how to structure a sentence so that your reader knows exactly what you're saying, it's a powerful feeling. Second, grammar and punctuation constitute the rules of the road. They're our baseline agreements about how to read, define, and structure a sentence. And when you know how to use these rules to express your ideas clearly, you're in control of your reader's experience.

What a Sentence Is and Why It Matters

If you want to control your reader's experience, you have to write sentences in which the grammar expresses your meaning effectively. And that means that you need to know what constitutes a sentence. Often when students who are fluent in English make basic structural errors, the errors are actually a sign of a problem in their thinking. When a writer hasn't thought through his idea completely, he can end up with sentence fragments; when he hasn't sorted out the main point he's making and how relationships in a given sentence function, he can end up with confusing or run-on sentences.

Let's look at this pair of sentences to see how they reveal a logical problem.

> The Creature, living and dying alone. He becomes more sympathetic.

Though the first phrase has a subject, you can't call it a sentence. Although *living* and *dying* look like verbs, they're actually adjectives that describe the Creature. One simple way to fix a fragment like this is by connecting it to what comes before or after. After all, there's probably a reason the two phrases are next to each other. Start by thinking about how the fragment connects to what's nearby. What relationship are you trying to set up? In this example, the relationship is one of cause and effect: The student is saying that the *effect* of seeing the Creature living and dying alone *causes* the reader to feel sympathy for him. Once he's clarified that, it's easy to fix the problem. Here's the revision.

> When the reader sees the Creature living and dying alone and friendless, she feels sympathy for him.

Fragments often signal a missing idea link. By figuring out what the sentence is really about, the student sees that the reader is the actual subject of the sentence and she is the one feeling sympathy. This lets him resolve both the grammar problem and the thinking problem. Instead of just trying to fix the grammar, it's always a good idea to step back and ask yourself, *What am I really trying to say here?*

Comma Splices

Comma splices happen when you put too many ideas and phrases into a sentence but you're missing the necessary punctuation. When a sentence has more than one point in it, you need to make sure that the relationships between those points are clear, and punctuation is a crucial way of indicating those relationships. If you leave out necessary punctuation or use the wrong kind, it tells the reader that the sentence isn't under your control.

Here's an example of the kind of sentence that students often call a run-on but that teachers call a comma splice.

> Frankenstein's Creature becomes a killer, it isn't his fault.

Teachers call this a comma splice because a **comma is used to connect—or splice together—two complete sentences. The comma splice is problematic because a comma alone cannot connect two complete sentences.** In this example, the sentence before the comma is complete: *Frankenstein's Creature* is a subject; *becomes* is a verb. The sentence after the comma is also complete: *It* is a subject; *isn't* is a verb. You'll also hear these two pieces of a comma splice called *independent clauses*: They are *independent* because they can stand on their own, which is another way of saying that they are complete sentences. A phrase that cannot stand on its own as a sentence is called a *dependent clause.*

As we've said, grammar issues are often red flags for thinking issues. In the case of the comma splice, the thinking issue is about **connections between ideas**: When you try to connect two separate and complete sentences by throwing in a comma, you're omitting necessary information about how those two sentences and the ideas they express are connected.

You can fix a comma splice by:

- using a conjunction and a comma to link the ideas.
- splitting the sentence into two separate sentences.
- joining the two separate sentences with a semicolon, a long dash, or a colon.
- subordinating one of the independent clauses to the other one.

Conjunction Plus a Comma

As you probably know, a *conjunction* is a word that glues sentences together such as *and*, *or*, and *but*. We said earlier that a comma can't link two independent clauses. An exception is made when you use a conjunction *and* a comma together—but this exception only stands if *both* the conjunction *and* the comma appear. The comma isn't optional; it's mandatory.

There are seven conjunctions that give the comma the power to link two independent clauses.

> For
> And
> Nor
> But
> Or
> Yet
> So

A handy acronym to remember this list: When you write the words in this order, their first letters spell FANBOYS.

Each of these seven conjunctions can join two complete sentences—but as you can see from the sentences below, they aren't interchangeable. It's useful to know exactly how each of the conjunctions operates so you can make the best choice.

> Frankenstein's Creature becomes a killer, **and** it isn't his fault.
>
> Frankenstein's Creature becomes a killer, **but** it isn't his fault.
>
> Frankenstein's Creature becomes a killer, **for** it isn't his fault.
>
> Frankenstein's Creature becomes a killer, **yet** it isn't his fault.
>
> Frankenstein's Creature becomes a killer, **or** it isn't his fault.
>
> Frankenstein's Creature becomes a killer, **nor** it isn't his fault.
>
> Frankenstein's Creature becomes a killer, **so** it isn't his fault.

The choice of conjunction changes the relationship between the first idea ("Frankenstein's Creature becomes a killer") and the second one ("it isn't his fault"). Here's how that works in each instance.

> Frankenstein's Creature becomes a killer, **and** it isn't his fault.

When you use *and* between two ideas, it's a simple plus sign. "Thing one and thing two are both happening"—that's all *and* can tell you. This is great if you want a list ("I want cake and ice cream") or if the whole point is that two things are happening rather than just one ("I took the train because it was cheaper and because it was faster") but not so good if there's actually a more complicated relationship between the two ideas.

> Frankenstein's Creature becomes a killer, **but** it isn't his fault.

When you use *but* between two ideas, you're setting up an opposition. Sometimes that opposition also includes a distinction. In this sentence, for instance, you're essentially saying, *Yes, the Creature does kill a bunch of people, but we must take into account the idea that it wasn't his fault.* All the words in italics are unstated: The *but* does all the work. When you use *but* in this way, you're doing several things: setting up an opposition between two ideas, distinguishing between these ideas, and indicating which of the two is, in your opinion, the correct point of view.

But can also be simply oppositional.

> Victor knows he should write to his family, **but** he doesn't.

In this case, *but* simply means, "He does the opposite." No distinction is being made.

> Frankenstein's Creature becomes a killer, **yet** it isn't his fault.

Yet and *but* function similarly: They both set up an opposition. The difference is about nuance. Where *but* is a very clear, strong division, *yet* is weaker—it gives a feeling that the two conditions could be considered together in some way. If that's the idea you want, you need to rewrite your sentence. You might, for instance, change it so it reads: "Frankenstein's Creature becomes a killer, **yet** it is wrong to hold him solely accountable." As you can see, what follows the *yet* has a less oppositional relationship to the first idea in the sentence than the clause that follows the *but* does.

> Frankenstein's Creature becomes a killer, **so** it isn't his fault.

> Frankenstein's Creature becomes a killer, **for** it isn't his fault.

When you use *so* and *for* between two ideas, you're setting up a very particular relationship: *cause and effect*. Both these words convey the idea of "in order to." We don't use *for* this way in contemporary English (we use *because* instead), but that's how it was designed. In this example, you don't want to use *so* or *for* because you'll end up with a sentence that contradicts itself. The idea that the Creature becomes a killer in order for the killing to not be his fault makes no sense. Here's how you could use *so* correctly: "Frankenstein's Creature becomes a killer, **so** he loses his sense of himself as innocent." There's no real reason to use *for*; it just sounds old-fashioned and odd. *So* is a better choice when you're setting up a cause-and-effect relationship. (More information on comma splices can be found in the Appendix.)

Other Sentence-Level Issues

Tense

Tense is a confusing issue for students, especially when they're writing about literary texts. While it may seem logical to refer to events in a text that was written in the past by using the past tense, that's not how it's done. When you're talking about events in a literary text, no matter when it was written, you need to use the present tense. (This is called *literary present tense*.) The reason for this is that the text itself—the book or document—exists in the present day, and as readers we're encountering the characters and the ideas now, today. Here are some examples.

> Victor Frankenstein sets out to create life.
>
> In her discussion of the Angel of the House, Virginia Woolf emphasizes the ways that the Angel obstructs women.
>
> Darwin's theory suggests that plants adapt to their environments over many generations.

There are two exceptions to this rule. Here's the first: If you're including biographical or historical information about an event that has already happened and has ended, you use the past tense.

> When Virginia Woolf wrote "Professions for Women," only a small percentage of women were in the workforce.

Here's the second exception: if you're setting up a time line of events and you want to make it clear that one thing happened before another. An easy way to do this is to use present-perfect tense. This form is constructed by using the past tense of the main verb along with the present tense of the verb *to be*, and it creates a time condition that *starts* in the past and *continues* into the present. Here are some examples.

> I have lived here for ten years.

In other words: "I started living here in the past, ten years ago, and I still live here now, today." In the essay on *Frankenstein*, you could use the present perfect like this.

> Victor has been working on making a wife for the Creature for a while when he decides that he can't continue, which enrages the Creature.

It's also possible to stay in the present tense simply by using time words that establish sequence. Here's how that might look.

> When Victor agrees to make a wife for the Creature, the Creature tells him that he will be watching and waiting.

Time words like *when* eliminate the need for the past tense because they do the same work: They establish an order for the events being discussed.

The more you write with this convention in mind, the more natural it becomes, but if it's new to you, you'll need to check your paper to make sure you aren't using the past tense.

Passive Voice

As we've said, active voice shows the subject doing the action; passive voice does not.

> **ACTIVE VOICE:** She flew the plane.
> **PASSIVE VOICE:** The plane was flown.

While the active voice gives information about the pilot, the passive voice tells you nothing about how it flew. For all the reader knows, the plane flew itself.

Passive voice drives teachers crazy because students often employ it (consciously or unconsciously) to avoid being clear and direct. If, for instance, you write this sentence, you're dodging an important question.

In e.e. cummings's poem "next to god of course america i," the issue of patriotism is raised.

Who raised this issue? When you use active voice, you're speaking directly rather than hiding behind fuzziness. And since you've done all of this process work that let you figure out exactly what you want to say, there's no need to fudge things.

The easy way to locate passive voice is to remember that most English sentences are organized in this order: subject, verb, object.

She [*subject*] flew [*verb*] the plane [*object*].

But passive sentences are organized like this.

Object, verb.

The plane [*object*] was flown [*verb*].

Once you've identified instances where you use passive voice, ask yourself who did the action you're talking about and rewrite the sentence to recast it in active voice. If you don't actually know who did the action, you need to go back to the text to figure it out.

ANOTHER WORD FOR THESAURUS

Another problem that comes up for students is repeating the same terms over and over. Using a thesaurus can help you avoid word repetition, but it can also get you into trouble. Thesauri are useful because they offer alternatives to words that you're overusing. But they can cause problems for you because the words they offer aren't always synonyms: Though they're closely related, they may not mean exactly the same thing. And as you know from close reading, words that may be similar enough for casual use can turn out to have very different nuances. So while it's often useful to use a thesaurus to find or recall words, if the words you find are new to you, or if you aren't sure of all of their meanings, look them up before putting them in your paper.

Another tip: Don't consult a thesaurus to look for a bigger, longer, "fancier" word to replace a simpler, shorter word. There's no reason to throw in fancy words to make yourself sound smarter. (In fact, if you use fancy words incorrectly, you'll look less assured.) You'll sound plenty smart if you're getting your ideas on the page and working with the text. It's much more effective to convey a complex idea in clear language than it is to wrap it up in complicated, unclear words or syntax.

Filler Words and Sentences

When you're working at the sentence level, you also want to be on the alert for filler words. These are words that aren't doing anything but making your paper longer. Often students use filler in an attempt to pad papers that are too short. (This doesn't work: Your professor will notice.) You shouldn't need filler words—close reading means you'll have plenty to say—but you may still be in the habit of including them. Here are some examples.

> For centuries, human beings have struggled with the question of how to be a good person. We can see this struggle in Mary Shelley's classic novel *Frankenstein*.

This kind of very general language, which is almost always found in the opening lines of an essay, usually occurs because students think an introductory paragraph should operate like a funnel, with a wide opening that then narrows down. And in fact, as you know from our discussion of what needs to be in an opening paragraph, you *are* presenting an overview rather than opening with a specific phenomenon you plan to look at. But that's quite different from an opening that starts with an enormous general statement or otherwise goes really, really big.

Another kind of filler that often makes its appearance in the opening paragraph is the use of multiple unnecessary words to describe the text that the paper will be talking about.

> Mary Shelley's famous and horrifying novel, which she wrote in England in 1818, tells the story of a major character named Victor Frankenstein who decides to create a human being.

Close to half of the words in that sentence are filler. Here's all you need.

> Mary Shelley's 1818 novel tells the story of Victor Frankenstein, who decides to create a human being.

There's no reason to include:

- an aesthetic description of the text.
- a separate clause to describe where and when the text was written.
- the word *character* (and any descriptors that go with it). When you're discussing a work of fiction, the reader assumes that the people you talk about are characters.

Here's another filler-laden opening move.

> Mary Shelley's novel *Frankenstein* is an awe-inspiring and terrifying look at the human condition, a classic of its kind.

Instead of talking about the text, this move fills space by praising the author. There's never any reason to compliment the author (or, indirectly, the professor who assigned the reading) in an analytical paper.

But filler can be found throughout the text, not just in the introduction. For example, this is another form of complimenting the author that you should avoid.

> Mary Shelley's subtle use of language means that every word must be considered carefully.

This doesn't do any analytical work, and it's often used as a stand-in for actual close reading. You don't need to tell your reader that the author of the text is capable of doing interesting things with language: You need to explore those things and say something about them.

Unnecessary explanations and definitions are also a form of filler.

> The organization of a cell, that is, the way it's put together, is very important.

Nothing is surprising or unexpected about how the word *organization* is being used here, so there's no reason to define it. It's just filler. In fact, the whole sentence is filler: If something is important, tell your reader why. Don't delay by dedicating a whole sentence to importance.

Once you're aware of these common filler words and phrases, they're easy to cut. This is another place where reading aloud is really useful (or you can ask a friend to read your essay aloud to you).

WHO VS. THAT

One small issue that's worth paying attention to is the use of *who* vs. *that*. While both words are connectors and are used similarly, there is a major difference: **That refers to objects; who refers to people.**

> This is the bus *that* I used to take to work.

> This is the co-worker *who* changed my life.
>
> If you refer to your co-worker or any other human being or category made up of human beings (firefighters or farmers or authors or nurses or acrobats) by the word *that*, you are reducing that person or group of people to the category of things. People deserve to be referred to as people.

The process we've shown you here will sustain you through all kinds of writing in all kinds of courses, all the way through college and beyond. Each essay will be a new challenge, and though the process will never be easy—it's hard for professors and other professional writers, too—the more you do it, the easier and more comfortable it gets.

This process is also useful for another kind of writing you'll likely need to do both in college and afterward: application essays, grant applications, and job letters. In an online exclusive (found at www.writersdigest.com/thinking-on-the-page), we discuss how the principles in *Thinking on the Page* can be applied to this type of writing.

THE FINAL POLISH:
A GUIDE FOR GRAMMARPHILES
AND PERFECTIONISTS

Now that you've done all this work, it makes sense to expend a bit more time doing one last check for grammar and formatting perfection. Here are some of the tools you need to do that.

AVOIDING SENTENCE FRAGMENTS

In chapter twelve we discussed what a sentence is and why it matters. Knowing what a sentence is and what it isn't will help you steer clear of sentence fragments.

Let's start by reviewing what makes a phrase a grammatically legal sentence. **A phrase is a sentence if it expresses a complete idea and has a subject and a verb.** (As you'll remember from chapter one, a subject is the person *doing* the action of a sentence; a verb *is* that action.) *George Washington governed* only has three words, but it's a perfectly fine sentence. It may not be particularly interesting or informative, but it's grammatically correct, even without an object. (A version of that sentence with an object would be *George Washington governed the United States.*)

A sentence fragment is a combination of words that can look like a sentence but that lacks either a subject or a verb.

This is a fragment.

> Looking around the room.

That's because there is no *subject* doing the looking and there's no complete thought.

This is also a fragment.

> The swimming boy.

That's because even though there is something that looks like a verb (*swimming*), it's not actually functioning as a verb here. Instead, it's doing the work of an adjective, which is to modify or describe the boy. What kind of boy is he? The swimming kind.

Fragments almost always result from words that seem like verbs but aren't functioning as verbs in a given phrase. One way to spot a fragment is to keep an eye out for verbs that end in *-ing*. When a verb is in this form, it can't sustain a sentence on its own because it's not actually *functioning* as a verb. For this reason, another verb needs to be included in the sentence. For example, this sentence is not complete.

> falling off your bike

But this one is.

> falling off your bike hurts

Falling off your bike hurts is a complete sentence because the addition of *hurts* means that the sentence has both a subject and a verb. *Falling* isn't a verb here; *hurts* is.

While *falling* may look like a verb, it's helpful to remember that a verb ending in *-ing* only functions properly when it's used with another verb, such as a form of the verb *to be*. For example, this is a complete sentence.

> He is living alone.

This sentence has all the necessary information; it's a complete thought, with a subject and a verb. If the first verb is missing, the clause is not a complete idea. For example, this fragment doesn't have a verb and it's not a complete idea.

> Living alone the Creature.

As soon as you notice that the sentence doesn't actually provide a concrete and complete piece of information, you can fill in the missing pieces and fix your fragment.

To find fragments, start by highlight the *-ing* verbs. Then check to see if a form of *to be* or another verb is near it. If not, see what follows or precedes the fragment to figure out what the missing piece or idea is. Once you train yourself to recognize fragments, it's easy to fix them. You just have to ask yourself what you want to say about, for example, looking around the room or the swimming boy. (You probably knew at some point in the process what you wanted to say, but that meaning didn't make it onto the page.)

FIXING COMMA SPLICES

As we said in chapter twelve, while sentence fragments are missing something, comma splices occur when there's too much going on—when you use a comma to connect two complete sentences. In chapter twelve, we showed you how to fix a comma splice by using a conjunction and a comma to link ideas. Here are some additional ways to prevent comma splices.

Splitting the Run-On Sentence into Two Separate Sentences

Students often like this approach because it's straightforward. But while this method solves the grammatical issue, it often leads to short, choppy sentences and it may not address the more important question of the real connection between the two ideas. In the case of our example, for instance, when you split the two clauses, you get this.

> Frankenstein's Creature becomes a killer. It isn't his fault.

And while a casual reader might keep reading, since nothing is obviously wrong there, a more engaged reader (for instance, your professor) might start asking, *Okay, so he's a killer, and it isn't his fault … but how do those two ideas relate to each other?*

The two-sentence method can be useful if you want to emphasize what's going on in each sentence separately rather than emphasizing the connection between them.

> Frankenstein's Creature becomes a killer. In his isolation, he festers.

The fact that these sentences work fine independently is a sign that they really didn't need to be together in the first place. But often, a comma splice occurs because there truly is a relationship between the two sentences that isn't yet clear. That's why the other methods of fixing a splice may be more useful to you.

Joining Independent Clauses with a Semicolon, an Em-Dash, or a Colon

Although the rules of grammar don't allow a comma to connect two independent clauses, the semicolon, the em-dash (also known as the long dash), and the colon *are* allowed to do this. These three forms of punctuation (written ; — and : respectively) do similar jobs, but they have some subtle differences that are useful to understand.

The *semicolon* connects two independent clauses that are talking about the same issue but in slightly different ways.

> When Virginia Woolf talks about the Angel of the House, it seems that there is one angel for all the houses. Later, however, it becomes apparent that each woman has her own angel.

Each of these independent clauses is a complete sentence: They can stand alone and are grammatically complete. But when you combine them with a semicolon, the relationship between them is highlighted.

> When Virginia Woolf talks about the Angel of the House, it seems that there is one angel for all the houses; later, however, it becomes apparent that each woman has her own angel.

It's important to remember that the **semicolon always connects two independent clauses**. Any phrase that comes after a semicolon must be able to stand on its own as a sentence. For example, this sentence is grammatically perfect.

> I love dogs; it's their owners I can't stand.

But this version is not.

> I love dogs; all kinds, big ones, little ones, long haired, or short haired.

That's because there's no subject or verb in the phrase after the semicolon.

And that kind of sentence is where the *colon* comes in. The **colon indicates that what follows is an explanation, an amplification, or a list relating to your**

first independent clause. Here's an example of a colon used to alert the reader that what's coming next is an explanation of the phrase before the colon.

> Victor Frankenstein is never clear about what it is he's trying to create: At times he speaks about it as if it will clearly be a human, while at other times he suggests it will be an amazing new species.

Colons can also be used to indicate that a list is coming—and a list does not need to be a complete sentence.

The em-dash also sets off whatever follows it. Like a colon, it indicates that an amplification, an explanation, or a list is coming. The main difference is that it does so more emphatically. An em-dash says to the reader, *Pay attention; I'm about to say something important.*

An em-dash can be used singly or in pairs. Here's an example of a single em-dash in a sentence.

> Although Victor Frankenstein looks human, he has forgotten the key aspect of humanity—relationships with others.

In this example, the em-dash both amplifies and explains "the key aspect of humanity." You could use a colon here instead, but the em-dash sets off and strengthens the phrase that follows it more than a colon would. That's appropriate here because this is a key idea in the student's essay.

Here's an example of a pair of em-dashes.

> Despite their enmity, what Victor and the Creature have in common—a need to have a relationship with someone who knows their history—is greater than what separates them.

When you use em-dashes in a pair like this, you're emphasizing the information between the dashes. It's almost like a billboard saying, *Pay attention here.*

But don't just whip through your paper and correct all the comma splices by swapping in a semicolon, a colon, or an em-dash. Every time you use one of these forms of punctuation, you're saying, *These two sentences can each stand on their own. However, I, the author, think that they belong together, so I don't want to divide them by putting a full stop (a period) between them.* And once you've made that decision, you also need to choose which form of punctuation to use to demonstrate the exact way that the sentences belong together. For instance, consider this comma splice.

> Victor Frankenstein never fully decides what he's making in his grand experiment, this uncertainty comes into play at the Creature's birth and throughout his unhappy life.

In this case, all you have to do to make the sentence work perfectly is to replace the comma with a semicolon.

> Victor Frankenstein never fully decides what he's making in his grand experiment; this uncertainty comes into play at the Creature's birth and throughout his unhappy life.

As we said above, the semicolon connects two independent clauses that are talking about the same issue but in slightly different ways. Here, as you can see, the two independent clauses both talk about Victor's uncertainty, but they make different points.

On the other hand, in our original example sentence, this isn't the case. Here's the sentence with a semicolon.

> Frankenstein's Creature becomes a killer; it isn't his fault.

This sentence is grammatically correct, but it doesn't make a lot of sense because the two clauses aren't actually about the same thing.

Subordinating One Independent Clause to the Other

Another way to fix a comma splice is to change one of the clauses so that it's no longer independent. The simplest and most useful way to do that is by *subordination*. **When you subordinate something, you're putting it below something else.** Thus, for example, the CEO of a company has many *subordinates*—people who work beneath her. But even if you've never heard these terms, you're familiar with the concept. For example, you know that this phrase isn't a complete sentence.

> Since I started school

That's because although this phrase has a subject (*I*) and a verb (*started*), the word *since* sets up the reader or listener to expect the phrase to continue. "Since you started school …" what? (If this reminds you of what we said earlier about fragments, it should: In both cases the words start an idea but don't complete it. The phrase remains incomplete because some necessary pieces are missing.)

Since subordinates this clause, requiring the clause to relate to something else. And that means it can't stand on its own: It needs an independent clause to be a whole sentence. If this were a corny romantic comedy, the subordinate clause would say to the independent clause, "You complete me." The subordinate clause needs a second phrase, like this.

> Since I started school, I've learned a lot about myself.

Now you have a complete sentence.

Don't be thrown off by the fact that the "linking" word is actually at the beginning of the sentence rather than in the middle. The grammatical relationship is still one of subordination. The clause that starts with *since* is *dependent* on the second clause: It can't stand on its own.

If you find yourself facing a comma splice, the problem may be that you haven't used necessary subordination. You mean for one clause to be subordinate to the other, but since you haven't made that clear with a subordinating term, the two clauses look equal (and poorly linked).

Lots of words subordinate. One important category is *time words*, which clarify *time relationships* between two clauses. Time words include *after, before, when*, and *during*, in addition to *since*.

Other subordinating words set up other relationships. For example, *although* functions very much like *but*. Unlike *but*, however, *although* subordinates. That's the grammatical difference between the two. There's also a subtle difference in meaning when it comes to how the distinction is set up. Take a look at how our *Frankenstein* sentence works when you use *although* to subordinate one of the clauses.

> Although Frankenstein's Creature becomes a killer, it isn't his fault.

The *although* says, *While I must admit that the Creature did kill a lot of people, really it isn't his fault.*

Although, in other words, subordinates the phrase it's attached to in two ways: It makes it grammatically dependent on its partner phrase, and it also signals that the sentence's *real* point of view is in the other phrase.

OTHER COMMA RULES

Fundamentally, the comma's job is to **separate elements in a sentence**. If you're using a comma, it's because two parts of a sentence need to be set off from each other to avoid confusion or misreading. Here's an example you may have seen.

> Let's eat, Grandma.

> Let's eat Grandma.

The first sentence is very different from the second. In the first, you're encouraging your grandmother to dig in; in the second, you're urging your readers to make a meal out of Grandma. The comma makes the difference. The version without the comma reads as if Grandma were the *object* of the verb *to eat*. Inserting the comma separates *Grandma* from the verb and lets the readers see that in this case, *Grandma* is the person being spoken to.

Commas and Introductory Clauses

Commas are frequently used to set off the introductory piece of a sentence (known as the *introductory clause*) from the rest of the sentence. Here's an example of a sentence with an introductory clause set off by a comma.

> When cummings describes the speaker as drinking "rapidly," it makes it seem like the speaker needs to clear his throat or get the taste of slaughter out of his mouth.

The comma makes the reader pause just a bit and assimilate the introductory point (the sentence is talking about the effect of *rapidly*) before moving on to the big idea the sentence wants to convey.

Often an introductory clause will start with one of the subordinating phrases we mentioned earlier. This is another reason you need a comma: Subordinated introductory clauses can't stand on their own. The comma signals that the real meat of the sentence is coming next.

To check for missing commas after an introductory clause, try one of these two methods.

- Highlight the opening word of your sentence. If it's a word that subordinates, you'll need a comma at the end of the phrase.

- Read the sentence aloud, and see if and where you pause naturally.

Commas and Essential Versus Nonessential Information

Commas also separate the pieces of a sentence that are *essential* from the pieces that are not. This nonessential information may be interesting or nice to know, but it isn't *essentially* what the sentence is about. To see how this works, take a look at this sentence.

> Victor Frankenstein, who was born in Switzerland, goes to Ingolstadt to attend the university.

The main purpose of the sentence is to inform the reader about where Victor went to school. The information contained in the phrase "who was born in Switzerland" isn't essential. The commas set off the nonessential information from the rest of the sentence. It's useful to think about the commas on each side of the phrase as little hooks: If you were to grab on to each comma and yank that phrase out, what's left would be a perfectly logical and complete sentence. It would read like this.

> Victor Frankenstein goes to Ingolstadt to attend the university.

Sometimes students punctuate a sentence that contains nonessential information in this way.

> Victor Frankenstein who was born in Switzerland goes to Ingolstadt to attend the university.
>
> OR
>
> Victor Frankenstein, who was born in Switzerland goes to Ingolstadt to attend the university.
>
> OR
>
> Victor Frankenstein who was born in Switzerland, goes to Ingolstadt to attend the university.

But none of these punctuation choices does the job of separating the nonessential information from the rest of the sentence. With no commas, the sentence is very hard to read (try reading it aloud to see what we mean), and with just one comma, the job you wanted the commas to do in the first place is incomplete.

Nonessential information can appear at the end of a sentence as well as in the middle. When it comes at the end, it's set off by just one comma. Here's what that variant looks like.

> Victor loses contact with his family while he's working on his grand experiment, which he later admits was a bad sign.

The main job of the sentence is to convey that Victor fell out of touch with his family while he was working on his creation. The fact that he admits that losing touch was a bad thing is interesting but again, nonessential.

Improving Your Comma Usage

Commas are the most frequently used form of punctuation, which means that trying to fix every one of them at once can be overwhelming. The best way to proceed is to choose one paragraph in your essay at a time to focus on.

- Print out the paragraph so you can see it by itself, and highlight each comma.
- Then go back, and ask yourself these questions.
  - What job is this comma doing?
  - Is it a job a comma is allowed to do? (Remember, commas can't link two independent clauses.)
  - Do you need a comma there? If not, do you need something else?

When you come to the end of your paragraph, assess what you've found. If you see that you're consistently making one kind of error, go through the rest of your paper and look specifically for that problem.

PREVENTING CHOPPINESS

Choppiness occurs when a number of very short sentences follow each other. This paragraph, for instance, is very choppy.

> Victor Frankenstein thinks of himself as a scientist. But he isn't. If he were a scientist, he would do things differently. He would decide exactly what he is making before he starts. He would be prepared for the experi-

ment's result. He would be curious about that result. He would not run away from his creation.

As you can see, all of these short and simply constructed sentences one after another make the author sound like a child, even though the ideas contained in the sentences aren't childlike.

The mechanical issue here is that most of these sentences are short and often constructed the same way (*he would, he would, he would*). The thinking issues are a lack of connections between ideas and a lack of subordination that create hierarchies among ideas. When each sentence sounds more or less alike, everything seems equal, so your reader doesn't know what to focus on or how things go together. Reading a very choppy paragraph made up of sentences that are all constructed the same way is like being poked in the arm over and over again.

When students write choppily, it's usually because they're trying to control the words on the page by keeping the sentences short and simple. This can happen to any writer; it often happens to non-native speakers, who, reasonably enough, want to avoid using complicated syntax they may not have fully mastered. But this isn't the way to maintain control of your sentences: Ironically, choppiness actually signals a lack of control.

The fastest way to check for choppiness is to read any section you're worried about out loud. Short, repetitively structured sentences are easier to hear than see. If you find a choppy patch in your draft, you can fix it by applying the lessons about subordination from the comma splice discussion.

- Start by reminding yourself why the sentences are next to each other in the first place. What's the relationship between ideas?
- Decide what sentences need to be totally rewritten and which ones can be subordinated or combined. The goal is to create longer, more complicated sentences that convey your ideas more clearly.

Here's what that might look like with the example we just looked at.

> Although Victor Frankenstein thinks of himself as a scientist, he really doesn't act like one. If he were a scientist, he would decide exactly what he is making before he starts. And instead of running away when the experiment turns out differently than he had hoped, he would be curious about what he had made. He would not run away from his creation.

As you can see, the paragraph is now much easier to read. The subordination and sentence combination make the ranking of ideas and the relationships between sentences much clearer.

Even if your sentences aren't super short, it's useful to keep an eye out for clusters of sentences that are all structured in the same way. Many writers have a pet structure they like to use, which can lead to overuse. The fix is the same as with choppiness: Using subordination and varying your conjunctions more will let you build sentences with a variety of setups.

For instance, students often over-rely on addition words (*and, also, in addition, as well*) to link their ideas. Here's what that looks like.

> The Creature considers himself to be good, but he continually does bad things. He murders Victor's little brother. In addition, he murders Henry Cleval. And finally he murders Victor's wife Elizabeth as well.

This could be rewritten like so.

> The Creature considers himself to be good, but he continually does bad things. Not only does he murder Victor's little brother; he also murders Victor's friend Henry Cleval and Victor's wife Elizabeth.

If you read this version out loud, you'll see that it flows better. That's because instead of a series of short sentences that are constructed more or less the same way and rely on only one kind of link (essentially a plus sign), the revision has a variety of connections. It's still a list of the Creature's victims, but it feels like it was constructed by someone who was looking at the big picture, not just adding things as they came to him.

Another commonly overused structure is starting every sentence the same way. One example of that is always starting sentences with the name of the protagonist or the author of a given text. Here's what that kind of repeated setup can look like.

> Victor Frankenstein decides he can create life from death. Victor works for a long time assembling body parts. Eventually, Victor puts them all together. Victor animates his creation. Then Victor panics.

A good way to avoid this is to use time words. These words do two things for you: They vary the beginnings of your sentences, and they also help guide your reader through your paragraph by creating an order of events. Here's a new version of the section.

> When Victor Frankenstein decides to create life, he also decides to use body parts from dead people. After years of work, he finally assembles the parts into a whole person and animates them. He panics, however.

You'll notice that even in the revised form, we kept that last *he*. Nothing is inherently wrong with starting a sentence this way; you just don't want to start all of your sentences like that. When you have more options, you can make decisions about where you really do want to use that setup.

Overusing a word or phrase—whether it's at the beginning of a sentence or not—is also something to keep an eye out for. If you keep hitting the same note over and over, the reader will find it dull and may stop hearing what you're saying. Here's a section from the *Frankenstein* paper that overuses the word *humanity*.

> While Victor's humanity is not technically in doubt, the Creature's humanity is. His humanity is compromised from the start, both by the way that Victor conceives the experiment and by the way Victor responds to him when he's born. But a close look at that response reveals that Victor's humanity is equally compromised.

As the highlighting shows, the student has used the same word four times in four lines. Sometimes, of course, only one word is available to you, and you have to use it repeatedly. But most English words have more than one form. Here, for instance, the overused word is a noun, but it also has a different, related noun form (*human*) and an adjective form (also *human*, as in the phrase "human decency"). By using some alternate forms, swapping in a word that does the same work, cutting out the original word where it's not really needed, and altering his sentence structure, the student cuts back on the repetition.

> While Victor's humanity is not technically in doubt, the Creature's is. His status—is he a person, or is he a monster?—is compromised from the start, both by the way that Victor conceives the experiment and by the way Victor responds to him. But a closer look at Victor's response reveals that Victor himself lacks some crucial traits that define a human being.

To catch word repetition, try reading your draft out loud. The ear is much pickier than the eye: While the eye slides right over the word, the ear hears each repetition as an ever-louder thump. While reading your work aloud can be painful (because there's no hiding from what you hear), it's a great diagnostic tool. And it's better to hear problems when you can still fix them than to leave them for your reader to discover.

POLISHING AND FORMATTING

After you've worked through your paper at the essay level, the paragraph level, and the sentence level (see chapter twelve), you have one small set of things left to check. These are polishing moves: the final tweaks that make your paper read professionally and smoothly. Students who are in a rush often skip this step, but that's a mistake: When a professor encounters sloppy mistakes like, for instance, the spelling of the author's name, he may have a hard time reading past that to see the excellent work that you've done. Don't let these tiny issues get in your way!

As we said above, it's important to make sure that you're using the citation style your professor prefers and to check to make sure your polishing choices align with that style. Common styles include MLA, Chicago Manual of Style, APA, ASME, and CSE. The style your professor prefers will depend in part on his area of expertise. (English professors tend to like MLA style; engineering professors often use ASME.) The citation style will dictate issues like the use of a title page, subheadings, where page numbers go, the use of charts and graphs, and other important formatting issues, so you definitely want to make sure you know the rules.

Here's a checklist of some standard polishing issues you want to be sure to address, regardless of which style you use.

Spelling Characters' and Authors' Names Correctly

It's easy to make a mistake on this front—and for professors, it's a pretty glaring one. It may cause your professor to think that you don't really know the text you're talking about. To make sure you've got it right every time, check the name in the text and then run a search of your document looking for that name. (If the name doesn't come up, you're probably not spelling it right.) Be sure to check place names and titles of texts as well—and make triple-sure you're spelling your professor's name correctly!

Getting Titles Right

In high school, you probably referred to your teachers as "Mr." or "Ms." In college, most professors are referred to as Professor (or Doctor). In some cases, your professor may encourage you to call him or her by first name; in other cases, your professor may not yet have a Ph.D. and may refer to him- or herself as "Mr." or "Ms." Regardless of what you call your professor in class, it's always best to use the most formal title available in your paper (and better to err on the side of overtitling than undertitling, so if you're not sure, go with "Prof."). One error you should definitely avoid: Do not refer to female professors as "Mrs." unless they explicitly tell you to.

Spelling Other Words Correctly

It's a very good idea to run a spell-check on your document—though remember, a spell-check program will not recognize words that aren't in its dictionary, like author and character names. (Your spell-check program may suggest *wolf* for *Woolf*, for instance, and will certainly have difficulty with an uncapitalized *cummings*.) Spell-check may also suggest words that are similar to words you've chosen but not the same. Be sure to search for misspelled words, but don't make suggested changes automatically; it's a good idea to shift back and forth to a dictionary as you go, to double-check anything you're unsure of. Turn off the autocorrect function as you type since the program knows far fewer words than you do and will often guess wrong about what you're going to say.

It's also a good idea to avoid grammar-check programs. These programs are, to put it bluntly, not very bright. They only recognize very simple sentence structures—so they're likely to dumb down your paper and make it less readable. Though it can be tempting to use a grammar-check program if you're not confident in your sentence constructions, it's much better to put in the hard work yourself.

Page Numbers

In every essay you hand in, be sure to number your pages. This is important not only because it looks professional but because it makes things easier for your professor: She can keep track of where things are in the essay, and, if the pages come loose from their staple, she'll know which order they go in. Page numbers also serve as a final check that you've included everything you meant to: Sometimes students leave a page out or include two pages that are the same by mistake. Checking your page numbers will help you avoid this.

In MLA format (the format most often used by English professors), the number goes at the top right corner of each page; there is no page number on the first page (there are no cover pages in MLA format). In the *Chicago Manual of Style* method, another commonly used format, there is a cover page without a number and then numbering starts with the first page. Other style methods may be different as well. Many professors ask you to include your last name with the page number, like this.

Smith 7

If you're not sure which style your professor prefers, be sure to check with her. (If your professor specifies a citation style, it's a safe bet that she'd like your page numbers to align with that style.)

Margins, Spacing, and Fonts

Students who are concerned about length often think that playing with margins, spacing, and font size will help them out. But professors notice when you use huge margins and triple-space your paper or, conversely, when you use 1.5" spacing and a tiny 8-point font. (The implication that your professor *won't* notice these things insults his intelligence—which is never a good idea.) Some professors have very particular formatting rules—check your class website, syllabus, or paper assignments for information on this. If your professor doesn't give you this information, here's the standard way to do it.

- Use 1" margins, top and bottom, left and right, on every page of your essay. (Block quotes are further indented.)
- Double-space your essay.
- Use a reasonable 12-point font (not Courier New or other stretched-out, giant fonts, and not Abadi MT Condensed or other tiny fonts).
- Either double-space between paragraphs or indent each new paragraph—not both.

Titles and Subtitles

Be sure to give your paper a meaningful title (not "Essay #2 or "*Macbeth* Essay" or "Capital Punishment"). What you're looking for here is a title that synthesizes what your essay is about. Good titles are hard to come up with precisely because they encapsulate your argument—which means you really need to know what you're talking about. Some titles do no more than describe your topic accurately. Here's an example.

Humanity in Mary Shelley's *Frankenstein*

This is fine: It gives your reader a clear idea of what you'll be talking about in your essay. But you can also give your title more style. A quote from the text can be a quick way to distill what you're talking about. For example:

"An Accumulation of Anguish": Humanity in Mary Shelley's *Frankenstein*

This is a richer, more interesting title, more likely to catch the reader's eye. Or you might use words or phrases of your own. For example:

Monsters, Worms, and Lonely Guys: Humanity in Mary Shelley's *Frankenstein*

Whatever you choose, be sure that it accurately expresses the core of your essay.

Subtitles are used in some formats but not in others. Essays in English classes rarely use subtitles; science writing almost always does. Be sure to check the format with your professor.

Staple!

Students often forget this simple step. Trust us: Professors hate it when you hand in a paper held together by tape or, worse, when you tear and fold over the corner. Until and unless all of your work is handed in electronically, stapling is a key final step. Invest in a good stapler, and use it. If your paper is so long that it can't be stapled, use a binder clip to hold it all together.

By the time you're worrying about your stapler, you're done. Congratulations!

CONCLUSION

The techniques we've shown you in this book will work for you in all kinds of courses—from English to architecture to engineering to psychology. And you can put them to work with all kinds of texts—not just books and class materials, but movies, political speeches, blogs, TV shows, scientific processes, court arguments … anything you're trying to understand. That means you can analyze just about anything you want, write about it if you need to, and feel confident that you're an informed participant in culture and politics—because instead of just consuming material, you're analyzing it.

Now that you've finished the book, we hope that, instead of sitting alone at your desk staring at a blank screen and feeling like everyone knows the secret but you, you can start to think of yourself as part of the enormous global community of writers—the community of people who make false starts and ask questions and go back to where they began, who revise and edit and fill in the missing parts and throw out stuff that's not working, who get frustrated and get stuck but keep working through it. In other words, we hope you'll see yourself as a person who thinks through writing.

At the beginning of this book, we told you that there are no bad writers—only writers who don't have techniques and approaches. If you've moved through this book step by step, trying out the methods we've offered along the way, you now have a whole host of approaches for reading and writing critically, closely, and effectively. In other words, if you thought you were a "bad writer" when you started this book, we hope you don't think that anymore. Now that you've learned that writing doesn't have to be a foreign language, and you've found some methods for figuring out what you have to say and how to say it, maybe you've come to think of yourself as a writer.

INDEX

WD WRITER'S DIGEST

WRITER'S DIGEST
ONLINEworkshops
WritersOnlineWorkshops.*com*

Our workshops combine the best of world-class writing instruction with the convenience and immediacy of the web to create a state-of-the-art learning environment. You get all of the benefits of a traditional workshop setting—peer review, instructor feedback, a community of writers, and productive writing practice—without any of the hassle.

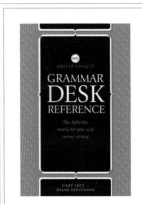

THE ONLY GRAMMAR GUIDE YOU'LL EVER NEED

Writer's Digest Grammar Desk Reference

BY GARY LUTZ AND DIANE STEVENSON

If you are new to writing, want to brush up on your grammar skills, or want to improve your work, turn to the *Writer's Digest Grammar Desk Reference*. You'll find in-depth information on grammar, punctuation, and usage and tips for avoiding common grammatical gaffes and usage mistakes.

Available from WritersDigestShop.com and your favorite book retailers.

To get started join our mailing list: **WritersDigest.com/enews**

FOLLOW US ON:

Find more great tips, networking and advice by following **@writersdigest**

And become a fan of our Facebook page: **facebook.com/writersdigest**